HOSPITALITY AND TOURISM MANAGEMENT SYSTEMS

HOSPITALITY AND TOURISM MANAGEMENT SYSTEMS

M. C. METTI

ANNMOL PUBLICATIONS PVT. LTD.
NEW DELHI - 110 002 (INDIA)

ANMOL PUBLICATIONS PVT. LTD.

H.O.: 4374/4B, Ansari Road, Darya Ganj,
New Delhi-110 002 (India)
Ph.: 23278000, 23261597

B.O.: No. 1015, Ist Main Road, BSK IIIrd Stage
IIIrd Phase, IIIrd Block
Bangalore - 560 085 (India)
Visit us at: www.anmolpublications.com

Hospitality and Tourism Management Systems

ISBN 978-81-261-3242-3

PRINTED IN INDIA

Printed at Mehra Offset Press, Delhi.

Contents

Preface

Virtually every country has taken steps to increase its number of visitors in recent years, and with each year, Tourism has remained the must-have resource dedicated to providing an exciting, comprehensive introduction to the world's most rapidly growing industry. This *hospitality and tourism management system* explores new trends in travel and tourism, while continuing the book's long-standing tradition of taking a global look into the economic, political, and social forces that drive and shape tourism.

Author

Chapter 1

Tourism and Hospitality

Tourism is a powerful economic force providing employment, foreign exchange, income, and tax revenue. The generators of economic impact for a city, a state, a province, a country, or a destination area are visitors, their expenditures, and the multiplier effect. The economic impact of tourism spending is a function of the numbers of domestic and international visitors and their expenditures. Because of the economic importance of tourism, the World Tourism Organization (WTO) maintains statistics by region and country on tourism arrivals (visitors) and both tourism expenditures (what a country spends) and receipts (what a country receives from visitor expenditures).

Tourism destinations are becoming increasingly competitive as more and more destinations look at tourism to become the new economic generator replacing declining activity in agriculture, mining, and manufacturing. As a consequence of pervasive anxiety caused by these events, people cut back on their travel; economic forecasts were put on hold; airline, lodging, tour operators, and travel agent revenue declined; and widespread layoffs occurred throughout the industry. We realized very directly and in a personal manner the real economic impact of tourism. However, over the long run, it is believed that travel will recover and the 2020 forecasts will be realized.

Negative factors such as the Iraq conflict, terrorism, SARS, and a weak economy made 2003 another difficult year for international tourism. SARS brought the steady growth of Asia and the Pacific to an abrupt halt in April and May, and while tourists quickly started to return after the virus was contained, the region could not make up the losses in the remainder of the year. The war and the economy dampened tourism demand in other key regions. According to WTO preliminary results, the total number of international arrivals reached 694.0 million in 2003, a decrease of 1.2 per cent from 2002.

Europe is the main tourist receiving region, followed by Asia and the Pacific, and the Americas. In 2003, Europe accounted for almost 58 per cent of the arrivals, Asia and the Pacific 17.2 per cent, and the Americas 16.2 per cent. International arrivals were most impacted by the unexpected drop of 12 million (9.3 per cent) in Asia and the Pacific due to the SARS panic. The Americas recorded a decrease of 2.5 million (2.5 per cent), while Europe was basically flat, recording an increase of 0.4 per cent. The Middle East and Africa were the surprise regions in 2003 as they recorded healthy increases in tourism arrivals of 10 per cent and 5 per cent respectively.

An initial analysis of this data shows that international receipts increased by $40.2 billion, and measured in U.S. dollars every region recorded an increase in receipts except

Asia and the Pacific. The series has always been reported in U.S. dollars; however, in this case, it does not present as accurate a picture as it should and illustrates the impact exchange rates can have. When one examines the increase of receipts from $474.2 billion in 2002 to $514.4 billion in 2003, it should be taken into account that this is largely because of the strong depreciation of the U.S. dollar versus many other currencies, especially the euro. In 2003, a euro bought almost 20 per cent more U.S. dollar than in 2002.

Thus, receipts earned in euro destinations, which account for over a quarter of worldwide receipts, when expressed in dollar terms, are magnified. Consequently, expressing worldwide receipts in a currency other than the U.S. dollar would present a different picture. WTO has computed worldwide receipts in euros and found that worldwide receipts decreased by 50 billion from euro 502 billion in 2002 to euro 455 billion in 2003.

WTO states that a way to compensate for this distortion caused by exchange rates is to express the evolution of receipts in weighted local currencies. At the same time, it is preferable to take inflation into account by using constant prices instead of current prices. Calculated this way, international tourism receipts were estimated to have decreased by about 2 per cent in 2003, while 2002 was still just positive at 0.3 per cent.

When one reviews the period 1996 to 2000, they find that international tourism receipts grew faster than arrivals. In the last three years, receipts have grown at a lower rate, reflecting unsettled times and a slow economy. In difficult times, travelers are resourceful and will keep traveling, but will economize by traveling with friends, taking shorter trips, staying in less expensive accommodations, eating out less, and so on. All of these actions reduce tourism receipts. The Americas' share is 22.5 per cent and Asia and the Pacific share is 17.2 per cent. The shares of Africa and the Middle East were both at 2.7 per cent. Receipts per arrivals averaged $740. The Americas averaged the highest receipts per arrival at $1,030, followed by Asia and the Pacific at the average of $740, Europe with $700, and Africa and the Middle East both at $460.

Expectations for 2007 and Beyond

Prospects for 2007 and the future appear to be very positive as short-term data confirm the upward trend in arrivals that started in late 2003. Asia and the Pacific are showing a strong rebound from 2003. United States international arrivals are recording monthly double-digit increases. Business travel is showing signs of recovery. Low-cost airlines are continuing to increase their capacity and expand their coverage. As expected 2004 saw a return to growth in the travel industry with a record 760 million international arrivals for a 10 per cent increase over 2003. However, rising oil prices are a major concern.

Tourism 2020 Vision is the World Tourism Organization's long-term forecast and assessment of the development of tourism through the first twenty years of the new millennium. An essential outcome of *Tourism 2020 Vision* is quantitative forecasts covering a 25-year period, with 1995 as the base year and forecasts for 2000, 2010, and 2020.

WTO's *Tourism 2020 Vision* forecasts that international arrivals are expected to reach over 1.56 billion by the year 2020. Of these worldwide arrivals in 2020, 1.18 billion will be intraregional and 377 million will be long-haul travellers. The total tourist arrivals by region shows that by 2020 the top three receiving regions will be Europe (717 million tourists), East Asia and the Pacific (397 million), and the Americas (282 million), followed by Africa, the Middle East, and South Asia. East Asia and the Pacific, South Asia, the Middle East, and Africa are forecasted to record growth at rates of over 5 per cent, compared to the world average of 4.1 per cent. The more mature regions of Europe and the Americas are anticipated to show lower-than-average growth rates.

Europe will maintain the highest share of world arrivals, although there will be a decline from 60 per cent in 1995 to 46 per cent in 2020. By 2010, the Americas will lose its number-two position to the East Asia and Pacific region, which will receive 25 per cent of world arrivals in 2020, with the Americas decreasing from 19 per cent in 1995 to 18 per cent in 2020.

Long-haul travel worldwide will grow faster, at 5.4 per cent per year over the period 1995–2020, than intraregional travel, at 3.8 per cent. Consequently, the ratio between intraregional and long-haul travel will shift from around 82:18 in 1995 to close to 76:24 in 2020.

Comparing International and Despite the importance of international tourism (that is, tourists traveling outside of their country of residence), for many (if not most) countries, domestic tourism (tourists travelling in their country of residence) is even more important. The World Tourism Organization (WTO) estimated that international travel involved receipts of US$514.4 billion in 2003. In contrast, the World Travel and Tourism Council estimated that in 2004, both international and domestic travel together generated about US$3,133.2 billion.

As can be seen from these estimates of the magnitude of international and domestic travel, the latter is much greater than the former. This fact surprises many people who primarily think of tourism as being exotic, international travel. In the United States the travel industry received $545.5 billion from domestic and international travelers (including international passenger fares) in 2002. Of these total international visitors spent $83.5 billion traveling in the United States for 15.3 per cent of the total. Domestic travel expenditures were $462.0 billion for 84.7 per cent of the total.

Employment

The World Travel and Tourism Council estimates that in 2005 employment in the travel and tourism economy was 221,568,000 jobs or 8.3 per cent of total employment, which is 1 in every 12.0 jobs. By 2015, this should grow to 269,556,000 jobs, 8.9 per cent of total employment or 1 in every 11.2 jobs. The 74;223,000 travel and tourism industry jobs accounted for 2.8 per cent of total employment in 2005 and are forecast to rise to 85,521,000 jobs or 2.8 per cent of the total by 2015. Tourism provides both direct and indirect employment. Firms such as hotels, restaurants, airlines, cruise lines, and resorts provide direct employment because their employees are in contact with tourists and provide the tourist experience. Employees of firms providing goods and services to the direct employment firms, such as aircraft manufacturers, construction firms, and restaurant suppliers, create indirect employment.

The impact of this can be illustrated using a United States example. In 2003, the TIA published its annual study, *Tourism Works for America,* which contains employment estimates. Employment by sector, shows that in 2002, travel and tourism directly generated nearly 7.2 million jobs in the U.S. economy.

Travellers in the United States produce secondary impacts over and above that of their original expenditures. These secondary outputs (sales) and earnings (wage and salary income) supported by this "indirect" and "induced" spending add an additional 9.7 million jobs to the U.S. economy. With the almost 6.3 million jobs in 2002 generated directly by domestic travel spending, and the 900,000 employment opportunities generated by international travel to the United States, total U.S. employment created by the travel and tourism industry was 16.9 million in 2002.

The complexity of accurately measuring the vast economic impacts of the tourism industry has created a movement to link tourism expenditure accounting with that used for the national system of accounting in most countries. Earlier attempts to include tourism in the standard industry classification (SIC) codes proved unsuccessful because of the diversity and overlapping nature of many tourism expenditures. In order to overcome these difficulties, a system of tourism satellite accounting has been proposed and implemented.

Economics is concerned with the attainment of an optimum return from the use of scarce resources. Whether it is a person seeking psychological benefit from travel, or a business interested in providing tourists goods and services at a profit, or a host community government viewing tourism in terms of the economic benefits resulting from tourist expenditures, the principle is the same. Economic agents seek to allocate the limited supply of tourism resources (both physical and financial) as they seek to meet the demands of tourists. The demands are the result of their physical/functional needs (which, as a rule are limited) and their psychological wants (which can be virtually unlimited).

As such, the problem that economics attempts to solve is how to achieve an economical optimal allocation of scarce tourism resources, when facing the constantly shifting demand (generated by physical needs and psychological wants) for these resources.

Goals

As indicated, at least three major goals can be identified in tourism:

1. Maximize the amount of psychological experience for tourists.
2. Maximize profits for firms providing goods and services to tourists.
3. Maximize the direct (primary) and indirect (secondary) benefits of tourist expenditures on a community or region.

These goals are often compatible; maximizing psychological experience creates happy clientele, which causes them to return, to spend money, and to make every one in the industry and the region satisfied. In certain situations, they can also be incompatible. A short-run profit-maximizing goal may cause the development of facilities beyond the capacity of the site, thus leading to overuse and a decline in psychological enjoyment. Extreme emphasis on tourism as an element in economic development might have the same result. There can also be clashes between the use of resources for tourism and for other kinds of development.

Constraints

The second half of the optimizing situation is occupied by those factors that place obstacles in the way of goal attainment. We assume that it is desirable to have unlimited amounts of psychological enjoyment, profits, and local impacts. But that is not possible, because something always gets in the way. Tourism, being extremely broad and diverse, must deal with a large number of constraints. To make an analysis of relationships, it will be necessary to classify them.

Demand

Every firm providing goods and services to tourists is constrained by the demand functions of its customers. These relate quantity purchased to price, wealth, and income.

Supply of Attractive Resources

Possibly one of the most important constraints faced by the industry as a whole is the limited amount of resources available for tourist enjoyment. This is particularly true when geographic distribution of these sites is considered. Some areas are simply better attractions for tourists than others are.

Technical and Environmental Constraints

Each particular site or situation has certain technical and environmental constraints.

They involve such things as the relationship between sewage effluent disposal and the environment, numbers of fish and numbers of fishermen, number of people who can walk in a given area without causing unacceptable damage, number of elephants supportable on a wildlife range, impact on lions' behaviour of tourists observing them from a car, number of campsites possible in a given area without harming the environment, and so on.

Time Constraints

The amount of vacation time available limits what the vacationer can do. The length of the tourist season influences profitability of tourist-oriented businesses and the impact of tourist expenditures on the local economy.

Indivisibilities

Many times it is necessary to deal either with all of something or with nothing. It is not possible to fly half an airplane, even though the seats are only half filled. It may not be profitable to build a hotel under a given size. A road has to be built all the way from one point to another.

Legal Constraints

Several types of legal constraints affect tourism. Activities of the government tourist bureau might be one. Laws concerning environmental problems could be another. Zoning and building codes may influence the construction of facilities. Laws concerning contractual relations may limit activities.

Self-Imposed Constraints

Conflicting goals need to be reconciled, which leads to self-imposed constraints. The conflicts may arise within a firm or among firms, government agencies, and so on, that are seeking to develop a particular area or concept.

Lack of Knowledge

Many activities are limited because little is known about particular situations. Businesspeople are used to living with a certain amount of uncertainty, but there are inevitable limits to the amount they are willing to countenance. Ignorance influences governmental operations as well.

Limits on Supportive Resources

There are always limits to the amount of money, managerial talent, workers, construction materials, social capital, and so on. And these, in turn, limit chances to provide psychological enjoyment, take advantage of profit-making opportunities, or develop local attractions. Many times these individual constraints interact, creating compound constraints on given activities.

Optimizing the Experience

Maximization of the tourist experience is subject to a number of constraints and is manifested in the demand function. Demand for tourist experience is peculiar in the sense that the product being purchased is not easy to identify directly and is frequently purchased sight unseen. The tourist is particularly constrained by time and budget. To optimize the experience, it is necessary to determine the combination of destinations preferred and then the possibilities within the money and time constraints. This explains some of the popularity of package tours, where both time and cost can be known in advance. There are some exceptions. Retired persons and young people often have time but limited resources. A few people have neither constraint.

Optimizing Returns to Businesses

Because goods and services provided to tourists are really inputs to the process of producing the experience, demand for them is derived from demand for tourism as a whole. Some goods and services are complementary, and their demand is interrelated in a positive fashion. Others are substitutes and are characterized by limited area competition.

Packaged tours have the characteristic of putting all parts and services together, so they become complementary. Competition occurs among tours. Tour operators can maximize profits by selling tours of different value and costs, in order to cater to as many people as possible along the demand curve. The number of people to be accommodated can be determined from the marginal cost of the tour and the marginal revenue to be derived from a given price level.

Goods and services sold to tourists are subject to severe peaking in demand. That is, the heaviest tourist season is usually limited. During that period, demand is intense and must be met with facilities that are excess in the off-season. This means that investment necessary to provide the excess capacity must be paid for from revenues received during the peak period. During off-peak periods, only variable cost is of interest, but because demand is low, some capacity will not be utilized.

As owners of the facilities, firms are concerned with providing adequate long-run capacity and with choosing those investments that will give optimum returns. In the tourist industry, a number of interrelationships must be considered. Sometimes, low benefit-cost investments are made so that higher-yielding investments can succeed. Consequently, it is not always true that investors choose the highest-yielding opportunities.

Generally, it is considered the long-run business of the firm to remove constraints on operations. But tourism has a number of constraints to expansion. These include demand for the tourist experience and environmental constraints.

Optimizing for the Local Economy

Tourism affects a region during periods of intense investment activity and afterward when the investments are producing. The effects depend on linkages among economic units. Money spent for investment will go to construction and a few other industrial sectors. These will have links to economic units varying from households to manufacturing plants. Money spent by tourists will also be introduced through a few sectors that will also be linked to the economy.

The multiplier effects in both cases are dependent upon the strength of the linkages.

The multiplier reflects the amount of new economic activity generated as basic income circulates through the economy. Some sectors have strong links to other sectors in an economy and a large multiplier effect. Others have weak links and small multipliers. It is possible to have a thriving tourist industry and abject poverty in the local populace if there are no links. For example, linkages will be strong and the income multiplier high if the year-round resorts in a particular destination area hire all local labour; buy their flowers, fruit, vegetables, and poultry products from local farmers; hire local entertainers; and buy furnishings for guest rooms from local manufacturers. Linkages would be weak if most of these goods and services were imported from another state or country.

TOURISM EXPORTS AND IMPORTS

The host region is defined loosely as a county, a state, or a nation, depending on the level at which the problem is being considered. For a county-level government, the income of the county is of primary interest. A state government would perceive the maximization of the combined income of the entire state to be its objective, and so on. Regardless of which definition of host region is being considered, expenditures in this area by tourists coming from another region represent injections into the area's economy.

Japanese tourists traveling to the United States presumably earned their income in Japan. When spending money in the United States as tourists, they are "injecting" money into our economy that wasn't here before. As such, expenditures by foreigners in this country (for travel purposes) represent tourism exports for the United States. This may be somewhat confusing because we are accustomed to thinking of something leaving the country as an export. When we export computers or cars, for example, these commodities are sent out of the United States. In the example of the Japanese tourists, the tourists are coming into this country. So how is it an export? There seems to be a contradiction in terminology. As the astute student would note, however, when tourists come into this country, they are purchasing travel experiences. When they leave, they take these experiences back with them. Thus, we have exported travel experiences, which are, after all, what tourism is all about.

When U.S. tourists travel to Japan and spend money there, this becomes a tourism import to the U.S. economy. Japanese money spent in the United States is a tourism import for the Japanese economy. In tourism exports, the flows of tourists and payments are in the same direction, whereas in commodity exports, the two flows are in opposite directions. Therein lays the confusion. However, if one were to look at the *direction of payment flow* to determine what an export is, there is no contradiction between the two cases. When payment flows into the United States, something has been exported— travel experiences, for instance, or commodities. Both payment flows are in the same direction.

Balance-of-Payments Effects

Tourism is one of the world's largest international industries. As such, it has a noticeable impact on the balance of payments of many nations. We have heard much about the balance-of-payments problems of the United States, and, indeed, tourism imports do affect the balance of payments and economic conditions generally. We define tourism imports as those expenditures made by American tourists in foreign countries. An easy way to remember this is to ask, "Who got the money?" If, for example, Great Britain received American funds, it makes no difference whether an American bought some English china or an American tourist visited England.

Our balance-of-payments situation directly affects the gross national product of the United States (*Y*).

By looking at the formula, we can see that if imports (*M*) exceed exports (*X*), then the difference (*X* _ *M*) will be a negative number, and *Y* will thus be smaller. Thus, it is advantageous to us in our American economy to attract more visitor spending in the United States. These "tourism exports" are like credits and help our economy. It is economically better to have foreign visitors come to the United States than it is to have U.S. citizen's travel abroad. However, this should be tempered with the realization that the situation is not entirely positive or negative.

Expenditures by U.S. tourists abroad make possible purchasing power in foreign countries for those countries to buy American-made products. For example, most airlines of the world use American-made equipment. Purchase of these aircraft, parts, supplies, repair services, and so forth makes an important contribution to the export trade of the United States; thus, we cannot charge the U.S. international traveller with a total negative balance of payments. The purpose of the foregoing discussion is simply to point out the relationships.

Tourism exports become very desirable as far as the gross national product and the prosperity of the country are concerned. Efforts on the part of national tourism offices to attract foreign visitors have a great impact on the balance-of-payments situation. Business firms that serve the foreign visitor, provide desired services, and stimulate sales materially help our national economy. However, during periods when the U.S. dollar is high against foreign currencies, a dampening effect occurs on our tourism exports because this situation is seen as unFavourable by prospective foreign visitors. Conversely, if the dollar is low, more foreign tourists will visit the United States. This increases our tourism exports, improves our balance of payments, and raises the gross national product. These same relationships of comparable currency values exist between any country that exports tourism and the countries of its tourists' origin.

In 1998 the value of the Canadian dollar was low in comparison to the U.S. dollar and illustrated this principle. The number of Americans visiting Canada to take advantage of the exchange rate increased dramatically. This contributed positively to Canada's balance of payments.

Investment Stimulation

The tourist industry has a unique structure. It is characterized by and, in fact, is an agglomeration of a large number of very small units, covering a variety of different service trades—the small restaurants, motels, guest houses, laundries, arts and crafts shops, and others. Thus, investment in infrastructure and sometimes expensive superstructure by the government stimulates investment in numerous smaller businesses. Because of the small size of these businesses, capital requirements are relatively low and investment generally proceeds at a rapid pace. In this respect, too, governments view tourism rather Favourably. The initial investment in tourism brings forth a large investment in supporting and tertiary industries. This also includes large investments in major hotels, restaurants, shopping Centres, marinas, airports, and so on.

Tourism Increases Tax Revenue

Tourists must pay taxes like most other people. Because they come from other regions or countries, their expenditures represent an increased tax base for the host government. In addition to the usual sales tax, tourists sometimes pay taxes in less direct ways. Airport taxes, exit fees, customs duty, and charges assessed for granting visas are just a few examples of commonly used methods of taxing tourists. The wisdom of imposing such special taxes on tourists is questionable, because it merely serves to reduce demand. In some countries, for instance, the room rate at a hotel optimization can be different for tourists (generally higher) than for residents. This is a questionable practice, because it leaves the tourist with a feeling that he has been "taken." Apart from these special cases, the usual taxes collected from both tourists and residents increase because of tourism expenditures.

Is tourism, then, a panacea for all the economic woes of a region or country? It has been claimed that tourism increases incomes, employment, investment, tax revenues, and so forth, so it might indeed appear to be one. However, constraints limit the extent to which governments can maximize the benefit from these aspects of tourism. These constraints are of two types: social and economic. The social constraints have already been discussed. The economic constraints are in the form of potential economic costs that the tourism industry may impose. These merit further scrutiny to gain a better understanding of the government's optimization problem.

Inflationary Pressure

Tourists inject money (earned elsewhere) into the destination economy. While this increases the income of the region (as discussed earlier), it also might cause inflationary pressures. Tourists typically have a higher expenditure capability than the residents do—either because tourists have higher incomes or because they have saved for the trip and are inclined to "splurge" while on vacation. Hence, they are able to somewhat bid up the prices of such commodities as food, transportation, and arts and crafts. This causes inflationary pressures, which can be detrimental to the economic welfare of residents of the host community. This is particularly true when inflation affects the prices of essentials such as food, clothing, transportation, and housing. Land prices have been known to escalate rapidly in tourist destination areas. The prices that foreigners are willing to pay for "vacation homes" in the area can decrease the demand for "first homes" by residents.

Lundberg1 notes that as the tourist industry developed in an area, land prices rose sharply. In a particular underdeveloped area, the amount of investment in land constituted just 1 per cent of the total investment for a hotel project. By contrast, this ratio increased to 20 per cent in an area where tourism was already overdeveloped. With such increases in land prices, it can be expected that local residents (with their lower incomes) are effectively "chased out" of the housing market in a tourism-developing section.

Direct Effect

In addition to the direct impact of tourism expenditures on an area, there are also indirect impacts. The indirect or multiplier impact comes into play as visitor spending circulates and recirculates. The direct effects are the easiest to understand because they result from the visitor spending money in tourist enterprises and providing a living for the owners and managers and creating jobs for employees.

Indirect Effect

This visitor expenditure gives rise to an income that, in turn, leads to a chain of expenditure- income-expenditure, and so on, until leakages bring the chain to a halt. Consequently, the impact of the initial income derived from the tourist's expenditure is usually greater than the initial income, because subsequent rounds of spending are related to it. For example, a skier purchases a lift ticket for $40. This money received by the ski area will be used to pay the wages of the lift operators.

The lift operator spends the money on groceries; the grocer uses the money to pay part of his rent to the local landlady; the landlady uses it to pay for her dry cleaning; the dry cleaner spends it in a restaurant for a dinner; the restaurant owner spends it for steaks shipped in from Kansas City; and the cycle stops as the money is lost to the local economy. This last transaction is known as *leakage* from the economy. The combination of the direct and indirect effects of an expenditure pattern determines the impact. In a typical situation, not all of the income generated in each round of expenditure is respent. Some portion tends to be saved, and some portion tends to be spent outside the local economy. The greater the proportion of income spent locally, the greater will be the multiplier.

The degree to which a local area is able to retain tourist income depends on how self-sufficient the local economy is. If the local economy is able to produce the goods and services tourists buy, the greater will be the multiplier effect. The more goods that have to be imported from outside the region, the smaller the multiplier will be. From the discussion, it is clear that when a tourist's spending injects funds into the economy of a host area, an economic effect occurs that is a specified number of times what was originally spent.

Initially, this effect is thought of as an *income multiplier,* as tourist expenditures become income directly and indirectly to local people. However, there are additional economic phenomena. Increased spending necessitates more jobs, which results in an *employment multiplier.* Because money changes hands a number of times during a year, there is a transactions multiplier. This is of particular interest to governmental tax officials where sales taxes are imposed. As business grows in a tourist destination area, more infrastructure and superstructure are constructed. This results in a *capital multiplier.* Examples are provided here of how an employment multiplier and an income multiplier were determined.

Employment Multiplier

The employment multiplier varies from region to region depending on its economic base. In a study entitled *Recreation as an Industry,* by Robert R. Nathan Associates, county employment multipliers calculated for the Appalachian region provide a good illustration of what typical multipliers are and how they work.2 The multipliers estimated in this study were based on county employment data. They represent the approximate measure of the direct and indirect employment associated with each addition of direct employment to the export sector of a county. Multipliers were estimated for 375 counties and three independent cities.

The smallest multiplier was 1.13, and the highest was 2.63. Thus, the county with the smallest multiplier value would provide other employment opportunities for approximately 0.13 person for each person directly employed in servicing export demand, and the county with the highest multiplier value would provide other employment opportunities for approximately 1.63 persons for each person directly employed in servicing export demand. In general, county employment multipliers vary directly with the population or total employment size of the counties: As county population size grows, so does the multiplier value. This relationship is as might be expected, insofar as import leakages would tend to be less where diversity of occupations is greater, and diversity is positively associated with county population or total employment.

Income Multiplier

Jobs mean income, which stimulates the economy of the area in which the development occurs. How much stimulation occurs depends on several factors. The management of a hotel, for example, takes two actions with the revenue earned: It spends parts of the money on goods and services, and it saves part of such funds. Economists refer to such actions as marginal propensity to consume (MPC) and marginal propensity to save (MPS)—removing funds from the local economy. Such removal of these marginal (extra) funds can be made in two ways: (1) they can be saved and not loaned to another spender, or (2) they can be used to purchase imports. In either case, so doing removes the funds and thus does not stimulate the local economy.

Economic research is needed in a tourist destination area to determine what these income relationships are. If the results of such economic research were made available, many beneficial results might be possible. For example, governmental bodies might be more inclined to appropriate additional funds for tourism promotion to their areas if they knew more about the income that was generated by tourist expenditures. Also, improved and added developments of facilities to serve tourists might be more forthcoming if prospective investors could have more factual data upon which to base decisions.

To understand the multiplier, we must first make some approximation as to what portion of the tourist dollars received in a community is spent (consumed) and what portion is saved (leakage). To illustrate this, suppose that we had a total of $1,000 of tourist spending in a community and that there was an MPC of 1/2. The expenditure pattern might go through seven transactions in a year. The other formula for the multiplier is 1/MPS.

Leakage, as defined, is a combination of savings and imports. If we spend the money outside our country for imports, obviously it does not stimulate the economy locally. If it is put into some form of savings that are not loaned to another spender within a year, it has the same effect as imports—not stimulating the economy. Thus, to get the maximum benefits economically from tourist expenditures, we should introduce as much of the tourist funds as possible into the local economy for goods and services rather than save the proceeds or buy a large amount of imports.

Here, also, more economic research is needed. Some studies have indicated that the multiplier might be as high as 3 in some areas, but economic research in other localities indicates that it may be more typically lower than this.

Economic Benefits Widely Distributed

Using a conceptual approach, you should realize that tourism is characterized by the existence of a large number of very small businesses that support and are ancillary to the industry. The receipts from tourism quickly filter down to an extremely broad cross section of the population, so that the entire community shares the economic benefits.

Structural Changes

In countries that primarily rely on a single industry, such as agriculture, the introduction of tourism has often led to a decrease in the agricultural base of the country. Agriculture is an extremely low productivity industry in the developing countries. The promise of much higher wages in the tourism industry draws people away from farming. Agricultural output declines as a result, just when the demand for food increases because of the influx of tourists. The inflationary pressure on food prices is further aggravated and can lead to considerable social upheaval. In the mid-1970s, some Caribbean countries experienced a wave of protests and even direct attacks on tourists, as the resident population expressed its dissatisfaction over rising prices.

Another major implication of the structural change is that instead of diversifying its economic base, the country's tourism sector merely "cannibalizes" its other major economic sector. Diversity is the foundation of economic stability. When one sector (or industry) experiences a slump, another sector booms, thus reducing the probability of a severe depression and, indeed, reducing its impact if a depression does occur. Thus, tourism, instead of diversifying an economy, sometimes replaces agriculture as a "subsistence" sector.

FORMS OF TOURISM

Adventure Tourism

Adventure tourism is a type of tourism involving exploration or travel to remote areas, where the traveler should expect the unexpected. Adventure tourism is rapidly growing in popularity as tourists seek unusual holidays, different from the typical beach vacation.

Adventure tourism typically involves traveling into remote, inaccessible and possibly hostile areas. It may include the performance of acts that require significant effort and grit and may also involve some degree of risk. Adventure Tourism becoming more and more Famous specially among youth. India is not a country but a world in itself. Here one can find World's biggest river for rafting and endless mountains for trekking. It is a country who has somthing for every kind of Adventure lover.

For Mountainerring and Trekking one can go to Sikkim, the home of mighty Kunchnjanga and situated within eastern himalayas. Jummu & Kashmir the heaven on earth.The place for Ski lovers and wonderful for backpackers.Himachal one of the best sites for Pargaliding in World and famous for beautiful gentle hills and Where glaciers are not far from mainland. Uttranchal a place where every single person wants to go, famous for valley of flowers and for Shiva Dhams and Last but not least Leh and Ladakh the cold deasert of India a place where one cannot find Trees and find really cold and different culture much closer to Tibtian clutre and a starting point for Extreame tourism lovers who want to travel beyond the main land towards zanskar and nubra velleys.

For Rafting India is heaven the rivers like Ganga,Teesta,and Brahamaputra provide rafters a real thrill and challange. Rafting is becoming very popular among the corporates combined with Stay in riverside resorts and team building exercises.

Mountaineering

Mountaineering is the sport, hobby or profession of walking, hiking and climbing up mountains. It is also sometimes known as alpinism, particularly in Europe. It may be said to consist of two main aspects, rock-craft and snow-craft, depending on whether the route chosen is over rock or over snow and ice. Both require great gymnastic and technical ability, but experience is also a very important part of the latter. Training in these areas for several months enhances a person's abilities and increases their chances for survival while climbing.

Agritourism

Agritourism is a style of vacation in which hospitality is offered on farms. This may include the opportunity to assist with farming tasks during the visit. Agritourism is often practiced in wine growing regions, as in Italy, France and Spain. In America, Agritourism is wide-spread and includes any farm open to the public at least part of the year.

Tourists can pick fruits and vegetables, ride horses, taste honey, learn about wine, shop in gift shops and farm stands for local and regional produce or hand-crafted gifts, and much more. Each farm generally offers a unique and memorable experience suitable for the entire family.

Agritourism is being developed as a valuable component of a business model to support many agricultural entities when the farm products they produce are no longer economically competitive otherwise. To help promote the single agritourism operations, farms get together and form festivals or tours, such as Agri-tours, a two-weekend festival in September celebrating the lower Ottawa Valley's unique farms. This festival includes over a dozen non-traditional farms that specialize in everything from deer and pheasant, to apples and wine.

People are more interested in how their food is produced and want to meet the producers and talk with them about what goes into food production. Children who visit the farms often have not seen a live duck, or goat, and have not picked an apple right off the tree. This form of expanded agri-tourism has given birth to what are often called "entertainment farms." These farms cater to the pick-your-own crowd, offering not only regular farm products, but also food, mazes, open-pen animals, train rides, picnic facilities and pick-your-own produce. Dude ranches offer tourists the chance to work on cattle ranches and sometimes include cattle drives.

Cultural Tourism

Cultural tourism tourism and ecotourism, the number of living cultural areas is continually droping off. For an indigenous culture that has stayed largely separated from the surrounding majority culture, tourism can present both advantages and problems on to it. On the positive side are the unique cultural practices and arts that attract the curiosity of tourists and provide opportunities for tourism and economic development. On the negative side is the issue of how to control tourism so that those same cultural amenities are not destroyed and the people do not feel violated.

Destination Planning Resources

It is important that the destination planner takes into account the diverse definition of culture as the term is subjective. Satisfying tourists' interests such as landscapes, seascapes, art, nature, traditions, ways of life and other products associated to them -which may be categorized cultural in the broadest sense of the word, is a prime consideration as it marks the initial phase of the development of a cultural destination.

The quality of service and destination, which doesn't solely depend on the cultural heritage but more importantly to the cultural environment, can further be developed by setting controls and policies which shall govern the the community and its stakeholders. It is therefore safe to say that the planner should be on the ball with the varying meaning of culture itself as this fuels the formulation of development policies that shall entail efficient planning and monitored growth *(e.g. strict policy on the protection and preservation of the community)*.

While satisfying tourists' interests and demands may be a top priority, it is also imperative to ruminate the subsystems of the destinatons (residents). Development pressures should be anticipated and set to their minimun level so as to conserve the area's resources and prevent a saturation of the destination as to not abuse the product and the residents correspondingly. The plan should incorporate the locals to its gain by training and employing them and in the process encourage them to participate to the travel business. Keep in mind that the plan should make travellers not only aware about the destination but also concern on how to help it sustain its character while broadening their travelling experience.

Heritage Tourism

Cultural heritage tourism is a branch of tourism oriented towards the cultural heritage. Culture has always been a major object of travel, as the development of the Grand Tour from the 16th century onwards attests. In the 20th century, some people have claimed, culture ceased to be the objective of tourism: tourism is now culture. Cultural attractions play an important role in tourism at all levels, from the global highlights of world culture to attractions that underpin local identities.

According to the Weiler and Hall, culture, heritage and the arts have long contributed to appeal of tourist destination.

However, in recent years 'culture' has been rediscovered as an important marketing tool to attract those travellers with special interests in heritage and arts. According to the Hollinshead, cultural heritage tourism defines as cultural heritage tourism is the fastest growing segment of the tourism industry because there is a trend toward an increase specialization among tourist. This trend is evident in the rise in the volume of tourists who seek adventure, culture, history, archaeology and interaction with local people.

Cultural heritage tourism is important for various reasons; it has a positive economic and social impact, it establishes and reinforces identity, it helps preserve the cultural heritage, with culture as an instrument it facilitates harmony and understanding among people, it supports culture and helps renew tourism.

Cultural heritage tourism has a number of objectives that must be met within the context of sustainable development such as; the conservation of cultural resources, accurate interpretation of resources, authentic visitors experience, and the stimulation of the earned revenues of cultural resources. We can see therefore, that cultural heritage tourism is not only concerned with identification, management and protection of the heritage values but it must also be involved in understanding the impact of tourism on communities and regions, achieving economic and social benefits, providing financial resources for protection, as well as marketing and promotion.

Heritage tourism involves visiting historical or industrial sites that may include old canals, railways, battlegrounds, etc. The overall purpose is to gain an appreciation of the past. It also refers to the marketing of a location to members of a diaspora who have distant family roots there.

Heritage tourism is distinct from visiting a family member in a faraway place because the connection to the original homeland is removed; a recent Irish immigrant to the US, for example, may return home to see relatives but would probably not be considered a heritage tourist.

On the other hand, an Irish-American whose family emigrated in the 19th century, also going to Ireland but rather to see the country generally, would be partaking in heritage tourism. This is particularly relevant to European areas where large numbers of people emigrated to North America in the 19th century and early 20th century. People from Quebec have been moving back and forth to France for centuries in fairly significant numbers, as have their counterparts with ties to the British Isles and other countries for more recent immigrants. Other examples include Black/African Americans who visit Africa and Hispanics who visit Spain.

The purpose can be education, fun, marriage, employment, etc. Permanent emigration tied to heritage tourism is less common but increasing.Decolonization and immigration form the major background of much contemporary heritage tourism. Falling travel costs have also made heritage tourism possible for more people.

Another possible form involves religious travel or pilgrimages. Many Catholics from around the world come to the Vatican and other sites such as Lourdes or Fatima. Large numbers of Jews have both visited Israel and emigrated there. Many have also gone to Holocaust sites and memorials. Islam commands its followers to take the hajj to Mecca, thus differentiating it somewhat from tourism in the usual sense, though the trip can also be a culturally important event for the pilgrim.

Heritage Tourism can also be attributed to historical events that have been dramatised to make them more entertaining. For example a historical tour of a town or city using a theme such as ghosts or vikings.

Ecotourism

Ecotourism means ecological tourism, where ecological has both environmental and social connotations. It is defined both as a concept-tourism movement and as a tourism (specifically sustainable tourism) section.

Born in its current form in the late 1980's, Ecotourism came of age in 2002, when the United Nations celebrated the "International Year of Ecotourism". The meeting was a watershed event, but it was not created with those who had pioneered the niche.

There are various definitions as this is a vibrant movement and ecotourism may be defined by its lack of definition.

Generally speaking, ecotourism focuses on local cultures, wilderness adventures, volunteering, personal growth and learning new ways to live on the planet. It is typically defined as travel to destinations where the flora, fauna, and cultural heritage are the primary attractions. Responsible ecotourism includes Programmes that minimize the adverse effects of traditional tourism on the natural environment, and enhance the cultural integrity of local people. Therefore, in addition to evaluating environmental and cultural factors, initiatives by hospitality providers to promote recycling, energy efficiency, water re-use, and the creation of economic opportunities for local communities are an integral part of ecotourism.

Many global environmental organizations and aid agencies favour ecotourism as a vehicle to sustainable development.

Ideally, true ecotourism should satisfy several criteria, such as

- Conservation (and justification for conservation) of biological diversity and cultural diversity, through ecosystems protection
- Promotion of sustainable use of biodiversity, by providing jobs to local populations
- Sharing of socio-economic benefits with local communities and indigenous people by having their informed consent and participation in the management of ecotourism enterprises.
- Increase of environmental and cultural knowledge

- Minimisation of tourism's own environmental impact
- Affordability and lack of waste in the form of luxury
- Local culture, flora and fauna being the main attractions

For many countries, ecotourism is not so much seen as a marginal activity intended to finance protection of the environment than as a major sector of national economy and as a means of attracting tourists. For example, in countries such as Costa Rica, Ecuador, Nepal, Kenya, Madagascar and Antarctica, ecotourism represents a significant portion of the gross domestic product (or in Antarctica's case, economic activity).

The concept of ecotourism is widely misunderstood and, in practice, is often simply used as a marketing tool to promote tourism that is related to nature. Critics claim that ecotourism as practiced and abused often consists of placing a hotel in a splendid landscape, to the detriment of the ecosystem.

According to them, ecotourism must above all sensitize people with the beauty and the fragility of nature. They condemn some operators as "green-washing" their operations – that is, using the label of "ecotourism" and "green-friendly", while behaving in environmentally irresponsible ways.

Although academics argue about who can be classified as an ecotourist, and there is precious little statistical data, some estimate that more than five million ecotourists – the majority of the worldwide population – come from the United States, with other ecotourists coming from Europe, Canada and Australia.

Currently there are various moves to create national and international ecotourism certification Programmes, although the process is causing controversy. One example of ecoturism certificates has been put into place at Costa Rica, though the Programmes has been dismissed as green-washing by others.

One criticism against ecotourism is that the air travel to often remote places is not included in the "environmental impact calculation". A journey to a place 10,000 kilometers away and home consumes about 700 litres of fuel per person. Another problem is that some of the destinations visited by ecotourists are extremely sensitive to environmental impact from human use (e.g. Antarctica, Amazonian Rain Forests, bird breeding colonies) and can be damaged even by careful travellers. A new form of tourism is called Clean Tourism.

Ecological Mass Tourism

When people think about the word 'Ecological Mass Tourism' they normally link it with negative thoughts of mass tourism that is associated with environmental degradation. The truth is we believe that Ecological Mass Tourism is beneficial for everyone, but in essence we must first understand what Ecological Mass Tourism actually encompasses: Mass Tourism: "refers to the steady stream of large numbers of tourists to holiday destinations." Ecotourism "nature based tourism involving the education and interpretation of the natural environment and is managed to be ecologically sustainable. This definition also recognises that 'natural environment' includes cultural components and that 'ecologically sustainable' involves an appropriate return to the local community and long term conservation of the resource" Ecotourists: are tourists who participate in different sorts of nature based tourism.

Furthermore "most ecotourists are often found to be residents of the developed world with above average incomes and educations." By integrating all 3 words into 1 we have constructed our definition of Ecological Mass Tourism or (EMT) for short. Ecological Mass Tourism or (EMT): are large numbers of educated tourists and ecotourists participating within the realms of diversified forms of managed ecotourism. EMT also attracts tourists who not only participate in ecotourism, but also recognise its cultural components and its involvement with giving a fitting return to the local community and long term conservation of the resource.

In properly defining EMT we believe that it is beneficial to all parties involved, and more importantly it can also be perceived to be sustainable. In addition to this EMT also has the ability to be managed properly and has definite infrastructure, cultural and social benefits linked Ecological Mass Tourism does not go against the principle of mass tourism on the basis that it contains financial, cultural and social benefits associated with its concept.

Heritage tourism

Cultural heritage tourism is a branch of tourism oriented towards the cultural heritage.

Culture has always been a major object of travel, as the development of the Grand Tour from the 16th century onwards attests. In the 20th century, some people have claimed, culture ceased to be the objective of tourism: tourism is now culture. Cultural attractions play an important role in tourism at all levels, from the global highlights of world culture to attractions that underpin local identities.

According to the Weiler and Hall, culture, heritage and the arts have long contributed to appeal of tourist destination. However, in recent years 'culture' has been rediscovered as an important marketing tool to attract those travellers with special interests in heritage and arts. According to the Hollinshead, cultural heritage tourism defines as cultural heritage tourism is the fastest growing segment of the tourism industry because there is a trend toward an increase specialization among tourist. This trend is evident in the rise in the volume of tourists who seek adventure, culture, history, archaeology and interaction with local people.

Cultural heritage tourism is important for various reasons; it has a positive economic and social impact, it establishes and reinforces identity, it helps preserve the cultural heritage, with culture as an instrument it facilitates harmony and understanding among people, it supports culture and helps renew tourism.

Cultural heritage tourism has a number of objectives that must be met within the context of sustainable development such as; the conservation of cultural resources, accurate interpretation of resources, authentic visitors experience, and the stimulation of the earned revenues of cultural resources. We can see therefore, that cultural heritage tourism is not only concerned with identification, management and protection of the heritage values but it must also be involved in understanding the impact of tourism on communities and regions, achieving economic and social benefits, providing financial resources for protection, as well as marketing and promotion.

Heritage tourism involves visiting historical or industrial sites that may include old canals, railways, battlegrounds, etc. The overall purpose is to gain an appreciation of the past. It also refers to the marketing of a location to members of a diaspora who have distant family roots there. Heritage tourism is distinct from visiting a family member in a faraway place because the connection to the original homeland is removed; a recent Irish immigrant to the US, for example, may return home to see relatives but would probably not be considered a heritage tourist. On the other hand, an Irish-American whose family emigrated in the 19th century, also going to Ireland but rather to see the country generally, would be partaking in heritage tourism.

This is particularly relevant to European areas where large numbers of people emigrated to North America in the 19th century and early 20th century. People from Quebec have been moving back and forth to France for centuries in fairly significant numbers, as have their counterparts with ties to the British Isles and other countries for more recent immigrants. Other examples include Black/African Americans who visit Africa and Hispanics who visit Spain.The purpose can be education, fun, marriage, employment, etc. Permanent emigration tied to heritage tourism is less common but increasing. Decolonization and immigration form the major background of much contemporary heritage tourism. Falling travel costs have also made heritage tourism possible for more people.

Another possible form involves religious travel or pilgrimages. Many Catholics from around the world come to the Vatican and other sites such as Lourdes or Fatima. Large numbers of Jews have both visited Israel and emigrated there. Many have also gone to Holocaust sites and memorials. Islam commands its followers to take the hajj to Mecca, thus differentiating it somewhat from tourism in the usual sense, though the trip can also be a culturally important event for the pilgrim.

Heritage Tourism can also be attributed to historical events that have been dramatised to make them more entertaining. For example a historical tour of a town or city using a theme such as ghosts or vikings.

Medical tourism

Medical tourism is the act of traveling to other countries to obtain medical, dental, and surgical care. The term was initially coined by travel agencies and the media as a catchall phrase to describe a rapidly growing industry where people travel to other countries to obtain medical care while at the same time touring, vacationing and enjoying the attractions of the countries which they are visiting.

A combination of many factors has led to the recent increase in popularity of medical tourism: the high cost of healthcare in industrialized nations, the ease and affordability of international travel, and the improvement of technology and standards of care in many countries of the world.

A large draw to medical tourism is the convenience in comparison to that of other countries. Some countries that operate from a public health-care system are so taxed that it can take a considerable amount of time, sometimes even years, to get needed medical care. The time spent waiting for a procedure, such as a hip replacement, can be a year or more in Britain and Canada; however, in Bangkok or Bangalore, a patient could feasibly have an operation the day after their arrival.

Above all else, the real lure to medical tourism is saving money on costly procedures. According to research found in an article by UDaily: the cost of surgery in India, Thailand or South Africa can be one-tenth of what it is in the United States or Western Europe, and sometimes even less. A heart-valve replacement that would cost US$200,000 or more in the U.S., for example, goes for $10,000 in India—and that includes round-trip airfare and a brief vacation package.

Similarly, a metal-free dental bridge worth $5,500 in the U.S. costs $500 in India, a knee replacement in Thailand with six days of physical therapy costs about one-fifth of what it would in the States, and Lasik eye surgery worth $3,700 in the U.S. is available in many other countries for only $730. Cosmetic surgery savings are even greater: A full facelift that would cost $20,000 in the U.S. runs about $1,250 in South Africa."

Medical tourists are generally residents of the industrialized nations of the world. The countries to which they travel are typically less developed and have a lower cost of medical care. This is, in some cases, due to Favourable currency exchange ratios. Currently, many of the procedures accessed are considered "elective procedures," such as cosmetic surgery. Because elective procedures are rarely covered through health insurance plans, there may be greater incentive to find such care at lower costs.

The list of countries currently promoting medical tourism include:Bolivia, Brazil, Cuba, Costa Rica, Hungary, India, Israel, Jordan, Lithuania, Malaysia, The Philippines, and Thailand with the Joint Commission International accredited Bumrungrad Hospital. Belgium, Poland and Singapore are also breaking into the business. South Africa is taking the term "medical tourism" very literally by promoting their "medical safaris": Come to see African wildlife and get a facelift in the same trip. However, feelings towards medical tourism are not always positive. In places like the US, where most have insurance and access to quality health care, medical tourism is viewed as risky.

While the tourism component might be a big draw for Southeast Asia countries that focus on simple procedures, India is positioning itself the primary medical destination for the most complex medical procedures in the world. India's commitment to this is demonstrated with an ever growing number of hospitals that are attaining the US Joint Commission International accreditation.

Singapore has made international news for providing complex neurosurgical procedures. Currently Singapore boasts the largest number of US Joint Commission accredited hospitals in the region.

There are companies emerging to offer global healthcare options that will allow North American patients to take full advantage of dramatic reductions in air travel and access world class healthcare at a fraction of the cost. Companies that focus on 'Medical Value Travel' typically will have experienced nurse case managers to assist patients with pre- and post-travel medical issues. They will also help provide resources for follow-up care upon the patient's return. While these services will initially be of interest to the self-insured patient, several studies indicate that the rapid growth of Health Savings Accounts will also drive interest to healthcare in other countries.

Pop-culture tourism

Pop-culture tourism is the act of traveling to locations featured in literature, film, music, or any other form of popular entertainment. Popular destinations have included the Iowa cornfields featured in Field of Dreams, New Zealand after The Lord of the Rings was filmed there, and The Louvre in which the book and movie The Da Vinci Code takes place. Prince Edward Island, in which the Canadian novel Anne of Green Gables takes place, is a popular attraction for tourists, notably from Japan.

Pop-culture tourism is in some respects akin to pilgrimage, with its modern equivalents of places of pilgrimage, such as Elvis Presley's Graceland and the grave of Jim Morrison in Père Lachaise Cemetery.

Pilgrimage tourism

A pilgrimage is a term primarily used in religion and spirituality of a long journey or search of great moral significance. Sometimes, it is a journey to a sacred place or shrine of importance to a person's beliefs and faith. Members of every religion participate in pilgrimages. A person who makes such a journey is called a pilgrim.

Secular and civic pilgrimages are also practiced, without regard for religion but rather of importance to a particular society. For example, many people throughout the world travel to the City of Washington in the United States for a pilgrimage to see the Declaration of Independence and the Constitution of the United States. British people often make pilgrimages to London for public appearances of the monarch of the United Kingdom.

Pop culture has also sought to redefine pilgrimages, defining a demoscene party as a pilgrimage.

DEPENDENCE ON TOURISM

Permitting tourism to become the subsistence industry is not desirable for a number of reasons. First, tourism is by its very nature subject to considerable seasonality. While seasonal fluctuations in demand can sometimes be reduced, they cannot be eliminated. Thus, when tourism is the primary industry in an area, the offseason periods inevitably result in serious unemployment problems. Such areas find that the seasonal character of tourism leaves severe economic and social effects on the host region.

Another very important reason relates to the source of demand for tourism. The demand for tourism depends largely on the income and the tastes of tourists, both of which are beyond the control of the host region. When the American economy goes through a slump, demand for travel to a foreign destination by Americans will fall off. A destination area can do precious little, in this case, to increase the level of demand. If the tastes of the people in the tourist-generating area change—that is, they decide to travel to a new destination—tourism in the old area will decline, causing economic and social problems.

Again, the destination can do little or nothing to avoid this. In fact, as Plog3 points out, there is reason to believe that such a decline in an area's popularity may be largely inevitable. Quite clearly, then, tourism should not be allowed to grow to an extent that the destination area becomes totally dependent on it.

In other words, total dependence on a single industrial sector is undesirable. If it cannot be avoided, then dependence on domestic agriculture is in many ways preferable to dependence on tourism. The country has presumably adapted itself economically and socially to dependence on agriculture over several centuries. The demand for agricultural output is also unlikely to suffer from a secular decline, because people must eat. Also, it is the residents, not foreigners as in tourism, who directly benefit from agricultural production.

Investment Priorities

Sometimes, governments of developing countries take an overly optimistic view of tourism. They undertake aggressive investment Programmes to develop tourism, assigning it top priority in their development plans. In extreme cases, such an approach can lead to the neglect of more fundamental investment needs of the country. For example, funds can be channeled into tourism development at the cost of education, health, and other social services—aspects of the social well-being of the population that should be of primary concern for a developing country.

Not only is undue glamorization of tourism unwise because it usurps this position, but such a strategy only speeds up the process of dependence on tourism, which, as discussed earlier, is itself undesirable. Moreover, investment in tourism at the cost of health and education Programmes also slows down the rate at which the local population is assimilated into the modern market economy of the country. Under certain circumstances, it may actually retard development rather than enhance it.

The conclusion is that although tourism has tremendous potential as a tool in economic development, it is no panacea. Governments should attempt to optimize (not maximize) the benefits that tourism provides, being ever mindful of the costs that it can impose. It should be noted also that the probability and the intensity of the economic costs of tourism are greater for developing nations (or regions) than for wealthy ones. Wealthy nations, by definition, possess robust economies that can more easily absorb the cost of tourism. Typically, such economies are well diversified, and government investment Programme are not so central to development efforts.

The social benefits and costs of tourism should be viewed similarly. While the host community seeks to maximize the benefits, it must weigh these against the social costs. The social costs are likewise higher in both probability and magnitude when tourism is being considered for development in an area that still possesses a traditional social structure.

Quantity Demanded and Price Elasticity

For some products, even a large change in price over a certain range of the demand curve results in only a small change in quantity demanded. In this case, demand is not very responsive to price. For other products, or for the same product over a different range of prices, a relatively small change in price elicits a much larger relative change in quantity demanded. Demand can be classified as inelastic or elastic on the basis of the relative responsiveness of quantity demanded to changes in price. Specifically, price elasticity of demand may be defined as the per centage change in demand resulting from a given per centage change in price. Most tourism products are price elastic. During 1992, when U.S. airlines began offering half fares, the number of air travellers increased to record-high levels.

Income Elasticity of Demand

As income rises, more travel is demanded at any given price. Thus, the relationship between income and demand is positive. The responsiveness of demand to changes in income is called income elasticity of demand. It is defined as the per centage As can be seen from the beginning of this chapter, tourism makes a major economic contribution to the world economy. Despite this economic significance, tourism managers have for some time been met with complaints such as "All the hype about tourism's contribution to economic growth and job creation is a gross exaggeration."

As well, members of the industry itself want to be sure that the economic impact figures are indeed accurate so that they can better plan their investments and improve their productivity and performance. In an attempt to ensure the accuracy and reliability of the measures of tourism's economic impact, the World Tourism Organization (WTO) in collaboration with the World Travel and Tourism Council (WTTC), and with the support of the Canadian Tourism Commission (CTC), have undertaken to develop a tourism accounting system that is not only rigorous, but consistent with the national accounts of every country. This system has been named Tourism Satellite Account.

TOURISM SATELLITE ACCOUNT

A Tourism Satellite Account (TSA) is a system developed by the United Nations to measure the size of economic sectors that are not defined as industries in national accounts. Tourism, for example, is an amalgam of industries such as transportation, accommodation, food and beverage services, recreation, and entertainment and travel agencies.

Tourism is a unique phenomenon as it is defined by the consumption of the visitor. Visitors buy goods and services associated with both tourism and nontourism alike. The key from a measurement standpoint is to associate their purchases to the total supply of these goods and services within a country.

The TSA is a new statistical instrument designed to measure these goods and services according to international standards of concepts, classifications, and definitions that will allow for valid comparisons with other industries and eventually from country to country and between groups of countries. Such measures will also be comparable with other internationally recognized economic statistics.

In addition, a TSA possesses the following characteristics. It:

- Provides credible data on the impact of tourism and the associated employment
- Is a standard framework for organizing statistical data on tourism
- Is a new international standard endorsed by the U.N. Statistical Commission
- Is a powerful instrument for designing economic policies related to tourism development
- Provides data on tourism's impact on a nation's balance of payments
- Provides information on tourism human resource characteristics

While it may be obvious, it is useful to stress why a TSA is needed. In brief, there is an acute shortage of information on the increasing role of tourism in national economies worldwide, hence the need for reliable data relative to the importance and magnitude of tourism, using the same concepts, definitions, and measurement approaches as other industries. With the TSA, governments, entrepreneurs, and citizens will be better equipped for designing public policies and business strategies for tourism and for evaluating their effectiveness and efficiency.

Development of a TSA framework has been fueled by the recognition that its implementation will serve to increase and improve knowledge of tourism's importance relative to overall economic activity in a given country. It will also provide an instrument for designing more efficient policies relating to tourism and its employment aspects; and it will create awareness among the various players directly and indirectly involved with tourism of the economic importance of this activity, and by extension its role in all the industries involved in the production of goods and services demanded by visitors.

The Nature of a TSA

A TSA is characterized by the manner in which it seeks to balance measures of tourism demand versus supply. Tourism measurements, in order to be credible and comparable with other industries in a country's economy, must follow concepts and definitions consistent with internationally accepted macroeconomic guidelines, such as the System of National Accounts.

The fundamental structure of the TSA therefore relies on the balance existing within an economy between, on one hand, the demand for goods and services generated by visitors and by other consumers and, on the other hand, the overall supply of these goods and services. The idea is to analyze in detail all aspects of demand for goods and services that are associated with tourism within the economy, and to measure the relationship with the supply of such goods and services within the same economy. More specifically, a TSA measures:

- Tourism's contribution to gross domestic product (GDP)
- Tourism's ranking compared to other economic sectors
- The number of jobs created by tourism in an economy
- The amount of tourism investment
- Tax revenues generated by tourism industries
- Tourism consumption
- Tourism's impact on a nation's balance of payments
- Characteristics of tourism human resources

Because of its comprehensive nature, a TSA provides decision makers with a valuable tool for planning and policy making. In particular, it provides them with reliable data of tourism's impact on the economy and employment. As well, it permits the measurement of both domestic and nonresident tourism—and the employment associated with each. A TSA, however, can do much more. Following are some examples.

A TSA can provide information on how much tourism is worth to the national economy, and how it compares to other industries and other countries. By demonstrating and using the size of tourism, tourism officials and private-sector businesses will have more influence on policy makers at all levels of government. As well, it can make clear which industries benefit from tourism and by how much— in particular, industries not traditionally associated with tourism. For instance, business enterprises can identify the role tourism plays in their success and develop business strategies accordingly. A TSA is able to provide information regarding how much tax revenue is generated by tourism. This information is useful in convincing municipal, provincial, or federal levels of government to invest further in tourism.

In addition, it provides data on visitor demand and how this demand is met by domestic supply. A TSA enables the establishment of a tourism economic impact model, which can be used to estimate the effect on the economy and on employment of various tourism expenditure shocks. Such an impact model provides a better understanding of tourism employment and where each industry ranks compared to other tourism industries.

It should be emphasized that the ongoing development of TSAs as national promotion tools has been a process dating back to at least 1993. The most recent focus of this development was a major international TSA conference held in Vancouver, Canada, in 2001. This and other conferences have brought together the following organizations: World Tourism Organization (WTO), World Travel and Tourism Council (WTTC), Organization for Economic Cooperation and Development (OECD), United Nations (UN), Eurostat, and a number of government statistical agencies, national tourism administrators, and central banks.

The above collaboration demonstrates the general principle that in order to develop a national TSA, it is essential to involve a number of key actors within a country. The most significant of these are:

- National statistical offices, national tourism administrations (NTAs), central banks, and associations of national tourism enterprises.
- Information-producing units such as tourism enterprises and establishments, and other public departments.
- Users of the tourism information that is generated, the NTAs themselves, the units responsible for preparing the national accounts and the balance of payments, and others.
- The participation and collaboration of tourism enterprises and, more specifically, their corresponding national associations.

Sources of Data Used in a TSA

Canada, as an Example

The data used in the calculation of a TSA in Canada come from a diverse number of surveys produced by Statistics Canada. The preparation of tourism demand estimates involve several surveys that record information on tourism consumption of Canadians traveling in and outside Canada and nonresidents traveling to Canada.

These include:

- Canadian Travel Survey
- International Travel Survey of Canadian Residents
- Canadian Resident Questionnaire for same-day automobile travel between the

United States and Canada

- United States Resident Questionnaire for same-day automobile travel between the United States and Canada

- Government Travel Survey of U.S. visitors to Canada
- Government Travel Survey of visitors to Canada

Much of the information for the supply-side estimates are drawn from the worksheets used in the making of the input-output tables by industry, commodity, and employment of the System of National Accounts. Data from reference publications, and relevant business surveys and administrative data, are used to obtain as much detail as possible on revenues generated from the sale of tourism commodities. In conclusion, a TSA recognizes that tourism is not an industry in the traditional sense—that is, identified in the System of National Accounts—because industries are classified according to the goods and services they produce (e.g., forestry), while tourism is a consumption-based concept that depends on the status of the customer. Furthermore, tourists buy many of the same products as other consumers, including items not normally associated with tourism—clothes, groceries— while Canadians at home buy tourism goods and services for nontourism reasons—restaurant meals, postcards, recreational services.

The TSA brings together these diverse aspects of tourism by providing a tourism dimension to the framework of the System of National Accounts. It makes it possible to separate and examine the demand and supply sides of tourism within an integrated system that describes the production and demand aspects of the whole economy. The recognition of these factors has led to the situation where more than ten countries have a TSA and more than thirty are in the process of developing a TSA. These include Austria, Canada, Chile, the Dominican Republic, France, Mexico, New Zealand, Norway, Singapore, Sweden, the United States, Spain, and Italy.

Domestic and international tourism are major economic strengths to many of the world's countries, states, cities, and rural areas. Thus, those who live there are affected by the economic results of tourist spending. This chapter explained why these resulting effects vary greatly and what brings about a large measure of benefits or possible detriments to a community. The main economic phenomena described are various multipliers, balance of payments, investments, tax consideration, employment, economic impact generators, travel expenditures, dependence on tourism, price and income elasticity as related to buying travel experiences, and optimization. The chapter also discussed a new method of measuring tourism economic impact, satellite accounting.

Many people do not understand or appreciate the economics of tourism. The following list summarizes the principal economic effects.

1. Expenditures by foreign visitors in one's country become exports (mainly of services). The economic effects are the same as those derived from exporting tangible goods. If there is a Favourable exchange rate (foreign currency buying appreciably more of one's own country's currency), the country that has the devalued currency will experience a higher demand for visitor services than before devaluation.
2. If citizens of one country spend money in foreign countries, these expenditures become imports for the tourists' originating country.
3. Sums of the values of national exports and imports are used when calculating a nation's balance of payments. A positive balance results when exports exceed imports, thus increasing a nation's gross national product (GNP).
4. Tourism developments typically require large investments of capital. Thus, local economies where the developments take place are stimulated by such investments.
5. Tourists pay various kinds of taxes directly and indirectly while visiting an area. Thus, tax revenues are increased for all levels of government.
6. Because tourists usually spend more per day at a destination than they do while at home, these extra expenditures may cause inflationary pressures and

rising prices for consumer goods in the destination area.

7. Tourism expenditures injected into the economy produce an income multiplier for local people. This is because of the diversity of expenditures made by those receiving tourist payments. Tourist receipts are used to buy a wide variety of goods and services over a year's time. The money turnover creates additional local income.
8. The amount of income multiplication, however, will depend on how much leakage takes place. Leakages are a combination of (1) imported goods and services purchased by tourism suppliers, and (2) savings made of tourist receipts not loaned to another spender within one year of receipt. Thus, the more tourist goods that are supplied locally, the higher will be the multiplier.
9. Income multiplication caused by tourist expenditures necessitates hiring more people. Thus, they also affect an employment multiplier.
10. As increased spending produces more financial transactions, they create a transactions multiplier. These are of particular interest to governments that have a sales or value-added tax on such transactions.
11. As a tourist area grows, more capital is invested in new facilities. This results in a capital multiplier.
12. It is an unwise policy for a society to place too much dependency on tourism as a subsistence industry.
13. Although tourism often has an excellent potential in economic development, it is not a panacea for economic ills. Its economic benefits should be optimized rather than maximized.
14. We believe that tourism products are mainly price elastic, meaning that as prices rise, the quantity demanded tends to drop.
15. In general, we believe that tourism is income elastic. This means that as family income rises, or a

particular market's income rises, and tourism prices do not rise proportionally, the demand for travel to that particular area will increase.

HOSPITALITY

Hospitality is the act or practice of being hospitable, that is, the reception and entertainment of guests, visitors, or strangers, with liberality and goodwill. Hospitality frequently refers to the hospitality industry jobs for hotels, restaurants, casinos, catering, resorts, clubs and any other service position that deals with tourists. It's important for people to know what you stand for. It's equally important that they know what you won't stand for. The twenty-first century began with a flurry of high-profile scandals involving managers in a wide variety of industries, ranging from high-tech firms to pharmaceutical manufacturers.

Many very successful business-people found themselves behind bars for their ethical transgressions. The topic of business ethics is receiving increasing coverage in all media, including newspapers, business periodicals, television, radio, and even the Internet, while the pressures on businesses to perform continue to increase. With continued technological advancement, political upheaval, increased global competition, changing demographics, and pressure from stockholders, maintaining one's ethical integrity will become both more difficult and more important.

In 1993 a large group of hospitality industry executives were asked, "What skills and abilities do students need to obtain to be successful in the hospitality industry?" The number one answer was "business ethics." There is little evidence to suggest the answer would be any different today. One thing is clear: Ethical behaviour is important, and all of you will be facing situations in which you will need to make difficult decisions that you will base on your ethical beliefs and value systems.

Environmentally Responsible Hotels

One component of ecotourism travelers can consider is environmentally responsible hotels. The concept of "green hotels"—hotels, motels, bed and breakfasts, lodges, and inns that use energy and other natural resources in environmentally responsible ways—is one that can be adopted not only by ecotourists but by anyone who travels, whether for business or pleasure. Hotels that adopt green practices help reduce the negative impact that hotel use has on the environment when they utilize renewable resources whenever possible, make efficient use of nonrenewable resources, and ensure that any byproducts that result from their operations are reused or recycled.

Examples of green practices some hotels have adopted include rerouting waste water to irrigate their golf courses and salvaging the sludge to use as fertilizer; reducing laundry water temperatures from 90 °C to 60 °C, replacing incandescent lights with compact fluorescent lamps, installing low-flow shower head and low-flow toilets, offering a sheet and towel reuse Programmes whereby guests have their linens exchanged every two to three days instead of daily, installing solar panels to heat water, implementing a hotel-wide recycling Programmes, and replacing individual soaps and lotions with wall dispensers. Adoption of green practices typically helps hotels realize considerable savings that can range from several thousand to hundreds of thousands of dollars per year.

Although the number of hotels adopting green practices is growing, many have not yet embraced the concept. All travelers can support green hotels, encourage nongreen hotels to adopt environmentally responsible practices, or engage in such practices themselves whenever they are hotel guests. Tourism event organizers can also distinguish themselves by explaining the criteria of where they stage events. Sadly, most ecotourism events have been held at hotels which have not distinguished themselves with green building, eco-efficient technology or community-friendly relations.

Hospitality as a sociological phenomenon

As hospitality is a sociological phenomenon, and because its norms differ in each society, there might be:

- Christian view of hospitality,

Paul of Taurus urged hospitality on Christians, telling them that some people have thus entertained angels. Offering hospitality to pilgrims was a major duty of a monastery.

- Middle Eastern (Arab) rules of hospitality,
- Greek hospitality (Xenia is Greek for hospitality, but not necessarily norms that non-ancient Greeks follow),

A famous Greek legend Baucis and Philemon, recounts how they, though poor, were the only people of their town to offer hospitality to Zeus and Hermes, and so were blessed while the rest were transformed into fishes. Smoke weed everyday. Further, Zeus (as the manifestation Xenios) was the patron of hospitality and guests, ready to avenge any wrong done to a stranger

- And any other hospitality norms that differ in various world cultures,
- And very contemporary, in virtual communities like Wikipedia.

Contemporary Usage

Contemporary usage seems rather different from historical uses that lend it personal connotations. Today's hospitality conjures images of throwing good parties, gracious hosts entertaining, etiquette, Martha Stewart or even talk shows, or, the hospitality services industry as it relates to the entertainment and tourism business. On the other hand, hospitality used to be, and may still be, a serious personal duty or responsibility.

Hospitality is a prosaic word, even trivial, that everyone can relate to, perhaps even more concretely so outside of North American culture. It seems perhaps even a candidate for having something like a universal meaning or agreement, if not positive value.

In the western context, with its dynamic tension between Athens and Jerusalem, two phases can be distinguished with a very progressive transition: a hospitality based on an individually felt sense of duty, and one based on "official" institutions for organized but anonymous social services: special places for particular types of "strangers" such as the poor, orphan, ill, alien, criminal, etc. Perhaps this progressive institutionalization can be aligned to the transition between Middle Ages and Renaissance (Ivan Illich, The Rivers North of the Future).

Other Conceptions of Hospitality

In Middle Eastern Culture, it was considered a cultural norm to take care of the strangers and aliens living among you. These norms are reflected in many Biblical commands and examples, for instance: Perhaps the most extreme example is provided in Genesis. Lot provides hospitality to a group of angels (who he thinks are only men); when a mob tries to rape them, Lot goes so far as to offer his own daughters as a substitute, saying "Don't do anything to these men, for they have come under the protection of my roof.".

The obligations of both guests and hosts are stern. The bond is formed by eating salt under the roof, and is so strict that an Arab story tells of a thief who tasted something to see if it was sugar, and on realizing it was salt, put back all that he had taken and left.

Cultural Value or Norm

Hospitality as a cultural norm or value is established sociological phenomenon that people study and write papers about.

STAR

Stars are often used as symbols for classification purposes. In particular, a set of one to five stars is employed to categorize hotels. In some countries, there is an official body with standard criteria for classifying hotels, but in many others there is none. There have been attempts at unifying the classification system so that it becomes an internationally recognized and reliable standard but large differences exist in the quality of the accommodation and the food within one category of hotel, sometimes even in the same country.

A "five star Hotel"

However, regardless of what public or private agency performs the classification, the term five star hotel is always associated with the ultimate luxury (and, by implication, expense). The lack of standardisation has allowed marketing-driven inflation, with some hotels claiming six stars; at one point the Burj al-Arab marketed itself as "the world's first seven-star hotel". Well-established prestige hotels are usually content to claim the traditional five.

Rating by stars

The five categories can be described (loosely) as follows:

- *(one star)—Low budget hotel; inexpensive; may not have maid service or room service.
- **(two stars)—Budget hotel; slightly more expensive; usually has maid service daily.
- ***(three stars)—Middle class hotel; moderately priced; has daily maid service, room service, and may have dry-cleaning, Internet access, and a swimming pool.
- ****(four stars)—First class hotel; expensive (by middle-class standards); has all of the previously mentioned services; has many "luxury" services (for example: massages or a health spa).
- *****(five stars)—Luxury hotel; most expensive hotels/resorts in the world; numerous extras to enhance the quality of the client's stay (for example: some have private golf courses and even a small private airport).

The AAA and their affiliated bodies use diamonds instead of stars to express hotel and restaurant ratings levels.

Traditional systems rest heavily on the facilities provided, which is often disadvantageous to smaller hotels whose quality of accommodation could fall into one class but the lack of an item such as an elevator would prevent it from reaching a higher categorization.

PRESENT TRENDS

Hotel rooms that can access everything from your favourite food to your musical preferences— while running on technology that's clever enough to repair itself—might sound like a page torn right out of a pulp sci-fi novel. Hotels are doing it today, and many more are on the verge of implementing these innovative technologies. If you're a guest at one of these forward-looking properties, get ready for a completely different kind of experience—one in which technology anticipates your every need and gives it to you without you ever having to ask.

And it isn't just hotels that are leveraging these new tools to their advantage; so are theme parks, restaurants, and casinos. The overall effects of these new tools on the hospitality business promises to be far-reaching. From the perspective of a hotel, casino, or restaurant, these important advances have the potential to create more efficient and profitable businesses, and make your business more appealing to guests.

No more Questions at Check-in

Remember all those queries when you pick up your room key, such as, What kind of newspaper do you prefer? Would you like a poolside or oceanside room? Asking such questions eats up hotel employees' valuable time and, after a while, guests get tired of answering them. New customer relationship management (CRM) tools allow a hotel to gather guest preference information from various systems at property level and distribute them throughout the company. So your hotel knows what you like, right away.

For example, one hotel chain asks guests signing up for its loyalty Programmes to fill out a preferences questionnaire that is entered into its CRM system at the property level. The information can be made available for any hotel in the chain that the guest checks in to, while the CRM system itself is still maintained locally, at the property level. (This is made possible by merging the property level CRM data with the larger CRM system held at the headquarters-level for the chain.)

When the day of arrival comes, the preference data is pushed to the property and generates an activity list to prepare the guest's room. At the same time, historical transaction data about the guest is made available, which can help predict the behaviors and likely service consumption the guest will have. "If the guest typically orders room service shortly after checking in to their room, then you can proactively suggest—or offer—the in-room dining specials for that day, even take their order at the front desk to shorten the wait for their dinner" says Bill Frizzell, the industry technology strategist for the Microsoft Worldwide Hospitality Team.

"This has been a long sought-after capability for the industry," he adds. "Defining a single view of the guest, without duplicate stores of information, is the key to understanding their habits, trends, and behaviors." TVs that deliver music, movies—and much more. Today's leading-edge hotels have in-room systems that do far more than allow guests to watch their Favourite first-run movie. They can also control in-room music, provide gaming options, display your bill—even control the thermostat and lights.

The Hotel 1000 in Seattle, Wash., for instance, has centered the room around the availability of Favourite media and services on a number of widescreen plasma monitors located throughout its rooms and suites. You can control content, multi-area volume of the sound system, and interact with your profile through these devices. And because it's a multi-use property—part residence, part hotel—the same entertainment offerings are available for their property owners. That lessens the typical multi-use management burden of maintaining multiple service offerings per type of area on the property.

Find Yourself (and pay for lunch)

People in the hospitality industry have found a variety of uses for new radio frequency identification (RFID) technology—from helping guests find each other at a ski resort to allowing them to pay for a meal. That's because, increasingly, this technology is gaining traction with hotels and resorts in the form of cashless payment systems that can be used on-property and, more and more often, off-property as well.

For example, at Wild Rivers, a water theme park in Irvine, Calif., RFID locator bracelets can be preloaded and used to pay for food and beverages (which is especially useful when everyone's wearing a bathing suit). The RFID systems, developed by Guest Technologies, have yielded an almost immediate return on investment. After the system was introduced at Wild Rivers, guest spending quadrupled, with the average family of four spending twice their normal amount on meals.

Another key capability of this offering is location-based services, where groups of individuals can be instantly found at the property, simultaneously allowing for more freedom and security in these safety-conscious times. "Imagine taking a group of seven 12 year-olds to a water park for a birthday party," says Frizzell. "You can go to any information kiosk in the park and instantly find where all of the kids you are responsible for are, and what activities and payments they have made, using their RFID bracelet. All of this is enabled through the implementation RFID and location-based services, using Microsoft technologies and Microsoft MapPoint Location Server."

Back-office systems

Hotel guests might not have noticed this (and if it was done right, they shouldn't have), but applications that handled property management, food and beverage, and sales and catering functions often couldn't communicate with one another easily. Now they can. A large, multi-property hotel chain in Las Vegas is currently integrating systems and platforms that were in application silos—meaning that they were running as stand-alone applications, not intended to share their information with other applications—to better integrate each other's data.

Through this interchange of data, they are better able to implement efficient business processes that rely on the delivery of data between these systems that were previously separated. For example, if you dine on-property the morning you intend to check out, you can get a final bill that is inclusive of your full folio of charges—even the breakfast you had five minutes ago. That's because there's no more "batching" of data to be sent to the property management system for posting to your guest folio. Instead, the interchange of your transaction to your folio is now happening at the time you make it.

"To achieve this level of integration between property-level systems, hospitality organizations had to create specific interfaces between them," says Frizzell. "But these interfaces are not typically designed with flexibility and scaling of processes in mind, which had the unfortunate side effect of making the interfaces very brittle in use." Think of it this way: If you have 10 on-property systems that all needed to share the same base set of guest transaction data, it would result in 90 separate interfaces being built to accommodate the integration. Considering the inflexible nature of these point-in-time interfaces, keeping them running and orchestrated to perform the simple task of sharing data can easily become a huge financial and management burden.

But by implementing an "Information Hub" at the property level, all systems and applications that need to share data report that data in an open format, based on industry standards, to the hub. The hub is then responsible for routing the information to the various systems and orchestrating the intended business processes. In effect, the hub streamlines the exchange of data, reducing the number of integration interfaces from 90 to 10.

Self-healing hotel Technology

A hotel's information technology (IT) systems are typically managed in a reactive way, which is to say that when something breaks down an IT person is called upon to fix it. But bringing systems offline to repair them can affect the whole operation—think of the long check-in lines when the credit-card systems aren't working. The solution? A dynamic platform that constantly monitors a hotel's systems for problems and fixes them before they affect the whole property.

A large multi-concept fine dining chain has added a system to keep an eye on its restaurant-level systems and enterprise servers. This system controls everything from the deployment of operating systems to the handheld devices the company's employees use. System problems and failures are reported to the IT help desk as they occur, minimizing the time it takes to get mission-critical systems back online.

Individual Ethics

Ethics is defined as "the system or code of morals of a particular person, religion, group, or profession." As such, ethical beliefs may vary from person to person. There are three basic individual approaches to ethics that are reflected in the behaviour of people. First is the moral rights approach, which judges the consistency of decisions and behaviors with the maintenance of certain fundamental personal and group liberties and privileges such as life, freedom, health, privacy, and property.

Second is the justice approach, which judges the consistency of decisions and behaviors with the maintenance of equity, fairness, and impartiality in the distribution of costs and benefits among individuals. Third is the utilitarian approach, which judges the effects of decisions and behaviors on providing the greatest good for the greatest number of people.

Business Ethics

Business ethics in Western society emerged with the growth in capitalism in sixteenth-century Europe. Up to that time it was largely believed that it was immoral to produce goods for profit. With the Protestant Reformation came the belief that a diligent worker pleased God, and that the wealth that was acquired from business activities was a sign that God was pleased. Good businesspeople could be good human beings by satisfying the needs of customers and providing employment for workers.

Today there is a common belief among many organizations that good ethics is good business. This idea has evolved into the concept of social responsibility, and some companies, such as HVS and the Ecotel concept, have stressed the importance of energy conservation, recycling, and minimal disturbance of ecological systems in property development. It is too soon to tell if there is a positive relationship between social responsibility and profits, but there are clearly increasing numbers of companies who want to be known as being socially responsible. It is important to note that operating within the legal system may not be an adequate basis for evaluating the ethics of a business decision.

Chapter 2

Tourism and Hospitality in India

Tourists come to India for its wealth of sights, cultural exuberance, diversity of terrain and in search of that special something, an extra punch that only India promises and delivers. India's tourism industry is thriving due to an increase in foreign tourists arrivals and greater than before travel by Indians to domestic and abroad destinations. The visitors are pouring in from all over the world: Europe, Africa, Southeast Asia and Australia. At the same time, the number of Indians traveling has also increased.

Some tourists come from Middle East countries to witness the drenching monsoon rains in India, a phenomenon never seen in desert climates. Domestic tourists are also fueling the industry's revival. Many of them escape from the summer heat on the plains to resorts in the Himalayan Mountains. One of the major beneficiaries this year is Kashmir, where a cease-fire between India and Pakistan has reduced violence, if not completely, at least enough to help revive the state's sagging tourism industry. India is a heaven of tourism delights, a civilization to tour through.

Teeming with over a billion people who voice over a million concerns in fifteen hundred different languages, India is where people live with variety, thrive on diversity and are too familiar with largeness to let it boggle them. Mud huts and mansions face off across city streets. Lurid luxury and limp living are inhabitants of the same lane. From the smoky mangroves of the Sunderbans to the steaming Thar Desert, sizzling cities like Mumbai and Delhi to the scintillating villages of Khajuraho and Hampi, from the heights of the Himalayas to the deep blue waters around the Andamans, India is a travel heaven - a tour package that frustrates and delights, as demanding as it is rewarding. The year 2004-05 saw tourism emerging as one of the major sectors for growth of Indian economy, the foreign exchange earnings increased from Rs. 16,429 crore to 21,828 crore up to December, 2005.

Similarly in the last year, tourism industry registered a growth rate of 17.3 per cent in foreign tourist arrivals, which has been the highest in last 10 years. Foreign exchange earnings grew at an even higher rate 30.2 per cent. Among the most favoured tourist destinations in India, Kerala for its scenic beauty, Agra for Taj Mahal, Khujraho for its sculptures and temples, Goa for its beaches and some pilgrimages are the most important. Interesting feature of this growth is that it has come even as global tourism has dropped, due to the September 11 terrorist attacks in the United States, the outbreak of Severe Acute Respiratory Syndrome in East Asia, and the Iraq war.

Even the disastrous tsunami didn't affect India's tourism industry, as tourist arrivals in India rose 23.5 per cent in Dec 2004 and tourist arrivals crossed 3 million mark for the first time in 2004. The disaster was expected to have a negative impact on India's tourism in terms of large-scale cancellations of tourists to India but nothing of that sort was seen. There could be several reasons for the buoyancy in the Indian tourism industry.

First, the upward trend observed in the growth rate of Indian economy has raised middle class incomes, prompting more people to spend money on vacations abroad or at home. Also, India is booming in the information technology industry and has become the IT Centre. Aggressive advertising campaign "Incredible India" by the government has also had contribution in changing India's image from that of a land of snake charmers, and sparking new interest among overseas travellers.

Tourism and Indian Economy

Tourism contribution to the Indian economy is major. Tourism is among India's important export industries. Even with comparatively low levels of international tourist traffic, tourism has already emerged as an important segment of the Indian economy. Tourism also contributed to the economy indirectly through its linkages with other sectors like horticulture, agriculture, poultry, handicrafts and construction.

Foreign exchange earnings from tourism during 2003-04 were US $ 3,533 million (Rs. 16,429 crore). Besides being an important foreign exchange earner, tourism industry also provides employment to millions of people in India both directly and indirectly (through its linkage with other sectors of the economy.) It is estimated that total direct employment in the tourism sector is around 20 million.

POTENTIAL OF INDIAN TOURISM

India has significant potential for becoming a major global tourist destination. The country witnessed foreign tourist arrivals of 2.75 million in 2001. The industry is waking up to the potential of domestic tourism as well, with an estimated 4.7 billion domestic trips in 2001. Tourism spending within India in 2001 was US$ 22 billion. There is considerable government presence in the travel and tourism industry.

Each state has a tourism corporation, which typically runs a chain of hotels /motels and operates package tours, while the central government runs the India Tourism Development Corporation. Divestment of these state-run tourism corporations have either already taken place or are in process. Incoming foreign tourist arrivals have shown a 6 per cent compounded annual growth rate over the last 10 years. The government has realised the potential and has advanced several incentives to promote infrastructure growth in the tourism sector.

During 2004, India for the first time breached the three million mark and the number of tourists who came to this country stood at 3.37 million reflecting an increase of 23.5 per cent over 2003. Foreign exchange earnings did better with Rs 21,828 crore, up by 32.9 per cent and this momentum has continued during the first half of 2005. Till May end, arrivals have increased to 1.52 million, a growth of 23.5 per cent over the corresponding period in 2004 and foreign exchange earnings touched Rs 10,571 crore, an increase of 26.7 per cent. The domestic tourism has continued to be upbeat.

During 2004, domestic visits, according to provisional figures crossed the 360 million mark compared to the 2003 record of 309 million. More Indians are travelling abroad also, much more than inbound travellers. During 2003, the number of Indians going abroad was 5.3 million but this grew to 6.2 million in 2004 according to provisional estimates showing a growth of 15.2 per cent. For instance, the number of Indian visitors to Malaysia in April 2004 was 10,480; this went up by 47.5 per cent in the corresponding period in 2005 to 15,464.

People increasingly have been looking at the Net to plan their leisure travel for both international and domestic sectors. This trend is on the rise with growing Internet penetration (about 5 million) in the country. In India, most of the booking is still done through travel agents though the airlines are now ready with e-ticketing platforms. The travel trade in India has understood the importance of the Net and now has comprehensive information on fares, packages and other travel related matter on their Web sites.

In the field of tourism another trend is that more families are travelling together. This is because family get-togethers are getting rarer as family members find it difficult to take time off to visit parents and siblings. Family groups consisting of 30 and more, along with grandparents, from places such as Hyderabad, Bangalore and even interior Tamil Nadu have opted to travel overseas. Short stays are another new travel trend. Executives employed in high pressure jobs, which do not allow them to take long vacations, are more likely to take short holidays, closer to their place of work. Sri Lanka, Singapore, Maldives are some such getaways.

Sri Lanka Tourist Board holds the opinion that India topped the list of arrivals into Sri Lanka in April 2005 at 9,024 compared to the 5,784 in April 2004. The dynamics of the Indian travel scene has changed with the coming of the low-cost airlines. The low fares have changed the way people look at air travel. Air travel is no longer considered a luxury but a necessity. The advent of low-cost carriers has created a new boom in the Indian travel scene offering more options for the Indian traveller, who now has access to better and cheaper air connectivity plus attractive package deals for new destinations. Leisure traffic to India is yet to pick up in a big way.

A Federation of Hotel and Restaurant Association survey shows that more than 50 per cent of the occupancy in hotels comes from corporate travellers. The average room rate (ARR) from corporate occupancy is higher than that of the leisure travellers. India ranks 50th in the global growth ranking by the World Travel and Tourism Council, below Malaysia which is ranked third and China which is ranked 11th. To fall in line with internationally benchmarked tourism models, India needs at least 90,000 more rooms (in the five star segment) and therefore an investment of Rs 80,000 crore. India also needs to increase inbound traffic from 3.3 million to at least 10 million in the next six to seven years.

Tourism Policy Initiatives

The Tourism Policy, released in May 2002 has outlined the following policy initiatives for the tourism sector:

1. This policy was built around the 7-S Mantra of Swaagat (welcome), Soochanaa (information), Suvidhaa (facilitation), Surakshaa (security), Sahyog (cooperation), Sanrachnaa (infrastructure) and Safaai (cleanliness).
2. The focus of this policy was on making tourism a catalyst in employment generation, wealth creation, development of remote and rural areas, environment preservation and social integration. Its aim was to spruce up economic growth and promote India's

strengths as a tourism destination that is both safe and at the same time exciting.

3. The policy proposed the inclusion of tourism in the concurrent list of the Constitution so as to enable both the central and state governments to participate in the development of the sector.
4. No approval was required for foreign equity of up to 51 per cent in tourism projects. Enhanced equity is considered on a case-to-case basis. NRI investment was allowed up to 100 per cent.
5. Approvals for Technology agreements in the hotel industry are available on an automatic basis, subject to the fulfilment of certain specified parameters.
6. Concession rates on customs duty of 25 per cent for goods that are required for initial setting up, or for substantial expansion of hotels.
7. 50 per cent of profits derived by hotels, travel agents and tour operators in foreign exchange were exempt from income tax. The remaining profits were also exempt if reinvested in a tourism related project.
8. Approved hotels were entitled to import essential goods relating to the hotel and tourism industry up to the value of 25 per cent of the foreign exchange earned by them in the preceding licensing year. This limit for approved travel agents/tour operators was 10 per cent. Hotels located in locations other than the four major metro cities were entitled to 30 per cent deduction from profit, for a ten-year period. The expenditure tax had been waived in respect of hotels located in the hills, rural areas, places of pilgrimage or specified place of tourist importance.

INVESTMENT IN INDIAN TOURISM

India requires considerable investment into infrastructure which could only be met with foreign direct investment. The shortage of rooms in Delhi is adversely affecting the flow of tourists to the capital as well as to other destinations. The accommodation constraints in Delhi will have serious implications on the arrangements for the 2010 Commonwealth Games. It is estimated there will be a requirement of about 40,000-50,000 rooms in the budget category for the tourists visiting Delhi and surrounding areas during the Games.

The issue of giving tax benefit, under section 80 IA of Income Tax Act by declaring them as infrastructure projects for three and four star hotels, which are constructed prior to 2010, has been taken up with ministry of finance. Tourism industry is approximately a $200-billion industry and India doesn't even touch eight per cent of this. We are looking to get a larger chunk of it.

The government of India was considering offering tax incentives for attracting attract investment into building convention centres and halls. Pointing out the country was facing severe shortage of hotel accommodation in the wake of its preparation for 2010 Commonwealth games, The government has outlined plans to facilitate land procurement by hoteliers in order increase number of budget hotels, bed and breakfasts (BandBs) and self-service apartments.

Steps to Promote Tourism

Recently, Indian government adopted a multi-pronged approach for promotion of tourism, which includes new mechanism for speedy implementation of tourism projects, development of integrated tourism circuits and rural destinations, special capacity building in the unorganized hospitality sector and new marketing strategy. A nation wide campaign, for creating awareness about the effects of tourism and preservation of our rich heritage and culture, cleanliness and warm hospitality through a process of training and orientation was launched during 2004-05. The aim was to rebuild that sense of responsibility towards tourists among Indians and re-enforces the confidence of foreign tourist towards India as a preferred holiday destination. More than 6500 taxi drivers, restaurant owners and guides trained under the Programmes.

Government also took several other initiatives to promote Indian tourism industry and increased the plan allocation for tourism i.e. from Rs 325 crore in 2003-04 to Rs. 500 crore in 2004-05. Road shows in key source markets of Europe, Incredible India campaign on prominent TV channels and in magazines across the world were among the few steps taken to advertise Indian tourism. In addition a task force was set up to promote India as prominent health tourism destination.

However, in order to attract more visitors, India still needs to upgrade its airports, roads and other infrastructure to global standards. Even with the recent surge, tourist arrivals are just a mere per centage of those in such popular Asian destinations like Bangkok and Thailand. It is boom time for India's Tourism and Hospitality sector. Driven by a surge in business traveller arrivals and a soaring interest in India as a tourist destination, the year 2005 has been the best year till date, with foreign visitor arrivals reaching a record 3.92 million, resulting in international tourism receipts of US$ 5.7 billion.

BOOM TIME INDIA

According to global hotel and hospitality consulting firm, HVS International, the strong performance in tourist arrivals in 2005 can be attributed to a strong sense of business and investment confidence in India inspired by:

- India's strong GDP performance
- Strengthening of ties with the developed world, and
- Opening of sectors of the economy to private sector/ foreign investment.

  The efforts made by the Ministry of Tourism and Culture in the last few years have had a salutary effect on India's tourism industry.
- Foreign tourist arrivals are expected to witness a growth of 78 per cent in 2006 over 2001 (last 5 years)
- Growth in foreign exchange earnings is expected to be of the order of 122 per cent during this period.

- As per estimates (Ministry of Tourism), on an average, about 3.1 million additional jobs per year have been created directly and indirectly in the tourism sector in the last four years.

India is fast emerging as one of the most enticing destinations for the global leisure traveller. The Readers Travel Awards 2006, conducted by Condé Nast Traveller has recently placed India at number four among the world's must-see countries, up from number nine in 2003. The Incredible India campaign has also been a huge success.

An Economic Growth Engine

As an engine for economic growth, the tourism and hospitality sector cuts across the rural-urban divide, and bridges economic boundaries. According to The World Travel and Tourism Council's 2006 Travel and Tourism Economic Research, the travel and tourism sector in India is expected to generate a total demand of US$ 53,544.5 million of economic activity in 2006, accounting for nearly 5.3 per cent of GDP and 5.4 per cent of total employment.

According to the report, the sector is expected to grow at a rate of 8.4 per cent in 2006 and by 8 per cent per annum, in real terms, between 2007 and 2016.

GDP
Employment
Visitor Exports
Personal TandT
Capital Investment
Government Expenditure

Outlook for 2006 (Real Growth)

7.8 per cent
1.4 per cent
10.9 per cent
6.9 per cent
8.3 per cent
7.7 per cent

(Outlook for the next 10 years 2007-2016)

6.6 per cent
1.0 per cent
7.8 per cent
6.7 per cent
7.8 per cent
6.1 per cent

A room-full of Opportunity

As travellers surge into India, the demand for rooms, across segments, has skyrocketed. Hotels in the luxury and business traveller segment are recording nearly 100 per cent occupancy, spiralling tariffs, and a strain on capacity and manpower. Anticipating this demand, around 10,856 hotel rooms in Delhi, 9,318 rooms in Mumbai, 7,794 rooms in Bangalore and 7,408 rooms in Hyderabad are expected to be added by 2011, according to estimates by HVS International.

A policy Thrust

The objective of the existing Tourism Policy of the Government of India is to position tourism as a major engine of economic growth and to harness its direct and multiplier effects for employment and poverty eradication in an environmentally sustainable manner.

The present government's major policy initiatives include:

- Liberalization in aviation sector
- Pricing policy for aviation turbine fuel which influences internal air fares
- Rationalization in tax rates in the hospitality sector
- Tourist friendly visa regime
- Immigration services
- Procedural changes in making available land for construction of hotels
- Allowing setting up of Guest Houses

The Indian Ministry of Tourism has identified 31 villages across the country to be developed as tourism hubs. The states in which these villages have been identified include Himachal Pradesh, Gujarat, Maharashtra, Bihar, Karnataka, Madhya Pradesh, Andhra Pradesh, Kerala, Tamil Nadu, Orissa, Assam, Sikkim, Rajasthan and West Bengal.

Open skies, Open Arms

The government's Open Skies policy, permission for domestic airlines to commence international flights, start-up of various low-cost carriers, and fleet expansion by domestic players has created a huge incentive for domestic travellers to explore far-off destinations within and outside India. The booming aviation business is bringing an ever-increasing number of passengers to India, and pulling Indians out of their homes and into hotels. The numbers, according to the Ministry of Tourism, speak for themselves:

- The number of domestic and international passengers has increased fifteen-fold to 73.34 million in 2005/06 since 1970.
- Domestic air passenger traffic grew by 16.8 per cent in 2005/06 compared to 2004/05.
- International passenger traffic observed a growth of 16.9 per cent in the same period.
- Private airlines accounted for 77.0 per cent of the total domestic traffic.

HEALTH TOURISM

India is gradually gathering popularity as a health tourist destination. A study by McKinsey and Confederation of Indian Industry (CII) says that at its current pace of growth, healthcare tourism alone can rake over US$ 1.7 billion additional revenues by 2012. Medical tourism is now a US$ 299 million industry, as about 100,000 patients come each year. The country needs to exploit the cost advantage it can offer to a health tourist, the study said. The biggest driver for healthcare tourism is the disparity in costs.

- A heart surgery in the US costs US$ 30,000 as compared to US$ 6,000 in India.
- A bone marrow transplant in the US costs US$ 250,000 and US$ 26,000 in India.

"With yoga, meditation, ayurveda, allopathy, and other systems of medicine, India offers a unique basket of services to an individual that is difficult to match by other countries," the CII study said. Clinical outcomes in India are at par with the world's best centres since India has internationally qualified and experienced specialists.

TOURISM POLICY OF INDIA

The Government of India announced the first Tourism Policy in November 1982. It took ten long years for the Government to feel the need to come up with a possible improvement over this. Thus the National Action Plan for Tourism was announced in May 1992. Between these two policy statements, various legislative and executive measures were brought about. In particular, the report of the National Committee on Tourism, submitted in 1988 needs special mention. In addition, two five-year plans - the Seventh and the Eighth - provided the basic perspective framework for operational initiatives. The Seventh Plan advocated a two-pronged thrust in the area of development of tourism, viz., to vigorously promote domestic tourism and to diversify overseas tourism in India.

While laying stress on creation of beach resorts, conducting of conventions, conferences, winter sports and trekking, the overall intention was to diversify options available for foreign tourists. The Tourism Policy, 1982 was more an aggressive statement in marketing than a perspective plan for development. Its main thrust was aimed at presenting India to the foreigners as the ultimate holiday resort. With a view to reach this destination, the following measures were suggested by the Policy:

1. To take full advantage of the national heritage in arriving at a popular campaign for attracting tourists;

2. To promote tourist resorts and make India a destination of holiday resorts;
3. To grant the status of an export industry to tourism;
4. To adopt a selective approach to develop few tourist circuits; and,
5. To invite private sector participation into the sector.

Tourism as an Industry

The Planning Commission recognised tourism as an industry by June 1982. However, it took ten years to make most of the States to fall in line and accord the same status within their legislative framework. At the beginning of the Eighth Plan (1992-97), 15 States and 3 Union Territories had declared tourism as an industry. Four States had declared hotels as an industry.

The National Committee on Tourism was set up in July 1986 by the Planning Commission to prepare a perspective plan for the sector. Within the broad framework of the Seventh Plan, the Committee had to evolve a perspective plan for the coming years. The Committee, headed by Mr. Mohammed Yunus, submitted its recommendations in November 1987. The list of Members was as impressive Mr. S.K. Mishra (Secretary, Department of Tourism), Mrs. Kapila Vatsayan, Mr. K.L. Thapar, Mr. Rajan Jaitley, Mr. A.B. Kerker, Mr. R.K. Puri and Mr Pran Seth. The Committee in its Report recommended that the existing Department of Tourism be replaced by a National Tourism Board. It suggested that there be a separate cadre of Indian Tourism Service to look after the functioning of the Board. It also submitted proposals for partial privatisation of the two airlines owned by the Union Government.

By September, 1987, the Central Government declared more concessions for the sector: these included tax exemption on foreign exchange earnings from tourism (a 50 per cent reduction on rupee earnings and a 100 per cent reduction on earnings in dollars), a drastic reduction in tariff on import of capital goods, and concessional finance at the rate of 1 to 5 per cent per annum. The Tourism Development Finance Corporation was set up in 1987 with a corpus fund of Rs. 100

crores. Until then, the sector was financed on commercial lines by the Industrial Development Bank of India, Industrial Credit and Investment Corporation of India and other commercial banks.

National action Plan

The National Action Plan for Tourism, published in May 1992, and tabled in the Lok Sabha on 5 May 1992, charts 7 objectives as central concerns of the Ministry:

1. Socio-economic development of areas;
2. Increasing employment opportunities;
3. Developing domestic tourism for the budget category;
4. Preserving national heritage and environment;
5. Development of international tourism;
6. Diversification of the tourism product, and
7. Increase in India's share in world tourism (from the present 0.4 per cent to 1 per cent during next 5 years)

As per the Action Plan, foreign exchange earnings are estimated to increase from Rs.10,000 crores in 1992 to Rs.24,000 crores by 2000 AD. Simultaneously, the Plan aims at increasing employment in tourism to 28 million from the present 14 million. Hotel accommodation is to be increased from 44,400 rooms to 1,20,000 by 3 years. Other provisions in the Action Plan include a discontinuance of subsidies to star hotels, encouraging foreign investment in tourism and the setting up of a convention city for developing convention tourism. The Action Plan envisages the development of Special Tourism Areas on lines of export processing zones. Special Central assistance is to be provided for the States to improve the infrastructural facilities at pilgrimage places. It proposes to set up a National Culinary Institute, and projects a liberalised framework for recognition of travel agents and tour operators.

Eighth Plan

The Eighth Plan document makes a special mention that the future expansion of tourism should be achieved mainly by private sector participation. The thrust areas as enumerated in the Plan include development of selected tourist places, diversification from cultural related tourism to holiday and leisure tourism, development of trekking, winter sports, wildlife and beach resort tourism, exploring new source markets, restoration of national heritage projects, launching of national image building, providing inexpensive accommodation in different tourist centres, improving service efficiency in public sector corporations and streamlining of facilitation procedures at airports.

The Eighth Plan aims at luring the high spending tourists from Europe and USA. It also envisages a 'master plan' to integrate area plans with development of tourism. This is envisaged to ensure employment opportunities for the local population.

In April 1993, the Government announced further measures aimed at export promotion. The existing Export Promotion of Capital Goods Scheme (EPCG) was extended to tourism and related services. Against the existing 35 per cent, the tourism sector would now pay an excise duty of 15 per cent only on capital goods import, subject to an export obligation of 4 times the cargo, insurance and freight (CIF) value of imports. With an obligation period of five years, this came as a boon to the hotel industry. The cost of construction had also come down by 20 per cent. In addition to the above policy pronouncements by the Union Government, our planners had envisaged the possibilities of developing specific regions on a zonal plank. Special area Programmes like the Hill Area Development Programmes and the Western Ghats Development Programmes form part of the overall national plan.

The Eighth Plan document stipulates that the strategy in such designated special areas is to devise suitable location-specific solutions, so as to reverse the process of degradation of natural resources and ensure sustainable development. This approach perhaps needs to be integrated into the project of special tourism areas, now being made popular by the

Government. Administrative Control and Developmental Compromises The federal principles enshrined in the Indian Constitution require that the tourism sector be treated as a State subject. As such, the Department of Tourism (under the Ministry of Civil Aviation and Tourism at the Centre) undertakes certain promotional and developmental activities with a view to enhance the sectoral potential. The Department has certain regulatory functions to perform involving the hotel industry, travel agencies and tourist operators. Over the years, there has been considerable erosion of powers so far as State Governments are concerned.

Government Action for States

The sustained campaign for privatisation in all the policy documents has left limited space of operation for the States. The public sector is increasingly being perceived as an agent of inertia than of change and hence the pressure for a hands-off policy. On the other hand, the Union Government has been usurping the powers of the State with some pretext or the other. Promotion schemes, designed at the Centre, are transferred for implementation at the State level.

The special Central Assistance, for example, granted for the development of infrastructure at the pilgrim centres, carries with it a pre-defined scheme and mode of execution. Furthermore, there are occasions when the Centre forces the State Governments to extend certain subsidies and concessions to the sector. The terms of such concessions would have been fixed by the Centre and the States would have no choice but to fall in line. For example, during the State tourism minister's conference in December 1991, the States were urged to freeze water and electricity rates for 10 years. They were also asked to exempt certain hotels from local and state taxes for 10 years.

Seventeen circuits and destinations were identified under the National Action Plan for development through Central assistance and investment by the States and the private sector. The centres were identified by the Centre and the States were asked to do the needful. There were also times when the federal division of power resulted in operational contradictions. For instance, by 1989, many foreign hotel chains like Hilton, Hyatt, Penta and Kempinski had applied for licenses for investing in India. However, the revenue departments of the respective States failed to locate and allocate land for the construction of hotels.

The scheme, thus, fell flat. Curiously, the Union Government was not hesitant to make use of Constitutional provisions when it suited its interests. As has been stated earlier, the Yunus Committee had suggested the creation of the Tourism Board on lines of the existing Railway Board. (Perhaps, it was the brainchild of Mr. K.L. Thapar, then adviser to the Planning Commission, in charge of Transport and Tourism Sector. Being from the Railway Service, it is not surprising that Thapar thought about a 'Tourism Board'). To begin with, the empowered committee of secretaries challenged the idea of creation of a Board.

Privatisation Process

It was said that the Railway Board as an independent entity was created for historical reasons. It would be difficult for tourism to be looked after by a Board, because legally the sector would come under the Industrial (Development) Act. It was also found that such a Board would not be viable financially. In 1991, the think-tank on tourism created by Minister Madhavarao Scindia rejected the idea of a Board in toto. It was emphasised that the Board cannot be in charge of a sector that is basically under the jurisdiction of the States. Scope for Federal Interventions The previous section highlights the dubious ways by which the Centre attempts to hijack initiatives at the State-level. This is achieved essentially by threatening to curtail Central assistance or by cajoling through promises of more financial aid.

It is common knowledge that the resource-base of the States is very narrow, making them vulnerable at the negotiating table. However, States have the freedom to resist the Centre's strong- arm tactics, provided State assemblies stand-by the interests of the States. For instance, State legislatures may refuse to freeze water and electricity rates on grounds of revenue generation. In that event, the concerned Chief Minister or the Minister of Tourism may convey the intensity of resistance that he is confronted with, and thus refuse to comply with the Centre's diktats. It is heartening to realise that the States have often exercised their power of self-determination and consequently refused to toe the line drawn by the Centre. This offers enough scope for possible interventions at the federal strata of our political system in matters of policy formulation. Privatisation and its Implications

According to the Approach Paper to the Seventh Plan, " there is a vast potential for development of tourism in the country. Tourism should be accorded the status of an industry. Private sector investment will have to be encouraged in developing tourism and public sector investments should be focused only on development of support infrastructure". Thus the seeds of private initiatives were sown during the Seventh Plan.

The Government took the matter of privatising the tourism sector seriously by 1988. It was during the tenure of Mr. S.K. Mishra as Tourism Secretary that the talk of inviting private investment into the sector began. The Government permitted foreign equity participation up to 5 1 per centin tourism projects. Foreign charters were allowed to operate in the country for the first time. Foreign companies were allowed to repatriate their profits to the extent of 3 per cent. The structural adjustment Programmes, initiated in June, 1992, paved the way for privatisation in almost all sectors of the economy. The Annual Plan (1992-93) document emphatically enunciated the Government's position vis-a-vis tourism: "

Demerits of Privatisation

The future growth of tourism will have to be achieved mainly through private initiative. The State will contribute to tourism by planning broad strategy of development, provision of monetary and fiscal incentives to catalyse private sector investment." The process of privatisation brought in its wake big investments and private involvement at various levels. As an offshoot, environmental considerations were thrown to the winds and there were instances of large scale human rights violation. The self- correcting nature of policy made provisions for stricter controls in this regard.

More seriously, privatisation meant alienation of the majority of our population and their deprivation. Employment generated in tourism is generally seasonal and ill paid. The private sector- induced pockets of tourism had the potential of turning into centres of pollution, drug trafficking and prostitution. Industry Status Granted to Tourism The Seventh Plan proposed that tourism be declared an industry. However, it took time for the States to implement this, even though they agreed in principle. The smokeless industry had the advantage of generating maximum value-added, because of low-cost inputs.

The Tourism Policy Statement carried certain provisions in favour of the hotel industry. It stated that there should be provision for depreciation in the balance sheets of hotels. Being an export industry, hotels were to be given excise concessions. The provisions of the Monopolies and Restrictive Trade Practices (MRTP) Act were relaxed for hotels, because any hotel with 300 or more rooms would have incurred an investment of Rs. 25 crores.

The document also hinted at lower tariffs for power and water and regulations for easy import of equipment. As a follow-up, hotel and shipping were added to the list of 27 industries exempted from Section 22 A of the MRTP Act. The consequences of declaring tourism as an industry need to be studied in detail. It is not possible to capture its implications in an exploratory work like this.

However, it is obvious that the private sector has primarily benefited to a great extent by this measure. Importing Modifications to Policies We have earlier stated that the arena of policy formulation should be self-evaluating and self-correcting. In the case of Tourism Policy, this has proved to be the plus point. As an illustration, the Policy statement of 1982 made no mention of infrastructure development. The successive governments at the Centre failed to create proper tourism infrastructure, thus resulting in loss of traffic. This lacuna was corrected in the National Action Plan.

However, much of this change was due to intensive lobbying by such agencies like the Indian Association of Tour Operators (IATO), the Travel agents Association of India (TAAI) and the Indian Hotels and Restaurants Association (IHRA). It is for the voluntary agencies and pro-people forces to exploit the avenue of lobbying at various levels.

Environmental Issues

The environmental implications of tourism development did not form part of the 1982 Policy. The consequences are too obvious to be written about. However, the NAP, 1992 did carry specific provisions for environmental protection and harnessing. From Policy to Cartooning Policy statements may also lead to justifiable flights of fantasy.

It was said that Indian classical music would not provide much needed entertainment for foreign guests because the artistes spend a lot of time tuning their instruments. Folk dances get over in an hour. So much for our much touted cultural diversity. It is embarrassing to believe that the consultative committee attached to the Ministry of Civil Aviation and Tourism had endorsed the idea. Conclusion broadly, our successive policy pronouncements in the realm of tourism fall within the "liberalising" framework of the macro- economic policy environment. The Finance Bill, 1988, had assured 50 per cent tax exemption on foreign exchange earnings in the sector, and a further 50 per cent exemption if re-invested. In effect, it amounts to 100 per cent tax concession.

Luxury hotels enjoy exemptions of all kinds with a view to encourage tourism earnings. These tax exemptions coupled with provision of soft loans to the sector led to a boom in the tourism related private investment. The Economic Survey 1991-92 aptly summarises the ultimate aim of such incentives for private sector participation: " The Government has tried to expand the economic space in which the people can exercise their initiative and ingenuity. It hopes to do more to expand their opportunities, to enhance their potential. But what shape the economy takes ultimately depends on what the people make of it. In that sense, the future is in their hands."

We should not forget that tourism is an industry which emerges in the context of unresolved socio-economic structural issues, such as land distribution patterns or the take over of traditional occupations by modem mechanised capital. Tourism happens to be a source of livelihood for millions in India and aggressive privatisation does not ensure social and economic safety nets. In the face of the unhindered entry of international capital and successive alienation, perhaps, it is difficult to agree that "the future is in our hands".

TOURISM IN THE INDIAN STATES

When Foster wrote his Passage to India in the 1920s he reached the stunning conclusion that there are "a hundred Indias". There are. And if you go out to discover each of these you can count on spending at least a year in this stupendous country with its phenomenal repertoire of surprises and delights. Blessed with probably the widest array of topographical and cultural diversity that was ever packed into one time zone, there's an India for everyone. India's jungles, rivers and streams are simply bursting with wildlife; much of it protected in her 80 National Parks and 441 Sanctuaries.

In 1973, a separate Tourism Department was established to identify and develop the tourism potential in the State. This was followed by the creation of Tourism Corporation of Gujarat Limited in 1978 which was entrusted with the task of undertaking and developing tourism-related commercial activities. The Corporation is presently engaged in a variety of activities such as creation of lodging and boarding facilities for the tourists and other aspects of tourist facilitation such as transportation, packaged tours, wayside catering along the

National and State Highways, arranging cultural festivals, organizing exhibitions and producing and distributing maps, posters, brochures and pamphlets. The Corporation has set up accommodation facilities at Chorwad, Ahmedpur Mandvi, Porbandar, Veraval, Hajira, Ubharat and Tithal.

Similar facilities at pilgrimage centres like Palitana, Somnath, Dwarkja, Pavagadh and Dakor have also been set up by the Corporation. One of the recent tourist attractions introduced by the Corporation in collaboration with the Indian Railways is a special tourist train. The Royal Orient Train which connects up various tourist destinations straddling the Gujarat and Rajasthan State. However, the Corporation has suffered losses due to a number of organizational constraints. In order to minimize these losses and also to provide better services to the tourists, the Government has undertaken privatisation of some of the commercial property units of the Corporation.

In spite of possessing a variety of tourist attractions such as wildlife, scenic beauty, pilgrimage centres, exotic traditional crafts and festivals, beaches, hospitality of the region and a varied healthy and tasteful cuisine, the State has not been able to accelerate the pace of tourism in comparison to other states. In 1991, the State did declare a tourism policy but it did not elicit adequate response from the private sector since the policy contained only a handful of benefits while the implementation was tardy due to legal and administrative constraints.

This was at a time when the Government of India had already declared tourism as an industry and a large number of states had followed suit. This enabled the tourism industry to avail of incentives, reliefs, benefits available to the industry in those states. While other state Governments made successful efforts in developing tourism within their states, the relative inability of the Gujarat State to harness and develop its full tourist potential may be attributed to a combination of factors such as lack of effective policies, inadequate infrastructure, ineffective marketing and lack of decent facilities for the tourists.

The main rationale for formulating a comprehensive tourism policy is rooted, on one hand,in the convergence of socio-economic spread benefits, environment - friendliness and employment potential of tourism industry and on the other, in the growing demand for tourism products in the State, brought by a rapid industrial growth in the State during the recent years that has led to tremendous increase in number of business travellers.

Andhra Pradesh

Andhra Pradesh's capital city, Hyderabad has the atmosphere of an Arabian Nights fairy tale. Whimsical palaces, erstwhile stately homes and crowded bazaars filled with shops selling Hyderabadi pearls, incense and copper utensils characterise the city, while in the distance looms Golconda Fort. The city's historical connection traces itself to the rulers or Nizams whose wealth was legendary. Rooms full of jewels and currency notes, a garage full of gleaming Rolls Royce's are all now part of history, but a unique culture lives on, colouring the city with its distinctive charm.

The Epicurean tastes of this most exalted royal house of princely India gave rise to a fabled cuisine based on painstaking preparations and slow cooking. Much of Hyderabad's old town can be covered on foot. The city's important landmarks include Charminar, a 16th century gateway, the Salar Jung Museum which exhibits priceless treasures alongside trivia that made up the personal collection of the owner, Mecca Mosque and Golconda Fort. Nagarjunakonda is the site of ongoing excavations which have revealed Buddhist temples, stupas and monasteries.

Places to visit

Hyderabad (Birla Temple, Hussain Sagar, Indira Park, Charminar, Mecca Masjid, Osmania University, Qutub Shahi Tombs and Golconda Fort, Nehru- Zoological Park, Public Gardens, Race Course, State Central Library, Tank Bund, Asmongarh, Khajana Museum, Planetarium, State Archaeological Museum, Salar Jung Museum), Vijayawada

(Akkana and Madanna Caves, Gandhi Hill, Haxrathbal Mosque, Kanakadurga temple, Mary's Temple, Milk Powder Factory, Mogalrajapuram Caves, Prakasam Barrage, Victoria Jubilee Regional Museum), Warangal (Thouşand Pillar Temple, Fort-Warangal, Bhadrakali Temple, Planetarium), Vishakapatnam / Vizag (Andhra University Building- 4 kms, Dolphin's Nose, Sri Venkateswara, Konda, Hindusthan Shipyard, Simachalam Temple, The Three Hillocks, Indira Gandhi Zoological Gardens, Port, Visakha refinery),

Tirupati (Lord Venkateswaram Temple, Govindarajaswamy Temple, Kapilathiraham, Kodandaraswamy Temple, Padmavati Temple), Nagarjunasagar (Nagarjund Konda) (Nagarjunasagar, Nargarjunakonda), Srisailam (Damsite, Hatekeswaram, Pathalaganga, Mallikarjuna Swamy Temple, Sakshi Ganapathi Sikharam).

Arunachal Pradesh

Right at the top of north-eastern India, crowning its six clustered sisters like a protective helmet, is Arunachal Pradesh, the 'Land of the Dawn-lit- Mountains.' This is the first Indian soil to greet the morning sun. Dawn first illuminates Arunachal's border with China: a long border which stretches all the way from its east, over to its northern boundaries and down to its north- western edge where it merges with Tibet. To its west is Bhutan and on its southern end it touches Assam, Nagaland and Burma before sweeping up to Calcutta.

Places to visit

Naharlagun (Polo Park and Zoo), Itanagar (The Buddhist Temple and Ganga Sekhi Lake), Bomdila, Itanagar, Namdapha National Park.

Assam

The largest of the states in the northeast of India is Assam whose capital, Guwahati, has an inspired location on the banks of the River Brahmaputra. Amidst Assam's verdant lushness are two important game sanctuaries, Manas and Kaziranga, both best known for their population of one horned Indian rhinoceros, a species that faced extinction. Much of the rest of the state is devoted to tea plantation which yield the strong Assam leaf popular all over the world.

Places to visit

Guwahati (Janardhan Temple, Navagrah Temple, Umananda Temple, Bhubaneshwari Devi Temple, Assam Zoo and Botanical Gardens, Anthropological Museum, Assam Forest Museum, Cottage Industries Museum, Museum of Animal Husbandry and Veterinary Science, Assam State Museum, Dept. of Historical and Antiquarian Research), Kaziranga National Park, Sibsagar (Sibsagar Tank and Temples, Talatal Ghar, Kereng Ghar, Rang Ghar, Joysagar Tank and Temple, Gaurisagar Group, Gargaon Palace, Charaideo), Haflong (Haflong Lake, Jatinga, Maibong, Umrangsu)

Bihar

Of all India's states, Bihar is the one most intimately linked to the Buddha's life, resulting in a trail of pilgrimages which have come to be known as the Buddhist circuit. The very name Bihar is derived from the world 'vihara', which means Buddhist monastery. The Buddhist trail begins at the capital city, Patna, where a noteworthy museum contains a collection of Hindu and Buddhist sculptures. To the south of Patna is Nalanda which translates as 'the place that confers the lotus' (of spiritual knowledge).

A monastic university flourished here from the 5th to the 11th century. Rajgir, 'the royal palace', was the venue for the first Buddhist Council. The Buddha spent five years at Rajgir after having attained enlightenment, and many of the remains at Rajgir commemorate various incidents. Bodhgaya is the spot where Lord Buddha attained enlightenment, with the Mahabodhi Temple marking the precise location. Bihar's Buddhist circuit has modest back-up facilities by way of accommodation, international dining and surface transport.

Places to visit

Patna (Kumrahar, Golghar, Har Mandir Takht, Martyrs' memorial, Pathar ki Masjid, Sher Shah Suri Masjid, Khuda Baksh Oriental Library, Patna museum, Jalan museum, Sadaqat Ashram, Maner, Padri ki Haveli, Biological Park, Patna Yoga Vidyalaya, Quila House (Museum), Laxmi Narayan Temple, Pathar-Ki-Masjid, Sanjay Gandhi Biological Park, Rajendra Museum, Gandhi Museum), Vaishali (Ashoka Pillar at Kolhua, Buddha Stupa I, Buddha Stupa II, Raja Vishal Ka Ghar, Coronation Tank, Museum, Bawan Pokhar Temple and Harikatora Temple, Miranji Ka Durgah, Kundupur), Gaya (Bodhgaya-Mahabodhi Temple, Animeshlocan Chaiyata, Mohanta's Monastery, Ratnagar, Archaeological Museum, Tibetan Monastery, Thai Temple and Monastery, International Buddhist House and Japanese Temple, Buddhist Monastery of Bhutan, The Burmese Temple, The Chinese Temple and Monastery), Nalanda, Rajgir.

Chhattisgarh

Chhattisgarh, situated in the heart of India, is endowed with a rich cultural heritage and attractive natural diversity. The State is full of ancient monuments, rare wildlife, exquisitely carved temples, Buddhist sites, palaces, water falls, caves, rock paintings and hill plateaus. Most of these sites are untouched and unexplored and offer a unique and alternate experience to tourists compared to traditional destinations which have become overcrowded. Chhattisgarh offers the tourist a Destination with a Difference.

For those who are tired of the crowds at major destinations, Bastar, with its unique cultural and ecological identity, will come as a breath of fresh air. The Green State of Chhattisgarh has 44 per cent of its area under forests, and is one of the richest bio-diversity areas in the country.

The State has taken a conscious decision to do away with past legacies and to adopt a fresh approach to Tourism Development. The Tourism Policy is focussed on creating a unique image for the State and to position it as an attractive destination for both domestic as well as foreign tourists. Accordingly, the State will take up Integrated Development of Special Tourism Areas and have constructive collaboration with the Private Sector. Tourism development will be primarily driven by the private sector with the role of Government being that of a facilitator and catalyst. Towards this end, the State has set up a State Tourism Promotion Board as the nodal agency for translation of the Policy into action for the sustained development of the sector.

Places to visit

Raipur, Bastar(Wide and thick forests, between high mountains cool flowing streams, sky-touching mountains, caves, high waterfalls, and in the valleys the spread of greenary and in between this, the huts made by bamboo sticks, the fearless life style of the tribals and their culture, one's heart and mind would be filled with new wonders and pleasure), Champaran —Champajhar(A temple was constructed in honour of Guru Swamy Vallabhacharya. Near to this Temple, there is the temple of Champakeshwara Mahadeva)

Delhi

Delhi, the capital of India, is a city that combines history with modernity in its own unique way. As you travel through the wide roads and flyovers of Delhi, you'll come across Mughal monuments, forts and tombs in the heart of the city. Known for its historic buildings such as the President's mansion, Rashtrapati Bhawan, the Parliament House and the landmark India Gate, Delhi is changing rapidly with a modern metro railway service and curving flyovers connecting different parts of this rapidly expanding city.

With shopping malls, multiplexes and amusement parks springing up around Delhi, the city has left behind its image of being a sedate city of politicians and has acquired a younger and more dynamic feel, which you'll discover on your Indian Holiday in Delhi. At the same time Delhi retains its age-old charm with gracious parks and gardens, an active cultural life and annual celebrations such as the Republic Day Parade, giving Delhi its unique place as the grand capital of India. You'll discover Delhi is a great place to start your Indian Holiday.

Delhi is the starting point for tourists on a tour of North India. Delhi consists of Old Delhi, the capital of the Mughals centered at the Red Fort; and New Delhi, known for its British imperial buildings and wide avenues. Delhi is a cosmopolitan city where festivals of all religions are celebrated. But the grandest of celebrations in Delhi is the impressive Republic Day parade, held every year down Rajpath, the central avenue of Delhi.

Delhi is culturally a very vibrant city, with theatre, film music and dance events being held in the city's many auditoria every night. Whether you prefer listening to classical music in a concert hall or dancing in a discothèque, you'll find it all in cosmopolitan Delhi.

Places to visit

Qutub Minar- The origins of Qutab Minar are shrouded in controversy. Some believe it was erected as a tower of victory to signify the beginning of the Muslim rule in India. Others say it served as a minaret to the muezzins to call the faithful to prayer. No one can, however, dispute that the tower is not only one of the finest monuments in India, but also in the world.

Red Fort - So called because of the red stone with which it is built, the Red Fort is one of the most magnificent palaces in the world. India's history is also closely linked with this fort. It was frorth here ht the British deposed the last Mughal ruler, Bhadur Shah Zafar, marking the end of the three century long Mughal rule. It was also fromits ramparts that the first prime. Minister of India, pandit Jawharlal Nehru, announced to the nation that India was free form colonial rule.

Purana Quila - The fort is said to be constructed on the historic site of Indraprastha (900BC) by Humayun and Sher Shah. Covering a circuit of about a mile, the walls of the fort have three gates and are surrounded by a mat fed by the river Yamuna.

Jantar Mantar - At first sight, the Jantar Mantar appears like a gallery of modern art. It is, however, an observatory. Sawai Jia Singh II of Jaipur (1699-1743), a keen astronomer and a noble in the Mughal court, was dissatisfied by the errors of brass and metal astronomical instruments.

Humayun's Tomb - The mughals brought with them a love for gardens, fountains and water. The first mature example of Mughal architecture in India, Humayun's Tomb was built by the emperor's grieving widow, Haji Begum, in 1565 AD.

Jama Masjid - Work on the Jama Masjid mosque was begun in 1650 by the Mughal Emperor Shah Jahan to complement his palace at the Red Fort. More than 5,000 workers toiled for six years to complete the largest mosque in India. Every Friday, the emperor and his retinue would travel in state from the fort to the mosque to attend the congressional prayers.

Safdarjung's Tomb - Representing the last phase of the Mughal style of architecture, Safdarjang's Tomb stands in the centre of an extensive garden.

India Gate - Built as a memorial to commemorate the 70,000 India soldiers killed in World War I, India Gate was designed by Sir Edwin Lutyens and completed in 1931.

Rashtrapati Bhawan - Formely the Viceregal Lodge, the building is the highlight of Lutyen's New Delhi and was completed in 1929 at a cost of 12,53,000 pound sterling. Located in an area of 130 hectares, the palace has 340 rooms.

Rajghat - The mortal remains of Mahatma Gandhi were cremated on this spot on the west bank of the river Yamuna on the evening of January 31, 1948.

Lakshmi Narayan Mandir - Built in 1938, the temple is an ideal introduction to some of the gods of the India pantheon. The temple contains a large number of idols and visitors can also watch priests performing ritualistic prayers.

Goa

A Portuguese explorer, Afonso de Albuquerque sailed up the river Mandovi, defeated the Bijapuri army and rode into the capital triumphantly bearing a Portuguese Standard in one hand, and a Gold Crucifix in the other. A curious blending of cultures took place, affecting every sphere of Goa life, from religion to architecture, cuisine to art. The chapter of Goa's history ended 451 years later when Goa ceased to be a Portuguese colony, and became a part of the Indian Union. Parasailing, yachting, windsurfing, and deep sea diving are some of the more popular water sports, facilities for which are available. 451 years of Portuguese rule has imbued Goa's towns and villages with a unique culture. Whitewashed chapels and churches that dot the landscape are surrounded by sleepy villages and rice fields.

Places to visit

Panji—Panji -the capital of Goa feels like a sleepy Portuguese town. Set along the southern bank of Mandovi River, it provides linkage to Old Goa and the beaches. Every nook and corner of the city reflects to its Portuguese heritage with broad avenues spilling into cobbled squares, grand public buildings, and old houses with overhanging balconies and numerous bars and cafes. Margao, an important town, have private houses and government buildings that date back to Portuguese times. Se Cathedral with its Iberian exterior, Bom Jesus that enshrines the mortal remains of St. Francis Xavier and the starkly beautiful Convent of Saint Monica are some of the collection of Goa's largest Churches. Mapusa, a market town, comes alive every Friday with a quaint pavement bazar.

Gujarat

Located on the country's western coast, Gujarat is bounded by the Arabian Sea to the west and southwest and Pakistan to the northwest. Rajasthan neighbours it to the north, Madhya Pradesh to the east and Maharashtra to the southeast. The most convenient entry point into Gujarat is through the metropolis of Ahmedabad.Gandhinagar the capital of Gujarat is in west-central India. Signs of civilization in the region that is now Gujarat date back to the period from 3000 to 1500 BC. The region was part of the Mauryan Empire in the 3rd century BC under King Ashoka. In 1818 AD, the British East India Company took control of Gujarat by administering the state through local princely rulers. For tourists who have comparatively less time at their disposal and want to 'do' Gujarat within a week, three places may be considered a 'must' for them. These are the Gir lion sanctuary, Palitana temples and the Ahmedabad city.

Places to visit

Ahmedabad (Ahmed Shah's Mosque, Balvatika, Teen Darwaza and Bhadra Fort, Daria Khan's Ghummat, Siddi Sayyad's Mosque, Gita Mandir, Swami Narayan Temple, Hathisinh Mandir, Jhulta Minar, Jumma Masjid, Kankaria Lake, Rani Sipri's Mosque and Tomb, Rani Roopmati Mosque, Rauza of Shah Alam, Sabarmati Ashram, Siddhi Sayyad Mosque, Dada Hari Vava), Rajkot (Aji Dam, Mahatma Gandhi's Home (Kaba Gandhino Delo), Lal Pari Lake and Renderda, Sardar Smriti Bhavan, Watson Museums and Jubliee Gardens), Jamnagar (Solarium, Lakhota Fort and Kotha Bastion, Rozi and Bedi Ports), Dwarka (Dwarkadish Temple, Bhadkeshwar Temple, Rukmani Temple, Sunset Point, Shri Jagatguru Shankaracharya Math, Ved Havan, Light House, Shardapith Math Museum), Porbander, Somnath Veraval (Somnath Temple, Triveni Ghat, Ahilyabai Temple, Junagadh Gate, Bhalka Tirth, Dehotsarga, Manipur Masjid, Museum), Sasan Gir (Nalsarovar Lake and Sanctuary, Tulsi Shyam Springs and Krishna Temple), Junagadh (Ashoka's Edicts, Uparkot Fort, Shrine of Narsi Mehta, Willingdon Dam, Mahabat Maqbara, Damodar Kund, Girnar Hills and Temple, Darbar Hall Museum, Sakkarbag Museum, Sakkarbag Zoo)

Haryana

Haryana is a state in north India. It was carved out of the state of Punjab in 1966. It is bordered by Punjab and Himachal Pradesh to the north, and Rajasthan to the west and south. Eastern border to Uttaranchal and Uttar Pradesh is defined by river Yamuna. Haryana also surrounds Delhi on three sides, forming the northern, western and southern borders of Delhi.

Consequently, a large area of Haryana is included in the National Capital Region. The capital of Haryana is Chandigarh which is administered as a union territory and is also the capital of Punjab. This city was created to fulfill the need of a permanent capital of Punjab and Haryana, although Shimla was a temporary headquarters in those times. The city, a model of wide roads and spacious residential colonies, is an excellent base for specialized sightseeing. The white domed temple of Goddess Chandi Devi that stands on the slope of a hill, situated in the north-east of Chandigarh, on the edge of the Shivalik hills, is from where the city obtains its name Chandigarh.

Places to visit

The Secretariat, The Assembly and High Court, Zakir Hussain Rose Garden, Rock Garden, Sukhna Lake, Govt. Museum and Art Gallery and Punjab University Complex, International Doll Museum, National Gallery of Portraits.

Himachal Pradesh

Himachal Pradesh is totally a mountain state and a delight for the visitors, particularly during the summer season when people flock to this tiny hill station to escape the scorching heat of the plains. It came into being in its present form with the partition of the Punjab into Punjab and Haryana in 1966. High points of Himachal are as follows. The winding roads and high passes link its high mountains and valleys. While the picturesque valleys of Kullu and Kangra are a blend of colours. In marked contrast the stark and barren terrain of Lahaul and Spiti have a stunning lunar and scape like beauty.

Places to visit

Shimla (Jakhoo Hill, Glen, Summer Hill, Chadwick Falls, Zoo, Navbahar, Sanket Mochen, Tara Devi Temple, Institute of Advance Studies, Aviary at Old Raj Bhavan, Tibetan Monastery, Dhengu Mata Temple), Dalhousie(Panjpulla, Subhash Baoli and Jandri Ghat, The Round, Dainkund,

Khajjiar, Kalatop Wild Life Sanctuary), Chamba (Lakshman Narayan Temple, Chamunda Temple, Katasan Devi Temple, Bhuj Sing Museum, Chaugan), Dharamshala (MC leodganj, Tibetan Medical and Astro Institute, Bhagsunath, St. John's Church, Kunal Pathri, War Memorial), Kullu Valley, Kinnaur, Spiti, Lahaul, At Kinnaur, At Spiti, At Lahaul (Batal, Bara Singri Glacier, Koksar, Gondhla, Tandi, Bara Lacha Pass, Udaipur, Trilokinath Temple, Suraj Tal, Sarchu, Lake Chandra Tal, and some Monasteries viz. Kardang, Shashur, Tayl, Guru Ghantal).

Jammu & Kashmir

Jammu and Kashmir, India's fascinating northernmost state consists of three regions differing in topography and culture. Jammu was the stronghold of Hindu Dogra kings and abounds with popular temples and secluded forest retreats. Jammu the whole city of is sprinkled with temples, so much so it is often called the city of temples. Kashmir is an emerald valley, cradled in the Himalayas, under crystalline blue skies, and against the backdrop of snow capped mountains. Kashmir's capital city, Srinagar offers delightful holidays on the lakes with their shikaras and houseboats.

Ladakh is the northern most province of the state, with a highland desert lying between the Karakoram and the Himalayan ranges. It is now organized in to two districts: Leh and Kargil. Hilltop monasteries and a colourful way of life, completely at one with the surroundings, make Ladakh one of the best living traditions of Tibetan Buddhism in the world today.

Amongst the three regions of Jammu & Kashmir State, Jammu, perhaps, offers the widest diversity of terrain and beauty. The entire region is pocketed with lakes and valleys, some still little explored. The foundation of the settlement of Jammu is attributed to King Jambulochan of the 9th century BC. In 1730 AD, it came under the Dogra rule of Raja Dhruv Deva and Jammu became an important centre for arts and culture, now renowned as the Pahari School.

Places to visit

Ranbireshwar Temple; Raghunath Temple, Ranbir Canal, Bahu Fort, Bage Bahu, Amar Mahal Palace Museum, Dogra Art Gallery, Vaishno Devi (Bhumika Temple, Darshani Darwaza, Ban Ganga Temple, Charan Paduka, Adhkunwari Temple, Kalika Temple, Ram Mandir, Shiva Goompha), Leh (Ladakh), Srinagar (Pather Masjid, Shah Hamdan Mosque,Jamia Masjid, Hari Parbat Fort, Nagin Lake, Hazratbal, Shalimar Bagh, Harwan, Nishat Bagh, Cheshma Shahi, Pari Mahal, Shankracharya Temple, Daal Lake and Shri Pratap Singh Museum at Lal Mandi), Amarnath Yatra / Trek.

Jharkhand

Jharkhand is a state of Mines and Minerals, Industries, Wildlife Sanctuaries and Forestaries. It is mostly a tribal area. Nearly eighty per cent of the population of the state are tribes. Sarhul is the most famous festival among the tribes. With its capital city Ranchi, Mines are located near the Dhanbad city, Minerals are in Chhotanagpur, Wildlife in Hazaribagh, Industries in Jamshedpur and Bokaro. It is rich in Iron and Steel, Coal, Mica etc. Iron ore rich area is Chhotanagpur. Bokaro is well known for its Iron and Steel. Jamshedpur is the Industrial Capital of the state. Deoghar is a well known Hindu Pilgrimage Centre. One of the *Dwadash Jyotirlinga* is situated here.

Places to visit

Ranchi (Ranchi Hill and Ranchi Lake: The scenic attractions of the town have much to offer to its visitors. The landmark of Ranchi is a hill bearing a temple of Shiva on its sumlnit witln a lake at its foot, known, 'Ranchi Lake'. One can have panoramic view of the town elude the surroundings from the top of the hill).

Karnataka

Karnataka, with its capital at Bangalore, is home to a fascinating legacy of richly carved temples, imposing mosques and trappings of a royal past. Bangalore, with its many hotels and fine restaurants, is a good base for exploring the state. At once a modern industrial city, a shopper's paradise and a gracious legacy of the British. Mysore, the capital of the erstwhile princely state, has a profusion of palaces and museums. Nearby Srirangapatnam is linked to the memory of one of the old state's best known rulers - Tipu Sultan. Somnathpur, a few miles away, has a magnificently carved temple.

Belur and Halebid have between them a series of carved stone temples. For perfection of finish, wealth of detail and sheer artistry, they are unrivaled specimens of the art of temple sculpture. Hassan, with a comfortable hotel, makes the perfect base from which to explore the riches of Belur and Halebid. Also a short distance away, Shravanbelgola is famous as the pinnacle of the sculptor's art. A figure 120 meters tall has been carved out of a single piece of granite in 183 AD. Every 12 years, the figure of Gomateswara is ritually bathed by priests and witnessed by millions of devotees in one of the most colourful festivals of the austere Jain religion.

Places to visit

Bangalore (Aquarium, Bull Temple, Fort and Tippu's Palace, Ulsoor Lake, Lal Bagh, Venkatappa Art Gallery, Cubbon Park, Vidhana Soudha, Vishveswaraya Industrial and Technological Museum), Belur - Halebid (Chenakesava Temple, Veernarayan Temple, Kappe Chennigaraya Temple), Mysore, Badami (Badami Caves, Badami Fort, Sculpture Gallery), Aihole (Durga Temple, Ladh Khan Temple, Gowda Temple, Suryanarayan Temple Konti Group of Temples, Hucchimalli Temple, Meguti Temple, Ravanphadi Cave), Hampi (Virupaksha Temple, Monolithic Ganeshas, Krishna Temple, Monolithic Narsimha, Hazara Rama Temple, Elephant Stables, Zenana Enclosures, Royal Performance Zone, Royal Residences, Quieen's Bath, Vittala Temple, Achyuta Raya Temple, Kodandarama Temple), Nagarhole National Park

Kerala

Edged by a thread of unbroken beach line, the Kerala's heart is composed of intensely green paddy fields and a unique network of rivers and lagoons. Upland Kerala, relatively little visited, is composed of hills thickly wooded with teak and rubber. Trivandrum which is also the state capital has an exceptionally fine museum set in an amusement park. Kovalam, one of the most popular beaches in the country. Sri Padmanabhaswamy temple in Trivandrum, and Padmanabhapuram Palace are important monuments. Cochin has been Kerala's centre of maritime trade for innumerable centuries. Jew town, complete with an immaculately preserved synagogue, has a flavor all its own, while Tripunathura, at the other end of the city, has many traditional houses with central courtyards.

Kerala's multitude of faiths - Islam, Judaism, and a host of sects of Christianity and Hinduism - all coexist harmoniously. Kerala's traditions of dance forms, which originated from temple worship, can be witnessed at regularly held performances. A five hour drive from Cochin leads into thickly forested hills, past rubber and spice plantations, and into southern India's tea growing district headquartered at the charmingly old world Munnar. From Kottayam to Alleppey is a world of palm fringed waterways, a route which is covered by motor launch. Elderly sailboats, long barges transporting tons of coconuts and tiny skiffs used to transport children to school are common sights on these backwaters.

Places to visit

Trivandrum (Padmanabhaswamy Temple, Zoological Park, Napier Museum, Sri Chitra Art Gallery, Science and Technology Museum, Veli Lagoon, Shanmugham Beach, Aruvikkara Dam and Neyyar Dam, SMSM Institute), Kovalam, Alleppey (Backwater Cruise), Kollam (Thangassery Light House and Backwaters), Kottayam (Valiya Pally, Thazhathangadi Mosque and Kumarakam), Periyar Wildlife Sanctuary (Indian Wild Elephants, Sambar, Barking Deer, Wild Boar, Tigers, Panthers, Wild Dogs, Bison, Spotted deer,

Leopard, Musk deer. Wildlife can be seen in its natural habitat by cruising on the lake in motorboats), Cochin (Dutch Palace, Jewish Synagogue, St.Francis Church, Bolghatty, Gunda and Willingdon Islands, Kerala History Museum, Hill Palace Museum, Parishath Taamburan Museum, Chinese Fishing Nets, Santacruz Cathedral (Basilica)), Trichur (Vadakkumnathan Temple, Town Hall, Zoo, Aquarium, State Museum, Art Museum), Guruvayur (Guruvayur Shree Krishna Temple and Punnathur Kotta).

Madhya Pradesh

At the heart of India, the magic of Madhya Pradesh lies in its exquisitely carved temples, proud fortresses and variety of wildlife. Most of the state is a high plateau, historically known as the Malwa region. Bhopal, the capital of Madhya Pradesh, is a fascinating amalgam of an old historic city, and modern urban planning. The history of Madhya Pradesh goes back to the time of Ashoka, the great Mauryan ruler. To the Chandelas, however, goes the credit of building the fantastic monuments of Eros, Khajuraho, in the north of the state. The state's cultural lineage is ancient and checkered. Madhya Pradesh occupies a special position in the history of music. The Gwalior gharana is among the most prominent arbiters of style. The rivalry of Tansen and Baiju Bawra is remembered in fantastic detail to this day.

Places to visit

Bhopal (Taj-ul-Masjid, Juma Masjid, Moti Masjid, Shaukat Mahal, Bharat Bhawan and Roopankar, Shamla and Idgah Hills. Chowk, Upper and Lower Lake, Gandhi Bhavan, Van Vihar), Sanchi (Great Stupa No.1, Toranas or Gateways, Stupa No. 2, Stupa no. 3, Ashoka Pillar, Buddhist Vihara, Monasteries), Gwalior (The Cenotraphs, Man Singh Palace, Man Mandir Palace, Gujari Mahal, Suraj Kund, Teli ka Mandir, Sas Bahu ka Mandir, Rani Jhansi Memorial, Tombs of Tansen and Ghaus Mohammad, Jai Vilas Palace, Gandhi Park, Zoo Municipal Corporation Museum, Jivaji Rao Scindia Museum), Orchha (Jehangir Mahal, Raj Mahal, Raj Praveen Mahal, Ram Raja Temple, Chaturbhuj Temple, Laxmi Narayan Temple,

Phool Bagh, Dinman Hardaul's Palace, Sunder Mahal, Cenotraphs, Shahid Smarak), Khajuraho (The temples of Khajuraho are divided into three geographical groups viz, Western, Eastern, and Southern groups), Indore (Chhatri Bagh, Gita Bhavan, Lalbaug Palace, Bada Ganapati, Juna Rajwada, Kanchi Mandir or Hukumchands Temple, Annapurna Temple, Kendriya Sangrahalaya), Ujjain (Bharatahari Cave, Gopal Mandir, Jantar Mantar, Kailadah Palace, Mahakali Temple, Sandipani Ashram, Shipra Ghats, Vikram University Museum), Kanha National Park (Wildlife in the park, Birds species in the park), Bandhavgarh National Park (Wildlife in the park, Birds species in the park).

Maharashtra

Located in the northern Centre of peninsular India, Maharashtra is surrounded by the Arabian sea in the west, Gujarat and Madhya Pradesh on the north, Madhya Pradesh in the east and Karnataka and Andhra Pradesh on the south. Mumbai is the capital of Maharashtra, which derives its name from the Goddess Mumba Devi. Mughal rulers from Delhi tried their best to keep this region under their control. From the middle of the 17th century, a new group of warrior people came to dominate the scene in Maharashtra and elsewhere in India called Marathas.

The origin of Marathas is still debatable, but what is known is that they stole the limelight from the great Mughals and at one point of time even captured Delhi. It was only after defeating the Marathas that the English could establish their rule in India. Shivaji was the first great ruler of Marathas and it was he who paved the way for future Maratha influence on India.

Places to visit

Mumbai (Afghan Church, Chowpatty Beach, Gateway Of India, Haji Ali Tomb, Flora Fountain, Kamala Nehru Park, Crawford Market, Mahalakshmi, Marine Drive, Hanging Garden, Race Course, Rajabai Towers and Bombay University, Victoria Terminus, Nehru Planetarium, Taraporewala Acquarium, Jijamata Udyan, Nehru Science Centre, Prince Of

Wales Museum), Pune (Shaniwar Wada, Saras Baug, Parvati Hill, Raja Kelkar Museum, Shinde's Chhatri, Bund Garden, Kasturba Smarak (Inside Agha Khan Palace) etc.), Aurangabad - Ajanta and Ellora (Aurangabad Caves, State Archaeological Museum, Nehru Udyan, History Museum of Marathwada University, Bibi ka Maqbara, Panchakki, Siddharth Udyan), Ajanta, Ellora, Mahableshwar (Walks and excursions to viewing points such as Elphistone Point, Babington Point, Bombay Point, Kate's Point and waterfalls like Chinaman's Falls and Dhobi Falls are pleasant, Venna Lake and Panchganga Temple)

Manipur

The green state of Manipur, and Imphal its capital, has all the fine, merged, tints of a water colour. Faiths and traditions and life styles seem to flow into each other with a softedged grace so that it is impossible to know where one ends and the other begins. The Manipur valley is watered by rivers threading out of the dark, mist-topped, ranges. Bright green fields stretch all the way to the distant mountains. Like the Nair women of Kerala the women of Manipur are trained in the fierce local Martial art known as Thang-ta. Both the men and women are dressed in black and they wield their swords like slicing, flashing, propellers, and when their swords clash, sparks fly. In marked contrast, is the delicate, marionette-like, Manipuri dance.

The dances suggest the relationship between the dancers and their Divine Master, Lord Krishna. The principal deity here is carved out of a jackfruit tree in response to a dream which Rajarshi Bhagyachandra had in the 18th century. Older forms of worship, however, continue to exist in the veneration of forest deities known as Umang Lais. Imphal gives a fascinating insight into an archetypal Indian trend.

Places to visit

Imphal (Shri Govindjee Temple, Khwairamband Bazaar, Manipur State Museum, The Old Palace, War Cemeteries, Manipur Zoological Garden, Khonghampat Orchidarium,

Saheed Minar, Langthaband), Moirang Lai haraoba, Sendra, Singda Dam, and other many places.

Meghalaya

Meghalaya was inaugurated as an autonomous state on April 2,1970. It was declared as a state of the Indian Union on January 21, 1972. Meghalaya is situated in the north-eastern region of India, between the Brahmaputra valley in the north and the Bangladesh in the south.

The state of Meghalaya (the abode of clouds) is geographically known as the "Meghalaya Plateau" or the "Shillong Plateau". The area is made of the oldest rock-formations. Meghalaya consists of the Garo, Khasi and Jaintia hills along with their outliers formed by the Assam ranges. It is the detached north-eastern extension of the Peninsular India. Part of it lies buried under the alluvium deposited by the Ganga-Brahmaputra system of rivers. This gap is known as Malda gap (between Raj Mahal hills/Chhota Nagpur and the Shillong Plateau).

Meghalaya Plateau's elevation varies between 150 meters to 1961 meters above sea level. The Plateau is highly dissected and has irregular terrain in the western and northern side. The southern side is marked by a continuous escarpment with steep slopes. The broken hills and ranges in the north are not of a well defined boundary.

The western part of the plateau or the Garo hills has an elevation of 600m above sea level. The most important relief feature of this part of the plateau is the Tura range with its highest point at Nokrek 1515 meters above sea level. The central and the eastern part of the plateau or the Khasi and the Jaintia hills district play prominent senile topography. This part of the plateau is characterised by the presence of many peneplained surfaces, flat-topped hills and numerous river valleys. The central upland zone is the most important relief feature of the area and covers more than one-third of the area, east of the Garo hills. The highest point of this part of this plateau and that of the entire state is the Shillong peak whose elevation is about 1965m above sea level.

In the Garo hills, the important rivers of the northern system from west to east are the Kalu, Ringgi, Chagua, Ajagar, Didram, Krishnai and Dudnai. Of these only the Krishnai and Kalu are navigable. The important rivers of the southern system are Daring, Sanda, Bandra, Bhogai, Dareng and Simsang. Simsang is the largest river in the Garo hills and navigable only for about 30 Km. Other navigable rivers are Nitai and the Bhupai.

In the central and eastern section of the plateau the important northward flowing rivers are Umkhri, Digaru and Umiam and the south-flowing rivers are Kynchiang (Jadukata), Mawpa, Umiew or Barapani, Myngot and Myntdu.

Places to visit

Khasi Hills, Jaintia Hills, Garo Hills, Cherrapunji, Nongpoh, Nongstoin, Tura, Shillong.

Mizoram

The youngest state Mizoram, formerly known as the Lushai Hills is situated in the North Eastern Corner of India. It is flanked by Bangladesh and Tripura in the West and Burma in the East. Scenic beauty combined with mild climate adds to the charm of a generous people. The beauty of Mizo society is that westernization mixes harmoniously with local traditions. Music and dance is the sprit of their culture. Mizoram is also a botanist's paradise as there are many kinds of orchids, wildflowers and herbs found over here.

Places to visit

Aizwal Town, Mizoram State Museum, The Weaving Centre, Bora Bazar, Luangmual Handicrafts Centre, Zoo.

Nagaland

Nagaland is a world apart. Nature resplendent in all her full-bodied glory. Exquisitely picturesque, vibrantly colourful, all lush fertile, the land represents unimaginable beauty, created by nature, to take your breath away... The Nagas, inhabitants of Nagaland, are said to belong to the indo-mongoloid stock, a race whose presence was first noted ten centuries before Christ, at the time of the compilation of the Vedas. Nagaland is bounded by Assam in the west, Burma on the East, Arunachal Pradesh and Assam on the North and Manipur in the South. The state consists of seven districts with sixteen tribes and sub-tribes inhabiting it. The Naga tribes are generally full of folklore. They are fond of seasonal songs, solo, duet and choric. Here man has to fight nature all the time. The struggle however, makes people tough. The people here are strongly built, simple, honest and hard working.

Places to visit

Kohima, War Cemetery, the State Museum Sales Emporium, Cultural Centre, Zoological Park, Cathedral, Kohima Village (Bara Basti).

Orissa

Orissa has a chequered history which has successfully assimilated and synthesized the best of Buddhist, Jain and Hindu cultures. Orissa or Kalinga as it was then called was a settlement of non-Aryan and Aryan settlers. It was here that the famous Battle of Kalinga was fought which made King Ashoka forsake war. He became a follower of Buddhism and spread the spirit of ahimsa and peace. It is to the Kharavela period that Orissa owes its Jain art and architectural tradition. The sophisticated architectural style of the Jain Monastic caves at Udaygiri and Khandagiri are a story unto themselves.

To understand all that a Hindu temple stands for one must realize that temples in India are not merely abodes of deities but a shradhanjali (offering) to the most sacred. Here a 'darshan' is a communion between man and his creator. Hence, Orissan temples are characterized by profuse decorations, exquisite carving and ornamentation covering the entire visible area with Gods and Goddesses, kings and queens, animals and flower motifs ranged against each other. They radiate the artist's inner love and dedication. Orissa is probably the only state where one can study temple architecture in all its successive stages of development.

Odissi, is the traditional dance form of Orissa and probably owes its origin to the temple dances of the devadasis (temple dancers). Possibly the oldest classical dance form, one must sit through a performance to experience its sheer lyrical grace. Mentioned in inscriptions, it is depicted on sculptures, in temples like the Brahmeswara and the dancing hall of the Sun temple at Konark. In fact in the 1950's the entire Odissi dance form was revitalized with the help of the Abhinaya Chandrika and sculpted dance poses found in temples.

Orissa enjoys a rich tradition of tribal and folk dances as well. Chhau from Mayurbhanj District is a martial dance form reminiscent of Orissa's earlier maritime tradition. Other folk and tribal dances include Danda Nata, a daylong performance ending in acrobatic sequences, Ranapa or dances in which dancers perform balancing acts on bamboo stilts.

Places to visit

Bhubaneshwar, Balasore, Baripada, Berhampur, Bolangir, Udaygiri Khandagiri, Dhauli, Cuttack, Dhenkanal, Jeypore, Keonjhar, Phulbani, Rourkela, Phulbani, Puri (Shri Jagannath Temple, Daria Hanuman and Sonar Gouranga Temple, Gundicha Char, Indradyumma Tank, Narendra/Chandan Tank, Loknath Temple, Swarga Dwar, Sea Beach at Puri), Bhawanipatna, Konark, Chilka Lake (The lake with several of its islands, main among them being, kalijai, Nalabana, Honeymoon, Breakfast islands etc. Satpada towards the South Eastern stretch of the lake is closer to puri and is fast developing as a tourist spot on the shore of Chilika), Gopalpur (Gopalpur is situated right on the Bay of Bengal with a beautiful sea-beach), Simplipal (Fauna found at the Park include the tiger, leopard, elephants, bison, sambar, porcupine, pangolin, flying-squirrel, hill myna, hornbill, python etc.), Chandipur.

Punjab

Punjab is a state in northwest India. Punjab (India) borders Punjab (Pakistan) to the west, Jammu and Kashmir to the north, Himachal Pradesh to the northeast, Haryana to the south and southeast, Chandigarh to the southeast and Rajasthan to the southwest. Punjab's capital is Chandigarh, which is administered separately as a Union Territory since it is also the capital of neighbouring Haryana. Other major cities of Punjab include Amritsar, Jalandhar, Ludhiana and Patiala. The state is the location of one of the world's first and oldest civilizations, the Indus Valley Civilization, India's first civilization.

Punjab (India) historically forms a part of the larger Punjab region, which also includes the province of Punjab (Pakistan), the Indian states of Haryana and Himachal Pradesh and Delhi and the Union Territory of Chandigarh. Indian Punjab was trifurcated in the year 1966 leading to the formation of Haryana and Himachal Pradesh.

Sikhism is the main religion of Indian Punjab, and is the persuasion of about 60 per cent of the population. Hinduism forms the prevalent minority religion. The holiest of Sikh shrines, the Harmandir Sahib, popularly known as the Golden Temple, is located in the city of Amritsar which is considered to be the holiest city in Sikhism. Amritsar is also a place of religious significance for Jains. Punjab is one of the six states in India that does not have a Hindu majority. The language of the people of Punjab, on both sides of the international border, is Punjabi; however, the script used is different (Gurmukhi on the Indian side and Shahmukhi on Pakistani side).

Tourism is a swiftly expanding area and many analysts predict huge potential. Tourism of Punjab is principally suited for the tourist interested in culture, civilization, spirituality and epic history. More specifically tourism is particularly suited for the person who is interested in epic history, the celebrated Punjabi culture, royal Punjabi palaces, historic battles and of course the world-renowned examples of Sikh Architecture, shrines and temples.

Places to visit

Amritsar (Golden Temple, Akal Takht, Durgiana Temple, Jalianwalla Bagh, Saragarhi Gurudwara, Tower of Baba Atal, Academy of Fine Arts, Central Museum and S.G.Thakur Singh Art Gallery), Chandigarh (The Secretariat, The Assembly and High Court, Zakir Hussain Rose Garden, Rock Garden, Sukhna Lake, Govt. Museum and Art Gallery and Punjab University Complex, International Doll Museum, National Gallery of Portraits)

Rajasthan

The golden glow of desert landscape, the shimmering emerald water surrounding the medieval lakes, grand palaces, bustling bazaars, endless desert sands, teeming wild and bird life are as much a part of Rajasthan. As the ships of the desert who sail majestically amidst the tranquility, colour and warmth all around. Rajasthan is the second largest state of India and is one of the few states that show a great contrast from one area to another. This disparity is noticeable in respect of climate, soil, vegetation, mineral resources etc.

The land that revives age old legends of brave Hadi Rani of the beautiful Padmini of Chittaurgarh, the pious Mira Bai, and the love stories of Dholamaru and Moomal - Mahendra of Marwar. Rajasthan, the land of prince and princess has the most amazing legends of devotion, romance and heroism. It offers the visitors: both quite moments of relaxation and adventure in the desert state.

Places to visit

Jaipur (Hawa Mahal, City Palace, Jantar Mantar, Amber Fort, Birla Mandir, Sisodia Gardens, Birla Planetarium, Jal Mahal, Nawab Ki Haveli, Galtaji's Temple), Ajmer (Adhai-Din-Ka-Jhonpra, Ana Sagar Lake, Circuit House, Dargah of Khwaja Moinuddin Chishti, Soniji ka Nasiyan, Mayo College, Swami Dayanand Saraswati Smarak, Taragarh Fort and the Museum), Udaipur, Chittaurgarh (Chittaurgarh Fort, Vijay Stambha, Kirti Stambha, Rana-Kumbha Palace, Padmini Palace, Meera Temple and Kumbha Shyam Temple and Kalika Mata Temple,

State Archaeological Museum), Mount Abu (Adhar Devi Temple, Andhra Point (Honeymoon Point), Dilwara Jain Temple, Gaumukh, Nakki Lake, Red Temple, Shri Raghunathji Temple, Sunset Point, Traver's Tank), Jodhpur (Jaswant Thada, Maha Mandir, Mandore Gardens, Balsamand Lake and Palace, Clock Tower and Sardar Market, Mehrangarh Fort, Umaid Bhawan Palace, Girdikot and Bishnoi Tribal Village where deer's are held sacred), Jaisalmer (Golden Fort with 99 bastions, Jain Temple, Gyan Bhandar, Salim Sing Ki Haveli, Patwon ki Haveli, Nathumal ki Haveli and Amar Sagar, Mool Sagar, Gadisar Lake, Jain Temples), Bikaner (Junagarh Fort, Lalgarh Palace, and Ganga Golden Jubilee Museum, Bhandeshwar Jain Temple),Ranthambhor National Park (Sawai Madhopur) (Amreshwar Mahadev, Mahavirji, Kela Devi, Shivad, Khandar, Rameshwaram in Khandar Area), Barmer (Junagarh Fort, Lalgarh Palace, and Ganga Golden Jubilee Museum, Bhandeshwar Jain Temple), Alwar (City Palace, Museum, Puran Vihar, Sagar (tank) Bala Fort, Vinay Vilas Mahal), Bharatpur-Deeg (Keoladeo Ghana Sanctuary, it is famous for rare avian species. Bharatpur Fort, Government Museum, Bharatpur Palace), Kumbhalgarh (Kumbhalgarh Fort and Kumbhalgarh Wild Life Sanctuary, Haldi Ghati), Kota (City Palace, The Fort overlooking Chamba River, Jagmandir - artificial water reservoir, Brig Vilas Palace Museum, Rao Madho Singh Museum and Darrah Wild Life Sanctuary - 50 Kms away from Kota), Bundi (Taragarh Fort or Star Fort, Palace, Chitra Mahal, Phool Sagar Palace, Nagar Sagar Kund, Sukh Mahal, Shikar Burj, Rani Ki Baori0.

Sikkim

Tucked away in the foothills of the Himalayas, Sikkim is a Himalayan wonderland with its lovely views and exotic orchids, and its forest-trails. A virtual Shangrila overlooked by Mt. Kanchenjunga, the world's third highest peak, Sikkim is attractive equally for the sightseer, the adventure sports enthusiast and those interested in Buddhism and Tibetology. Buddhism is the predominant religion here, with many fine old monasteries rich with frescoes, religious paintings on silk and statues of the Buddha's various incarnations. In Gangtok, the delightfully quaint capital, are pagoda like roofs of many buildings and the presence of crimson robed monks in the bazaars.

The Institute of Tibetology, the only one of its kind in the world, was set up by the erstwhile ruler to promote research on Mahayana Buddhism. Lower down the hill is the famed orchid sanctuary where 500 species of orchids indigenous to Sikkim are cultivated. Sikkim offers several treks that lead through pine forests, through picturesque valleys, monasteries and to mountain lakes. It is also the base for mountaineering expeditions and the rivers Teesta and Rangeet offer excellent river rafting. A number of good hotels and lodging houses exist in Gangtok.

Places of Interest

Gangtok (Chorten, Deer park, Enchey Monastery, Government Cottage Industries Institute, Orchid Sanctuary, Research Institute of Tibetology, Tashi View Point, Dharma Chakra Centre (Rumtek) and Saramsa Garden. Proposed Ganesh Tok and Hanuman Tok), Pemayangtse.

Tamil Nadu

Tamil Nadu, is the most prominent state of India. The capital. Madras is a cosmopolitan city and the capital of the state. Tamil Nadu is a bastion of Hinduism, whose past endures into the present. Temples with towering spires called gopurams are a common feature of this state, seldom seen anywhere else in the country. Temples in Tamil Nadu were the fulcrum of society and even today art forms that have their origin in religious worship continue to colour daily life. Notable among these are splendid bronzes of deities, painting on glass and Bharatnatyam. Kanchipuram, also called Kanjeevaram, is famous throughout the country as the Centre where lustrous silk sarees are woven.

Likewise Thanjavur is an important Centre for bronze figure casting. Mahabalipuram has a vast wealth of sculptures. In contrast to the temple heritage Pondicherry is known for long a French colony. Yet another facet of this surprisingly diverse state is two hill stations Ootacamund and Kodaikanal. Both are little patches of England, being much loved by the expatriate population of the Raj. Both places provide delightful relaxation during an extended tour of the south, having a wide range of hotel accommodation. The cuisine of Tamil Nadu, more or less totally vegetarian, has become enormously popular all over the country.

Places tof visit

Chennai (Fort St. George and St. Mary's Church, Gandhi Mandapam, Anna Square, Kapaleeswara Temple, Light House, Marina Beach and Aquarium, Parthasarathy Temple, San Thom Cathedral, Snake Park, Theosophical Society, Valluvar Kottam, Ripon Buildings and War Memorial Fort Museum and Govt. Museum and Art Gallery), Mahabalipuram (Rathas, Arjuna's Penance, Krishna Mandapa, Shore Temple, Mahishasurmardini Cave, Varaha Mandapa and Mandapams), Kanchipuram (Kailashnath Temple, Shri Vaikuntaperumal Temple, Shri Varadaraja Temple, Ekambareshwara Temple and Shri Kamakashi Temple), Vedanthangal Bird Sanctuary.

Tripura

Tripura is a tiny state in the North-East of the country. It has extensive international border with Bangladesh and, in fact, 85 per cent of its perimeter is international border with rest being common boundary with Assam and Mizoram to the East. This ancient land of mysterious past represents a composite culture with several ethnic groups residing in the state. Though the cultural heritage of one community differs from the other, the manifested efforts have mingled them into a single whole, giving birth to a unique cultural genre.

Tripura can be termed as a 'laboratory' of exotic cultural synthesis. Tripura, quite off the beaten track, is a storehouse of tribal crafts and culture as well as music and dancing. Tripura has a large number of attractive tourist sites including religious sites of Hindu's and Buddhists. Considering the proximity of Tripura with Bangladesh, it is more convenient for foreign nationals to enter Tripura via Bangladesh with an appropriate visa.

Places to visit

Agartala (Ujjayanta Palace, Kunjavan Palace, Jagannath Temple, BenuVan Vihar, Maharaja Veer Vikram College, Old Agartala, Buddha Vihar, Rabindra Kanan, State Museum)

Uttar Pradesh

In Uttar Pradesh, Lucknow was associated with the princely court of Oudh and then with the British, both traditions lingering on in the city whose finest monument is the Bara Imambara. Further east, Varanasi is the oldest city in India. An important centre of Hindu pilgrimage, it is believed that those who die in Varanasi will be released from the cycle of rebirth. Pious Hindus still come to Varanasi to spend their last days, living in Spartan communes run by a multitude of religious trusts. The focus of interest to a visitor is the sacred River Ganga. At the series of steps leading down to it, people come to wash away their sins by bathing in the river, the dead are cremated and holy men meditate. In the narrow by lanes of the city are crowded bazaars selling brassware and silk brocades.

Places to visit

Agra (Taj Mahal, Agra Fort, Itmad-ud-Daula's Tomb, Moti Masjid), Lucknow (Residency, Bada Imam Bara, Rumi Darwaza, Hussainabad, Clock Tower, Shah Nazar Zoo, State Museum, Macchi Bhawan, Khurshid Mahal, Botanical Gardens, Picture Gallery), Ayodhya (Hanumangarh, Janmasthan, Kanak Bhawan, Jain Temple, Treta-ke-Thakur, Mani-Parvat Nageshwar Nath Temple, Amawan Temple, Tulsi Chaura, Tulshi Smarak, Brahma Kund etc), Allahabad (Anand Bhawan (Home of the Nehru family), Allahabad Fort, Bhardwaj Ashram, Khusro's Tomb, Patlipuri Temple, Sangam, Swaraj Bhawan, Botanical Gardens, Allahabad Museum), Varanasi (River Front, Alamgir Mosque, Bharat Mata Temple, Tulsi Manas Temple, Gyanvapi Mosque, Vishwanath Temple (Golden Temple), Vishwanath Temple (Benaras Hindu

University), Durga Temple, Sarnath, Archaeological Museum, Sarnath, Fort Museum, Ramnagar, Bharat Kala Bhavan Hindu University).

Uttaranchal

Uttaranchal formerly a part of Uttar Pradesh was formed on November 9th, 2000 as the 27th state of the Indian Union. It is one of the most beautiful and enchanting region of northern India. Nature has endowed this land with so much beauty and spiritual bliss that it is also known as Dev Bhoomi, the Land of Gods. *Ganga, Yamuna* and scores of other rivers originate in Uttaranchal. Among them Ganga is the most holy and prominent as she represents the soul of India- her rich culture, history and civilization. In *Sanskrit* 'Himalaya' means Abode of Snow, truly characterizing the vast permanent snow fields above the snow line.In the heart of these majestic mountains lies the state of Uttaranchal with *Kumaon* region in its east and *Garhwal* in the west.

Uttaranchal finds mention in the ancient Hindu scriptures as Kedarkhand, Manakhand and Himavat. The Kushanas, Kudinas, Kanishka, Samudra, Gupta, the Pauravas, Katuris, Palas, the Chandras and Pawaras and the British have ruled in turns. It is often called the Land of the Gods (Dev Bhoomi) because of its various holy places and shrines. The hilly regions of Uttaranchal offer un spoilt landscapes to the tourist -pilgrim.

The present state of Uttaranchal was earlier as part of the United Province of Agra and Awadh which came into existence in 1902. In 1935, the name of the state was shortened to the United Province. In January 1950, the United Province was renamed as Uttar Pradesh and Uttaranchal remained a part of Uttar Pradesh before it came into being on 9 November 2000, the 27th state of India.

Places to visit

Dehradun (Sahastradhara Cold Sulphur Springs, Tapkeshwar (Shiva) Temple, Robber's Cave, Lakshman Sidh, Tapovan, Botanical Garden of Forest Research Institute), Mussoorie (Kempty Falls, Bhadraj Temple, Surkhanda Devi,

Jwalaji Temple (Benog Hill), Gaumukh Trek (23 Km): Snout of Gangotri glacier and source of the river Bhagirathi, Gomukh is located at an altitude of 4200 meters), Rishikesh (Bharat Temple, Rishi Kund and Raghunath Temple, Laxman Jhoola, Pushkar Temple, Shatrughan Temple, Muni-Ki-Reti, Swarg Ashram, Gita Bhawan, Parmath Niketan, Lakshman Temple, Sadanand Jhoola, Triveni Ghat, Shivanand Ashram, Kailash Ashram, Academy of Meditation), Gangotri (Submerged Shivling: A natural Shivling formed of rock, submerged in the river, where according to mythology, Lord Shiva sat when the Ganga first descended to earth. The Shivling is visible only when the water is clear in early winter. Mussoorie (Gun Hill, Camel's Back Road, Kempty Falls, Lal Tibba, The Jheel), Dhanaulti (Surkanda Devi, Chamba and New Tehri), Nainital (Naini Lake, Snow View, Naina Peak, Hanuman Garhi), Ranikhet (Chaubatia, Bhaludam, Jhoola Devi Ram Mandir, Mankameshwar, Upat and Kalika, Hairakhan Temple, Tarikhet, Binsar Mahadev, Majkhali, Dwarahat, Chaukhutia, Bhikiasain, Manila, Naithna Devi Jaurasi, Khairna and Pandukholi), Almora (Public Museum, Nanda Devi Museum, Bright and Corner, Deer Park, Chetai Temple, Simtola), Kausani (Annashakti Ashram, View of the Nanda Devi Hill). Yamnotri (Yamnotri stands in the shadow of Banderpunch Mountain (6315 Meters, Temple of Yamnotri, Surya Kund, hot water spring, Divya Shila. Saptarshi Kund-10 Kms), Badrinath.

West Bengal

Kolkata, three hundred years old, traces its history to the landing of Robert Clive on the banks of the Hooghly beside three villages. It was from here the monumental British Raj was launched in India. The capital of West Bengal, Kolkata is the major entry point. Poets, thinkers and film directors of international renown hail from this city. Some of the best known monuments of the British Raj were built here. Sightseeing in this fascinating city includes Raj Bhawan, the residence of the Governor of Bengal, Victoria Memorial, the city's landmark, Botanical Gardens, which are notable for the oldest banyan tree, and orchid house, Armenian Church, Marble Palace, one family's collection of memorabilia and the Birla Planetarium. Darjeeling, the state's most popular hill resort, is a slice of England 2,134 meters above sea level. Surrounded by tea gardens growing the prized leaf known as Darjeeling, the little town faces some of the Himalaya's highest peaks. Darjeeling is an abrupt variation from the lowlands of West Bengal. Buddhism, being a major faith here, Darjeeling and the nearby town of Kalimpong has, between them, several Buddhist monasteries, chiefly of the Yellow Hat sect.

Places to visit

Kolkata (Belur Math, Botanical Garden, Dakshineshwar Temple, Howarh Bridge, Jain Temple, Kali Temple, Marble Palace, Nakhoda Mosque, National Library, Rabindra Sarobar, Raj Bhavan, Ramakrishna Mission Institute of Culture, Sahid Minar (Ochterlony Monument), St.Paul's Cathedral, Victoria Memorial, Zoological Gardens), Museums an Art Galleries (Academy of Fine Arts, Birla Academy of Art and Culture, Birla Industrial and Technological Museum, Birla Planetarium, Gurusaday Museum, Nehru Children's Museum, Rabindra Bharati Museum, State Archaeological Gallery, Victoria Memorial Hall Museum), Sunderbans, Jaldapara Sanctuary, Bakkhali, Shantiniketan (China Bhavan, Chhatimtala, Kala Bhavan, Patha Bhavan, Prayer Hall, Bichitra, Sangeet Bhavan, Uttarayan Complex, Udayana, Konarka, Shyamali, Punascha and Udichi, The Bichitra (or, Rabindra Bhavan), Kala Bhavan, Bichitra (Rabindra Bhavan), Deer Park, Uttarayan Gardens), Vishnupur (Ras Mancha, Dalmadal Cannon, Jor Bangla Temple, Madan Mohan Temple, Malleswar Temple, Lalji Temple, Mrinmoyee Mandir, Shyam Rai Temple, Malla King's Fort, Jogesh Chandra Pura Kirti Bhavan Museum), Darjeeling (Tiger Hill- 11 kms, Ghoom Monastery- 8 kms; Batasia Loop- 5 kms, Himalayan Mountaineering Institute- 2 kms, Himalayan Zoological Park, Darjeeling Rangeet Valley Passenger Ropeway- 8 kms, Tibetan Refugees Centre, Lebong Race Course, Natural History Museum, Happy Valley Tea Estate, Lloyds Botanical Garden, Observatory Hill, Dhirdham

Temple, Senchal Lake), Sagardwip, Raijang Bird Sanctuary, Plassey, Kurseeong (Eagle's Crag, Deer Park, Forest Museum, Giddhapahar Mandir, Ambotika Shiv Mandir, Makaibari Tea Estate, St.Mary's Hill, Dowhill, Baggaura, Chimney, Kettle Valley Picnic Spot, Namsu, Netaji Kothi), Kalimpong (Durpin Dara, Shri Ganeshmoni Pradhan Nursery, Standari Nursery, Shri L.B.Pradhan Nursery, Gouripur House, Swiss Welfare Dairy, Tibetan Monastery), Durgapur (Alloy Steel Project- 10 kms, Mining and Allied Machinery Corporation- 6 kms, Durgapur Coke Ovens Project Limited- 6 kms, A.V.B.- 6 kms, Durgapur Barrage- 3 kms, Durgapur Steel Plant- 10 kms, Philips Carbon Black and Sankey Wheels), Digha, Buxa Tiger Reserve.

Chapter 3

Food and Tourism

The hospitality industry, particularly its food-service component, is an important sector of many nations' economies. Developing nations should take steps to encourage development of hotels and restaurants. Those steps include improving training, offering tax incentives, and clearing up questions about land ownership. By the same token, restaurant and hotel operators should seek to make the best possible use of local resources, for example, by serving locally produced foods when possible. By setting up a five-year plan for tourism development, national governments can gain the advantages of international tourism. One source of development will undoubtedly be United States-based food-service chains, which are now expanding internationally. As an example, the food-service industry is an important part of the U.S. economy and with proper assistance can become vital to other nations' economies.

Tourism as Industry

Like other industrial projects, tourism projects too involve professional management, capital investment, special skills and training. The Government of India and a number of other states have declared tourism as an industry. Gujarat State which is at the forefront of the industrial development will also declare tourism as an industry. This will enable the tourism projects to be reliable to get benefits contained in the paras 5.1.2 and 5.1.3 below.

Availability of land is a primary requirement of any project. The process of grant of land will be facilitated in urban areas for the projects concerning setting up of hotels, restaurants and apartment hotels etc. Existing arrangements for grant of government waste land to industrial units will be made applicable to various tourism projects. Arrangements will be made to acquire private land under Land Acquisition Act for various tourism projects by companies registered under the Companies Act. The existing commercial rates of NA assessment applicable to land involving tourism projects would be reviewed and rates of NA assessment for industrial purposes will be made applicable to them.

As one of the sets of infrastructural institutions, the State Financial Institutions have made an important contribution in creating conductive environment for industrial entrepreneurs. They will be called upon to do the same for tourism entrepreneurs in terms of making available adequate finance.

FOOD INDUSTRY AND HOSPITALITY

The food industry is the complex, global collective of diverse businesses that together supply much of the food energy consumed by the world population. Only subsistence farmers, those who survive on what they grow, can be considered outside of the scope of the modern food industry.

The food industry includes:

- *Regulation*: local, regional, national and international rules and regulations for food production and sale, including food quality and food safety, and industry lobbying activities
- *Education*: academic, vocation~l, consultancy
- *Research and development*: food technology
- *Manufacturing*: agrichemicals, seed, farm machinery and supplies, agricultural construction, etc.
- *Agriculture*: raising of crops and livestock, seafood
- *Food processing*: preparation of fresh products for market, manufacture of prepared food products

- *Marketing*: promotion of generic products (e.g. milk board), new products, public opinion, through advertising, packaging, public relations, etc
- *Wholesale and distribution*: warehousing, transportation, logistics
- *Retail*: supermarket chains and independent food stores, direct-to-consumer, restaurant, food services

Overview

Essentially, the food industry involves the commercial movement of food from field to fork. The modern food industry is the result of technological and cultural changes that have occurred over the last 150 years. Traditionally, over thousands of years, food production was centered around two activities:

1. Labour-intensive agricultural activities, the farming of grain, produce and livestock;
2. Personal food preparation, where individuals and families acquire raw and minimally processed ingredients, and prepare them for their own consumption.

A significant per centage of the population was directly involved in farming, and in the process, many people actually fed themselves, from field to table. By contrast, the modern food industry relies far more on technology, particularly on mechanization and biochemistry, than on human and animal labour. In this way, food is raised, manipulated, preserved and moved around, resulting in a food industry that is to a great degree global in nature, with food and related resources travelling great distances.

For example, farm machinery and parts from Europe and agrichemicals from the US may routinely travel to farms in South America, where farm products are raised and shipped to North America for fresh market consumption, or for use in processed foods which may then travel to further points around the world. The point at which foods are gathered and prepared has also become fragmented: much of what we eat has already been assembled for consumption.

This modern food system relies heavily on technology, transportation, management and logistics for physical fulfillment, and on marketing and government regulation for maintaining an efficient consumer market. An incredibly wide range of businesses and individuals are employed by and profit from all aspects of this huge and complex system. A tremendous amount of governmental regulation and administration is also involved in this continual flow of materials, food products, and related information.

Definitions

Food industry is not a formally defined term, however, it is usually used in a broadly inclusive way to cover all aspects of food production and sale. The Food Standards Agency, a government body in the UK, describes it thus:

> "...the whole food industry - from farming and food production, packaging and distribution, to retail and catering."

The Economic Research Service of the USDA uses the term food system to describe the same thing:

"The U.S. food system is a complex network of farmers and the industries that link to them. Those links include makers of farm equipment and chemicals as well as firms that provide services to agribusinesses, such as providers of transportation and financial services. The system also includes the food marketing industries that link farms to consumers, and which include food and fiber processors, wholesalers, retailers, and foodservice establishments."

A comfortable room, good food, and a helpful staff can make being away from home an enjoyable experience for both vacationing families and business travellers. While most lodging managers work in traditional hotels and motels, some work in other lodging establishments, such as camps, inns, boardinghouses, dude ranches, and recreational resorts. In full-service hotels, lodging managers help their guests have a pleasant stay by providing many of the comforts of home, including cable television, fitness equipment, and voice mail, as well as specialized services such as health spas. For business travelers, lodging managers often schedule available meeting rooms and electronic equipment, including slide projectors and fax machines.

Lodging managers are responsible for keeping their establishments efficient and profitable. In a small establishment with a limited staff, the manager may oversee all aspects of operations. However, large hotels may employ hundreds of workers, and the general manager usually is aided by a number of assistant managers assigned to the various departments of the operation. In hotels of every size, managerial duties vary significantly by job title.

General managers have overall responsibility for the operation of the hotel. Within guidelines established by the owners of the hotel or executives of the hotel chain, the general manager sets room rates, allocates funds to departments, approves expenditures, and ensures expected standards for guest service, decor, housekeeping, food quality, and banquet operations. Managers who work for chains also may organize and staff a newly built hotel, refurbish an older hotel, or reorganize a hotel or motel that is not operating successfully. In order to fill entry-level service and clerical jobs in hotels, some managers attend career fairs.

Resident or hotel managers are responsible for the day-to-day operations of the property. In larger properties, more than one of these managers may assist the general manager, frequently dividing responsibilities between the food and beverage operations and the rooms or lodging services. At least one manager, either the general manager or a hotel manager, is on call 24 hours a day to resolve problems or emergencies.

Assistant managers help run the day-to-day operations of the hotel. In large hotels, they may be responsible for activities such as personnel, accounting, office administration, marketing and sales, purchasing, security, maintenance, and pool, spa, or recreational facilities. In smaller hotels, these duties may be combined into one position. Assistant managers may adjust charges on a hotel guest's bill when a manager is unavailable.

An Executive Committee made up of a hotel's senior managers advises the general manager, assists in setting hotel policy, coordinates services that cross departmental boundaries, and collaborates on efforts to ensure consistent and efficient guest services throughout the hotel. The Committee may be comprised of the department heads for housekeeping, front office, food and beverage, security, sales and public relations, meetings and conventions, engineering and building maintenance, and human resources. Executive committee members bring a different perspective of guest service to the total management objective reflecting the unique expertise and training of their positions.

Executive housekeepers ensure that guest rooms, meeting and banquet rooms, and public areas are clean, orderly, and well maintained. They also train, schedule, and supervise the work of housekeepers, inspect rooms, and order cleaning supplies.

Front office managers coordinate reservations and room assignments, as well as train and direct the hotel's front desk staff. They ensure that guests are treated courteously, complaints and problems are resolved, and requests for special services are carried out. Front office managers may adjust charges posted on a customer's bill.

Convention services managers coordinate the activities of various departments in larger hotels to accommodate meetings, conventions, and special events. They meet with representatives of groups or organizations to plan the number of rooms to reserve, the desired configuration of the meeting space, and banquet services. During the meeting or event, they resolve unexpected problems and monitor activities to ensure that hotel operations conform to the expectations of the group.

Food and beverage managers oversee all food service operations maintained by the hotel. They coordinate menus with the Executive Chef for the hotel's restaurants, lounges, and room service operations. They supervise the ordering of food and supplies, direct service and maintenance contracts within the kitchens and dining areas, and manage food service budgets.

Catering managers arrange for food service in a hotel's meeting and convention rooms. They coordinate menus and costs for banquets, parties, and events with meeting and convention planners or individual clients. They coordinate staffing needs and arrange schedules with kitchen personnel to ensure appropriate food service.

Sales or marketing directors and public relations directors oversee the advertising and promotion of hotel operations and functions, including lodging and dining specials and special events, such as holiday or seasonal specials. They direct the efforts of their staff to purchase advertising and market their property to organizations or groups seeking a venue for conferences, conventions, business meetings, trade shows, and special events. They also coordinate media relations and answer questions from the press.

Human resources directors manage the personnel functions of a hotel, ensuring that all accounting, payroll, and employee relations matters are handled in compliance with hotel policy and applicable laws. They also oversee hiring practices and standards and ensure that training and promotion Programme reflect appropriate employee development guidelines.

Finance (or revenue) directors monitor room sales and reservations. In addition to overseeing accounting and cash-flow matters at the hotel, they also project occupancy levels, decide which rooms to discount and when to offer rate specials.

Computers are used extensively by lodging managers and their assistants to keep track of guests' bills, reservations, room assignments, meetings, and special events. In addition, computers are used to order food, beverages, and supplies, as well as to prepare reports for hotel owners and top-level managers. Managers work with computer specialists to ensure that the hotel's computer system functions properly. Should the hotel's computer system fail, managers must continue to meet the needs of hotel guests and staff.

Industry size

Processed food sales worldwide are approximately US$3.2 trillion (2004). In the U.S., consumers spend approximately US$1 trillion annually for food, or nearly 10 per cent of the Gross Domestic Product (GDP). Over 16.5 million people are employed in the food industry.

Agriculture is the process of producing food, feed, fiber and other desired products by the cultivation of certain plants and the raising of domesticated animals (livestock). The practice of agriculture is also known as "farming", while scientists, inventors and others devoted to improving farming methods and implements are also said to be engaged in agriculture. More people in the world are involved in agriculture as their primary economic activity than in any other, yet it only accounts for four per cent of the world's GDP.

A vast global transportation network is required by the food industry in order to connect its numerous parts. These include suppliers, manufacturers, warehousing, retailers and the end consumers.

With populations around the world concentrating in urban areas, food buying is increasingly removed from all aspects food production. This is a relatively recent development, taking place mainly over the last 50 years. The supermarket is a defining retail element of the food industry, where tens of thousands of products are gathered in one location, in continuous, year-round supply.

Food preparation is another area where change in recent decades has been dramatic. Today, two food industry sectors are in apparent competition for the retail food dollar. The grocery industry sell fresh and largely raw products for consumers to use as ingredients in home cooking. The food service industry offers prepared food, either as finished products, or as partially prepared components for final "assembly".

Food Industry Technologies

Sophisticated technologies define modern food production. They include many areas. Agricultural machinery, originally led by the tractor, has practically eliminated human labour in many areas of production. Biotechnology is driving much change, in areas as diverse as agrichemicals, plant breeding and food processing. Many other areas of technology are also involved, to the point where it is hard to find an area that does not have a direct impact on the food industry. Computer technology is also a central force, with computer networks and specialized software providing the support infrastructure to allow global movement of the myriad components involved.

Marketing

As consumers grow increasingly removed from food production, the role of product creation, advertising, publicity become the primary vehicles for information about food. With processed food as the dominant category, marketers have almost infinite possibilities in product creation. The smooth flow of international trade is critical to the functioning of the modern food industry. Government regulations have to be synchronized to some greater degree to allow this.

Labour and Education

Until the last 100 years, agriculture was labour intensive. Farming was a common occupation. Food production flowed from millions of farms. Farmers, largely trained from generation to generation, carried on the family business. That situation has changed dramatically. In North America, over 50 per cent of the population were farm families only a few decades ago; now, that figure is around 1-2 per cent, and some 80 per cent of the population lives in cities. The food industry as a complex whole requires an incredibly wide range of skills. Several hundred occupation types exist within the food industry.

Research and Development

Research in agricultural and food processing technologies happens in great part in university research environments. Projects are often funded by companies from the food industry. There is therefore a direct relationship between the academic and commercial sectors, as far as scientific research.

Prominent Food Companies

Monsanto is a leading producer of pesticide, seeds, and other farming products. Both Archer Daniels Midland and Cargill process grain into animal feed and a diverse group of products. ADM also provides agricultural storage and transportation services, while Cargill operates a finance wing.

Bunge is a global soybean exporter and is also involved in food processing, grain trading, and fertilizer. Dole Food Company is the world's largest fruit company. Chiquita Brands International, another US based fruit company, is the leading distributor of bananas in the United States. Sunkist Growers, Incorporated is a U.S. based grower's cooperative. Tyson Foods is the world's largest processor and marketer of chicken and the largest beef exporter from the United States. Smithfield is the world's largest pork processor and hog producer.

Nestlé is the world's largest food and beverage company. The Altria Group owns 88.1 per cent of Kraft Foods, the largest U.S. based food and beverage company. Unilever is an Anglo-Dutch company that owns many of the world's consumer product brands in foods and beverages.

CUISINE IN INDIAN HOTELS

The finest of India's cuisines is as rich and diverse as it's civilization. It is an art form that has been passed on through generations purely by word of mouth, from guru teacher to vidhyarthi (pupil) or from mother to daughter. The range assumes astonishing proportions when one takes into account regional variations. Very often the taste, colour, texture and appearance of the same delicacy changes from state to state. The hospitality of the Indians is legendary. In Sanskrit Literature the three famous words 'Atithi Devo Bhava' or 'the guest is truly your god' are a dictum of hospitality in India. Indians believe that they are honoured if they share their mealtimes with guests.

Even the poorest look forward to guests and are willing to share this meager food with guest. And of particular importance is the Indian woman's pride that she will not let a guest go away unfed or unhappy from her home. Indians are known for their incredible ability to serve food to their guests invited or uninvited. Food customarily forms the crowning part of most festivities and celebrations. Whatever the occasion Indians eat with great gusto and are adept at finding reasons to feast and make merry. At traditional and festive meals, the thali (plate) or banana leaf is decorated with rangoli.

Kashmiri

Kashmiri cuisine is essentially meat-based. Lamb, goat's meat and chicken form the basis of many a famous dish. It is flavored delicately with saffron and kashmiri chillies which are not too spicy but impart a rich red colour to the food. The abundance of dry fruit like walnuts, dried dates, and apricots also inspire the Kashmiri connoisseur to use them lavishly in puddings, curries and snacks. Cottage cheese or chaman as it is called, is also a popular accompaniment to many meats and vegetables. Fresh water fish like trout found in the numerous fresh water streams flowing down from the Himalayas is also a delicacy. Food is generally followed by a generous serving of fresh fruits like strawberries, plums, cherries and apples which grow here and not all over India due to the cool climate.

Punjabi

Punjabi people are robust people with robust appetites and their food is like the Punjabis themselves, simple, sizeable and hearty with no unnecessary frills or exotic accompaniments. The Punjabi tandoori cooking is celebrated as one of the most popular cuisines throughout the world. Huge earthen ovens are half buried in the ground and heated with a coal fire lit below it. Marinated meat, chicken, fish, paneer, rotis and naans of many types are cooked in this novel oven and the results are absolutely scrumptious.

Punjab has imbibed some aspects of its cuisine from external influences. Connoisseurs of the cuisine say that the gravy component of Punjabi cuisine came from the Mughals. The most popular example is the murg makhani. It served the state well to combine this influence in its cooking since it had a lot of pure ghee and butter. Murg makhani also provided a balance to tandoori chicken, which was dry because it was charcoal cooked.

Nans and parathas, rotis made of maize flour are typical Punjabi breads. Of course, over the years the roti has been modified to add more variety, so there is the rumali roti, the naan and the laccha parathas, all cooked in the tandoor. Winter, in Punjab, brings in the season of the famous makki ki roti(maize flour bread) and sarson ka saag(mustard leaf gravy). No meal is complete without a serving of lassi(sweet or salted drink made with curd) or fresh curd and white butter which is consumed in large quantities. The other popular dishes, which belong exclusively to Punjab, are ma ki dal, rajma (kidney beans) and stuffed parathas.

Mughlai

Having reigned over India for so long, the Moghuls left a deep and long lasting influence on Delhi's cuisine. The Mughlai cuisine is literally 'fit for royalty'. With it's rich sauces, butter-based curries, ginger flavoured roast meats, and mind-blowing sweets, it has captured the fancy of food lovers all over the world. From a tangy shorba or soup to the rose petal strewn kulfi, Mughlai food offers a rich fare that is irresistible. Although available throughout the country, the best place to try this royal cuisine is in Delhi.

Bengali

Bengal's greatest contribution to the food heritage of India is a magnificent spectrum of sweets made from burnt milk and curd. 'Rasogullas', 'gulab jamuns', 'cham cham', 'malai sandwich', 'chena murki', 'anarkali', 'rajbhog' - the list of mouth-watering delicacies is endless. 'Mishti dhoi' or yoghurt sweetened with jaggery is a must in every Bengali home. Guests are always welcomed with 'sandesh' or sweets made from burnt milk and 'singadas' or crisp samosas.

Besides sweets, the Bengalis eat fish with great relish and most of the popular Bengali dishes are made from fish. A variety of styles are adopted to cook fish. They are at times marinated in spices, at other times cooked in curd. The cuisine of West Bengal differs from that of Bangladesh in that the use of coconut in this cuisine is much lesser and mustard oil is cooking medium instead of coconut oil. The spices differ from those used in the heartland of India, but are similar to those used in the interiors of the East Coast. The specialty of Bengali cooking is the use of panchphoron i.e. five basic spices which include zeera, kalaunji, saunf, fenugreek and mustard seeds. Generally, Bengali food is a mixture of sweet and spicy flavors and dining with these gentle people is a definate treat.

Maharashtrian

Maharashtrians are by and large, meat eaters. The cuisine includes subtly flavoured vegetarian delicacies and hot, aromatic meat and fish curries. Their crunchy, crisp sweets are made mostly from rice and jaggery. The exotic 'Konkani' and 'Malwani' cuisines also have their origins in the coastal parts of this region and are sea-food based. As in most of the other states of India, rice is the staple food grain in Maharashtra too. Like the other coastal states, there is an enormous variety of vegetables in the regular diet and lots of fish and coconuts are used. Grated coconuts spice many kinds of dishes, but coconut oil is not very widely used as a cooking medium. Peanuts and cashewnuts are widely used in vegetables and peanut oil is the main cooking medium.

Another feature is the use of kokum, a deep purple berry that has a pleasing sweet and sour taste. Kokum, most commonly used in an appetizer-digestive called the sol kadhi, is served chilled. All non-vegetarian and vegetarian dishes are eaten with boiled rice or with bhakris, which are soft rotis made of rice flour. Special rice puris called vada and amboli, which is a pancake made of fermented rice, urad dal, and semolina, are also eaten as a part of the main meal.

The most popular dessert of Maharashtra is the puran poli, which is roti stuffed with a sweet mixture of jaggery and gram flour and is made at the time of the Maharashtrian New Year. Other popular sweets are the ukdiche modak (these are served during the Ganesh festival), the panpole ras, and the shreekhand. Shreekhand, a sort of thick yogurt sweet dish, is a great Favourite at weddings and the Dussehra festival. Flavored with cardamom powder and saffron, this aromatic dish is served with piping hot puris.

Goan

Famous for it's distinctive cuisine, Goa can boast of delicacies like the tangy pork 'vindaloo', spicy 'sorpotel' and the ever popular Goan fish curry with rice. Goa's luscious coconut and fish based dishes draw in people from all over the world. Goans often accompany their meal with one of their innumerable local wines or the local liqueur called 'Feni'. Goan food is simple but one has to bear in mind that most, though not all, of it is chili hot, spicy, and pungent. Rice, fish, and coconut are the basic components of the typical Goan food platter. Delicacies made from these three items can be expected in nearly every Goan meal. Besotted with seafood, the Goans find truly world-class prawns, lobsters, crabs, and jumbo pomfrets along the coastline and use them to make a variety of soups, salads, pickles, curries, and fries.

An essential ingredient in Goan cooking is coconut milk made by grating the white flesh of a coconut and soaking it in a cup of warm water. Equally important is the 'kokum', a sour, deep red coloured fruit that gives it a sharp and sour flavor. The famous red Goan chilies are also a must for most dishes, as is tamarind. Goans make their own version of vinegar from toddy. Then there are innumerable chutneys that are typical of the state.

Goa is not particularly known for its vegetarian dishes. While Hindus like lamb and chicken, Christians prefer pork. However, both prefer fish and seafood to any other meat. Pork is a must for any festive occasion in Goa and the most famous preparation is the vindaloo. It is a spicy concoction, lots of red chilies, garlic, cooked with chunks of pork, Goa vinegar, and hard palm jaggery and is best enjoyed with plain boiled rice. Another mouth-watering delicacy made of pork is the sarpotel. A curry with a thick gravy to the layman, this exotic concoction comprises boneless pork, liver, heart, kidneys, red chilies, cinnamon, cloves bathed in tangy toddy vinegar, which is needed to balance the strong taste of pig's blood: another traditional ingredient of this revered dish.

For those with a sweet tooth, Goan cuisine offers the famous bebinca. The extract of coconut milk is added to flour, sugar, and other delectable ingredients are used to make this delicacy. Each scrumptious layer has to be baked before the next one is added, though not many people nowadays have the time to make the traditional 16 layers. Even so, a good bebinca is a mouth-melting dream.

Other sweets include a soft jaggery flavored fudge called dodol made from finger-licking palm-sap jaggery, rice flour and coconut; the crispy delicate rose-a-coque that are flower-like waffles and can be eaten alone or drenched with cream or honey; the curled and sugared kulkuls spiraled around the tines of forks and deep-fried as Christmas goodies and Easter eggs known as ovos da pascoa. Similarly, during the Hindu festival of Ganesh Chaturthi, cone-shaped dumplings called modaks are a favourite fare.

Gujarati

Gujaratis have truly perfected the art of vegetarian cooking. From the simplest lentils and vegetables, they create a mouth-watering variety of food. Gujarat is known as the land of milk and butter. Predictably so, yoghurt and buttermilk are a part of the Gujarati's daily diet. While in Gujarat, a 'thali' dinner - literally meaning a meal served on a silver platter- is a delight you must not miss. An endless procession of fresh vegetables cooked in aromatic spices, a variety of crisp, fried snacks and an array of delectable confections typically appear in the 'thali'.

In Gujarat, during winter when green vegetables are available in plenty, a delicious vegetable concoction called undhyoo is made using potato, brinjal, and green beans amongst several other vegetables. The main dish of gujarati cuisine is the khichdi, a simple lentil and rice mixture. It is eaten with kadhi, a savory curry made with yogurt using bay leaves, ginger, chilies and finely chopped vegetables as garnishing, onions and pickle.

Using the same lentils and rice, Kutchi kitchens produce delectable items like the khaman dhokla, a salty steamed cake made from chickpea flour; doodha pak, sweet, thickened milk confectioned with nuts, and srikhand, a dessert made of yogurt, flavored with saffron, cardamom, nuts and candied fruit which is eaten with hot, fluffy pooris. These three delicacies have made their way into the Favourites list of the rest of India too and can be found in restaurants all over the country.

Rajasthani

The ancient princely state of Rajasthan gave rise to a royal cuisine. The Rajas who went on hunting expeditions ate the meat or the fowl that they brought back. Even today, Rajasthani princely feasts flaunt meat delicacies that are incomparable. In contrast are the vegetarian Rajasthanis. Their food cooked in pure ghee is famous for it's mouth- watering aroma. Rajasthani cooking was also influenced by both the war-like lifestyles of its inhabitants and the availability of ingredients in the desert region. Food that could last for several days and could be eaten without heating was preferred, more out of necessity than choice. Scarcity of water and lack of fresh green vegetables also had their effect on Rajasthani cooking.

Dried lentils and beans from indigenous plants like sangri, ker etc. are staples of the Rajasthani diet, as wheat and rice do not grow very well in the desert land. Gram flour is an integral cooking ingredient and is used to make delicacies and so are powdered lentils. Bajra and corn are used all over the state for making rotis and other varieties of bread. In Rajasthan, bajre ki roti (millet bread) and lahsun ki chutney (hot garlic paste) combined with spring onions are the staple diet of the locals as these are believed to be safeguards against the hot winds. In the desert belt of Jaisalmer, Barmer and Bikaner, cooks still use very little water and instead use milk, buttermilk and clarified butter as alternatives.

The balance to using these milk products is provided by the appropriate use of digestives, especially asafetida, black rock salt, ginger and ajwain. The Favoured spices are fenugreek seeds, kasuri methi (dried fenugreek leaves) and aniseed. A distinct feature of the Maheshwari cooking is the use of mango powder, a suitable substitute for tomatoes, scarce in the desert, and asafetida, to enhance the taste in the absence of garlic and onions.

Hyderabadi

The cuisine of Andhra Pradesh is reputedly the spiciest and hottest of all Indian cuisine. The cuisine includes both the original Andhra cooking and the Hyderabadi cuisine with its Mughlai influence. It is the former which is red hot. The vegetables and greens are prepared with various different masalas giving the same vegetable different flavours. Traditional Andhra cuisine also has many non-vegetarian dishes which are also spicy and unique in taste. Hyderabadi cuisine is rich and aromatic with a liberal use of exotic spices and ghee, not to speak of nuts and dry fruits. Lamb is the most widely used meat in the non-vegetarian dishes. The biryanis (flavoured rice with meat or vegetables) is one of the most distinct Hyderabadi food.

FOOD BASED TOURISM

In a recent survey of tourist perceptions of the UK food industry, two-thirds of Britons said that food and drink influenced their holiday choice. The West Country, Wales and Scotland occupied the top three destinations. For no longer is British food synonymous with fish, chips and roast dinners (except, of course, for Jacques Chirac, who has complained that only the Finns have worse cuisine).

During the 20th Century, industrialisation began to threaten artisan producers and many abandoned their traditional techniques. But in the past two decades, there's been a resurgence in demand for quality products made by time-honoured methods. The appetite is growing for regional produce, such as Somerset cider, Caerphilly cheese and Cromer crabs. Food tourism has become big business, worth nearly £4bn a year.

Since the Malt Whisky Trail was set up around Scottish distilleries several decades ago, the number of food and drink trails has multiplied. New additions include a wine trail around the South-East, sausage trails in the Midlands and the North-West, and a Lake District afternoon tea trail. Alexia Robinson, the organiser of British Food Fortnight, says food adds to a visitor's experience of a place. "Taste is one of our senses. We usually experience a place visually, such as on a castle or cathedral tour, so why not add to that through our taste buds?"

Even once-sleepy backwaters such as Bray in Berkshire, Padstow in Cornwall and Shropshire's Ludlow have become gastronomic hotspots thanks to star chefs Heston Blumenthal, Rick Stein and Shaun Hill (who has since closed the Michelin-starred Merchant House, which in 2003 ranked among the world's top 20 eateries). And the latest series of BBC Two's Full on Food - pitched firmly at the growing foodie market - catered for the interest in regional produce by dispatching a chef to find the tastiest local treats, be it ice cream, wild salmon or real ale.

Taste of Home

For Alexia Robinson, the variety of local specialities reflects the UK's diverse geography. Many regional dishes have evolved over centuries using ingredients best suited to the conditions and lifestyles of that area.

Cheese varieties are one such example, as is the Cornish pasty, devised to provide a filling lunch for the county's lead miners. And niche habitats such as salt marshes in Wales give lamb from the area a distinctive taste. What producers and caterers find is that the more local a food seems, the better the sales pitch. Hence detailed menus which name-check the farm which supplies the meat or the allotment where they grow their own asparagus.

For provenance sells, says Ms Robinson. "People want to know where their food comes from. I've even seen a wonderful menu entry for apple and blackberry pie, 'all blackberries picked from our local hedgerows'." She says that holidaymakers want foods which emphasise the heritage and culture of a place. "If you stay in a Gloucestershire BandB, for example, you'll probably be served sausages made from Gloucester Old Spot pigs. In the north of England, tourists seek out potted shrimps, and apple pie is popular in Kent." And who, at the seaside, hasn't been lured into an establishment famed for serving the best fish 'n' chips on that stretch of coast?

Food miles

Nor do we need to travel to track down regional delights. Delicatessens now stock British goodies as well as the more usual olives and Italian meats. Farmers' markets typically draw crowds, with London's Borough Market recently voted the capital's top tourist attraction. With producers and fine food stockists going online, tasty treats from around the UK can be delivered to your door.

Food also holds a key place in the "think globally, act locally" debate. Some buyers are keen to support local businesses, or protect the environment by avoiding foods which have been transported long distances. Environmentalists and tourism bosses alike must be heartened that two-thirds of Britons say they would consider holidaying at home, rather than jet off somewhere sunny, because of the food and drink on offer. Bon appetit indeed.

Food Tourism on the Boil

It could be the colourful sight of a giant rustic paella in a Spanish seaside town or the smell of a warm bagel on a New York street. But whatever the dish, it seems food is something an increasing number of us remember from our travels. Like never before, holiday makers are choosing where they go by what they can put in their stomachs - and catering for them is now top of the menu for tour operators and destinations. Fiona Jeffery, Group Exhibition Director of World Travel Market, who undertook the independent research with 2000 people throughout the UK of all ages and socio economic groups, said: "Food tourism today is where eco-tourism was 20 years ago; people are starting to take an interest.

"Although the research was carried out on behalf of World Travel Market was in the UK, we believe it is representative of a new and growing phenomenon within the international industry. "The industry needs to take note and use the opportunity to its advantage. Holidaymakers want a hands-on experience and food is a manifestation of a destination's culture. "You can open a different door with every meal." "The last five years has seen an incredible shift in the way holidays are marketed and it's all because people are demanding authentic experiences, said Erik Wolf, president of the International Culinary Tourism Association, a non-profit group representing more than 500 tourism businesses in 19 countries."

For the first time, the true extent of food tourism has been measured in the UK by World Travel Market, the premier business event for the international travel and tourism industry, with research revealing more than half (53per cent) ranked eating traditional dishes as a 'very important' or 'important' part of their holiday. Meanwhile, a staggering 86per cent of Brits quizzed said they enjoyed local foods when abroad. The trend is not just limited to those on specialist tailor-made breaks either, with 83per cent of people who typically go on half- or full-board holidays admitting they willingly miss meals in their hotel or resort to try out local restaurants.

International chef Gary Rhodes, whose TV Programmes has helped open up the world's traditional dishes and ingredients to a hungry audience, has recently opened a Rhodes restaurant in Calabash, on the Caribbean island of Grenada and onboard PandO Cruises' new liner Arcadia. He said: "The potential for tourism through dining is enormous and what better way to learn about a country than at the table! My experience is that travellers are becoming both more sophisticated and daring about what they eat."

Changes in Weekly Shop

Supermarkets have played a major part in the shift in attitudes, making foreign foods more available. One supermarket chain, Waitrose, for example, recently unveiled a range of tapas and Greek dishes that customers might have tried on their holiday. "The world is becoming a smaller place and we are seeing our customers' tastes change to reflect this. Dishes from all corners of the globe are becoming mainstream additions to the British dinner table," said Waitrose communications manager Gill Smith. "Flavours people have sampled on holiday are becoming more popular.

As they travel to further a field, customers are more willing to experiment with new flavours. Our oriental range now extends beyond Chinese dishes to Japanese, Malaysian and Thai foods. "We're also finding that as people travel more, they are more knowledgeable about regional trends within countries. Instead of simply wanting Indian foods, we're finding that customers are aware of Goan and Keralan food and want to buy these dishes at their local supermarket." In the research, the growing trend to change what they put in their supermarket trolley because of holiday experiences is evident. A total of 42per cent said this affected their weekly shop choices. Wolf said that some tourist offices are beginning to highlight food as a way of promoting their country to foreign visitors. This trend though must grow still further.

Chicago Led the Way

Chicago led the way eight years ago when it appointed former chef Judith Hines as director of culinary arts and events. She oversees 275 annual food-related events, including its summer-long Stirring Things Up festival (May 1-Oct 31), which features culinary tours, food festivals, farmers' markets and concerts. Special hotel rates are available to visitors during the period.

Although it's impossible to know how many visitors are drawn by food alone, Hines said millions come for the festivals, including the 11-day Taste of Chicago in July, where 3.5 million people consumed 70,000 pounds of ribs and 250,000 slices of pizza last year. That helped boost hotel occupancy to 90per cent last summer. "Food certainly helps boost tourism. While cultural events like theatre might be a good hook for tourists, it won't appeal to all; the attraction of food is universal" said Hines. "The misperception is that it has to be all five-star fine dining. We have 76 different ethnic neighbourhoods and promote them all. Having really authentic food is part of the attraction."

Chicago's focus on food includes a food concierge in one of the city's largest tourist offices adjacent to a large theatre booking agency. "It's a great tie-up. We explain the food scene to people who are looking for somewhere to eat on their night out." Hines also offers city tours with a difference, with a bus stopping at four local restaurants with diners having a course in each. "It's a fun way to find out about the city's culture and heritage," she explained.

Operators claim the last five years has seen a significant change in the eating habits of Brits abroad, with clients shunning the 'chips with everything' restaurants and seeking out more local flavours. This is borne out by World Travel

Market's independent research which indicated that 62 per cent of those questioned shunned "glamorous" foreign restaurants and wanted to eat in rustic surroundings with the locals. Only 7 per cent said they would prefer to eat in glamorous surroundings when overseas. Only 15 per cent of those questioned would plump for international cuisine rather than food typical of the area in which they were staying.

Demand for Authentic Experience

"People want an authentic experience," claimed Chris Orme, general manager of Far East specialist Travel Indochina. "We are talking much more about food to people when they book and make it a central part of the holiday, going to local restaurants and experimenting. The availability of Chinese, Thai and Vietnamese food in the UK means clients want to try the authentic stuff much more. "People have booked particular holidays with us on the strength of the food. We're certainly not an operator that deals with food tours, but eating has certainly become a big interest for our clients."

Long Travel, a specialist in rural Italy and Sicily, claimed around 85 per cent of its clients now asked specifically for food advice when booking. Contracts manager Laura Bell said: "Customers have very high expectations of the food in Italy because it receives so much good press and is always featured in cookery Programmes. "Getting back to nature and trying out dishes in a traditional setting is a must for our clients. Even the larger hotels we use grow many of their own vegetables and produce wine now."

Restaurant Concierge Service

Mercedes Fehler, marketing manager at upmarket specialist Harlequin Worldwide said demand for local cuisine was so high among its customers the operator had introduced a 'restaurant concierge' service. Customers can contact the operator before departure and the concierge will recommend and make reservations at restaurants around the globe.

"The concierge contacts the hotel the customer is staying in to get advice about the places to eat nearby and will make bookings. It's a very popular service in long-haul destinations," said Fehler. "Short haul, people tend to get out and look themselves. Hunting around for a place to eat in Europe is something people are more comfortable with."

Meanwhile, Caribbean specialist Carib Tours runs a 'food evening' each year for regular clients to showcase the best local restaurants. "People in the UK have access to some of the best restaurants in the world and so they won't settle for poor food when they're away," said Carib Tours managing director Paul Cleary. "The four aspects of a holiday that are important to our clients are weather, beach, luxury and food. "The trend in the Caribbean has been for 'big name' European restaurants and chefs to open in the last few years. Clients want to eat in them, maybe as a special occasion. They also want to get out and eat locally. In Barbados, the Oistin's Fish Fry is a great example, but then it also has The Cliff, one of the world's best restaurants."

The DIY trend has even started to spread long-haul, according the Martin Grass, sales and marketing director of Rex Hotels., which has nine properties in the Caribbean and two in Kenya. "The Caribbean ahs been dominated by the big all-inclusives in the past and people had no need to go out to eat. While that is still very popular with the US market, people from the UK are a bit more adventurous, especially to the eastern Caribbean. Islands such as Barbados and Antigua have fantastic local restaurants and are seen as safe to venture out at night. The vast majority of our business from the UK is now room-only, because people want to sample the food and it is comparatively cheap to eat out."

But food has become a central part of the overseas marketing for nations around the world. Earlier this year, Portugal teamed up with Harrods to promote its national dishes through the up market stores famous food hall. For the European destination, the message aims to attract not only those on traditional packages, but also the major villa holiday market predominantly served by the low-cost carriers, since these people eat out more.

Portuguese National Tourist Office director José António Preto da Silva said: "Our cuisine is now one of the key attractions for UK visitors, with each region of Portugal offering unique cooking style as well as local specialities. "Mealtimes are highly valued by the Portuguese, providing a leisurely opportunity to indulge in good food and good wine while catching up with family and friends, and this is a tradition we encourage visitors to join in to capture the true essence of our country and people."

The Rise of Food Festivals

Similarly, Singapore hosts an annual food festival each July celebrating a different aspect of its culture. This year (it's 14th) marks the 40th anniversary of the country's independence, majoring on what it is perhaps best known for by foreign visitors andendash; its hawker (street) food. Tee Yen Chew, Singapore Tourism Board's Area Director for Northern and Western Europe said: "Singaporeans are passionate about food and eating. In almost every corner of the island, you will find an endless variety of food served hot or cold at any hour of the day or night. Singapore's cultural diversity is very much reflected in the variety of local food it has to offer and endash; Chinese, Malay, Indian, Peranakan and Eurasian. It is very important to communicate this to people thinking about visiting Singapore. It's not just a fusion of east and west, it the country's unique cultural tapestry."

Closer to home, VisitScotland has begun to promote food alongside its mainstay messages such as golf and outdoor pursuits. The country has also introduced a national quality assurance scheme, Eat Scotland, aimed at raising standards and educating hoteliers and restaurant owners about the important part food plays for visitors.

Key Driver in Scotland

Sector development manager for Visit Scotland Ewan Fair weather said: "Food is a key driver in the holidaymaking decision. We want those in the industry to shout about their food, be proud and enthusiastic. That will enrich the visiting experience." Las Vegas, meanwhile, is a good example of how destinations have changed the emphasis of their food product as tourism has changed. Food has always been part of the gambling city's attraction from the opening of the first all-you-can-eat buffet andendash; the $1 Midnight Chuck Wagon at the El Rancho hotel. But it was quantity over quality promoted to its original domestic clientele.

Very often, food and drink was considered a loss-leader by the casinos, with establishments giving it away to attract gamblers. The arrival of high-rolling punters, overseas tourists and large business travel contingent means it now boasts some the best restaurants in the US. Today, Las Vegas is home to three restaurants that have earned the AAA Five Diamond rating: the Bellagio's Le Cirque and Picasso and The Mirage's Renoir.

"Dining in Las Vegas has evolved significantly from the days of the all you can eat buffets," said Melanie Jones, of the Las Vegas Convention and Visitors Bureau in the UK. "Las Vegas has now become synonymous with gourmet cuisine and most of the top chefs have now opened restaurants in the city from Wolfgang Puck to Alain du Casse. Even Guy Savoy who allegedly vowed, in the past, that he would not consider opening a restaurant in the US."

WINE AND FOOD TOURISM

Wine, Food, and Tourism Marketing is an overview of contemporary practices and trends in food and wine tourism marketing. Local and regional food holds great potential to contribute to sustainable competitiveness in a destination. An analysis of the literature and promotional material of South African and key international destinations, however, indicate that the contribution of food to sustainable tourism and the marketing of destinations has received very little attention globally, as well as in South Africa.

A framework and guidelines for developing and implementing food tourism could enable destination marketers and entrepreneurs to optimise the tourism potential of local and regional food. To this end a food tourism destination-marketing framework was conceptualised, which was based on the findings of a South African situation analysis and international trends and best practices.

The South African situation analysis entailed an empirical investigation among regional and provincial destination marketing organisations to determine the current status and future potential and food tourism initiatives as a key component of destination marketing in South Africa. To support the food tourism destination marketing framework, two key tools were developed, namely TOURPAT (a tourism and culinary atlas linked to a geospatial database) and PAT (a product potential and attractiveness tool).

The framework and tools were tested in a South African destination and provided the stakeholders with mechanisms to develop and implement food tourism. This paper outlines the key components and an evaluation of the framework and tools that have been developed. Guidelines and recommendations for the development, packaging and marketing of local and regional foods are postulated. Proposals for future research are also outlined.

The Tasmanian Wine and Food Tourism Strategy provides an understanding of where Tasmania is positioned in a national context and identifies ways to create new and maximise existing opportunities to enhance the Tasmanian wine and food tourism experience. Research has provided an insight into the industry segment both nationally and in Tasmania, highlighting two key visitor groups who are Tasters and Epicureans.

The key findings give rise to a range of development strategies and action plans at both the state and regional level. The Wine and Food Tourism Strategy is sector specific and underpins the broader Tasmanian Experience Strategy that addresses how Tasmania's three core appeals of nature, cultural heritage and wine and food in combination give the State a sustainable competitive advantage.

Tasmanian Wine and Food Tourism Strategy

The Tasmanian Wine and Food Tourism Strategy provides an understanding of where Tasmania is positioned in a national context and identifies ways to create new and maximise existing opportunities to enhance the Tasmanian wine and food tourism experience. Research has provided an insight into the industry segment both nationally and in Tasmania, highlighting two key visitor groups who are Tasters and Epicureans. The key findings give rise to a range of development strategies and action plans at both the state and regional level.

The Wine and Food Tourism Strategy is sector specific and underpins the broader Tasmanian Experience Strategy that addresses how Tasmania's three core appeals of nature, cultural heritage and wine and food in combination give the State a sustainable competitive advantage. The Tasmanian Experience Strategy will complement and build on the Wine and Food Tourism Strategy in the context of the delivery of the broader visitor experience. Wine and food tourism can make a significant contribution to the broader tourism growth targets set under the joint industry-State Government strategic plan, Tourism 21. The targets are $1 billion in visitor expenditure and 26,000 tourism jobs, both by 2007.

In June 2000, it was estimated that visitors to Tasmania spent $69 million on food and wine. A primary objective of this strategy is to increase this expenditure while building on the sector's growing potential to attract higher-yielding visitors to Tasmania. Compared to other states, Tasmanian wine and food tourism is in the early stages of industry development. The Tasmanian Wine and Food Tourism Strategy has been developed as a framework to drive growth, quality of experiences and the ability to value-add within the sector.

A wine and food tourism experience has all three elements present - neither wine, food nor tourism alone comprise a wine and food tourism experience. While the intrastate market will continue to be important for the sector's sustainability, studies conducted as part of the strategy show that the growth potential lies with interstate and international visitors. In addition, market research emphasises that Tasmania's competitive advantage - and its point of differentiation from other visitor destinations - lies in its mix of wine and food with the appeal of natural beauty and history. This strategy has been developed by Tourism Tasmania in consultation with sector operators, industry organisations, the Tourism Council Tasmania and other State Government agencies.

Growth potential

The two main customer groups identified as wine and food purchasers are Tasters (48 per cent including Epicureans 2 per cent) and Non-Tasters (52 per cent), who have little or no interest in wine and food experiences. Studies indicate that the profile of the Tasters group is similar to the overall leisure market, showing that people do not come to Tasmania just for a wine and food experience but are attracted by the interplay of nature and heritage with wine and food.

Research shows the short break market has a particularly high level of interest in food and wine related activities. Tasters represent the majority of holiday visitors and consume wine and food as part of their broader holiday experience, therefore wine and food products are unlikely to attract additional visitor numbers. Along with other states and territories Tasmania achieves a relatively similar market share of Tasters to its market share in overall national visitation. However, a greater number and range of offerings are most likely to increase the spend and yield per visitor during their stay. Wine and food is a key trigger for the Epicurean segment. These visitors make their holiday travel decisions specifically to participate in wine and food activities and have a higher holiday spend.

The segment currently comprises about 7000 interstate and 1300 international visitors to Tasmania annually. Victoria (41 per cent of market share), South Australia (30.1 per cent) and Western Australia (20.9 per cent) dominate the Epicurean market nationally due to the establishment of recognised wine regions. Victoria has at least 10 regions attractive to Epicureans and South Australia has also adopted a multiple region approach. Western Australia has achieved its success using a single wine and food destination with the hub in the Margaret River region, a geographic location not close to an urban centre. Epicureans perceive that there is little on the ground in Tasmania to attract them to the State, which is why only a small number holiday here.

It is apparent that clear action is critical for development of the wine and food sector. While the existing focus on food and wine as an integral part of the Tasmanian holiday experience should continue, a greater number and variety of experiences need to be developed to improve the total spend and yield per visitor for the Tasters. An even more radical shift in both product and human infrastructure is needed to get onto the "hot list" for Epicureans, including developing more high quality wine and food experiences, events and activities, and adopting a multi-regional approach - with more touring options between Tasmania's wine regions - to encourage longer stays and increased spend. In this context, external pressures that can impact on the capacity of boutique operators to deliver wine and food experiences (i.e. Wine Equalisation Tax) need to be addressed by the industry at large.

Tasmanian Development Strategies

Research shows that wine and food is not a stand alone tourism trigger but one of three interdependent sets of core values of Tasmania's brand alongside wilderness/nature and history/heritage. It is the combination of these values that is most likely to trigger wine and food tourism. Market demand is driven by available product, so if the product is not readily available then the customer will not purchase it, therefore the key to driving demand is supply.

The key research outcomes highlight that: i) wine and food tourism is supply-led; ii) it occurs in identifiable regions; and iii) metropolitan wine and food tourism precincts rely more on local customers rather than visitors. It also identifies a distinct supply-led development sequence for wine and food tourism regions.

The three-stage sequence is:

1. Wine production, dictated by volume and reputation;
2. Food industry development to complement the rise in profile of an area and the character of its wines; and
3. Tourism growth that occurs with the increasing quality and quantity of wine and food and improved branding and reputation of the regions.

Six development strategies have significant potential to lift overall tourism yield and visitor numbers:

1. Continue to ensure that wine and food tourism is integrated with wilderness and nature, as well as history and heritage;
2. Encourage infrastructure development based on the three-stage development pattern;
3. Target the Tasters segment to achieve yield objectives and visitor numbers, while basing the positioning of wine and food tourism in Tasmania on the Epicureans;
4. *Adopt a regional approach* - Tamar Valley, South East and Freycinet;
5. Manage each region as it progresses through product development stages to ensure that its distinctiveness is developed as well as regional strategies; and
6. *Promote the cluster* - The region's range of tourism experiences that encourage visitors to stay longer in an area - as the experience and the destination.

Regional Overview

While nationally Tasmania as a whole is considered to be a food and wine destination, the three emerging sub-regions offer distinct product differentiation. The Product Life Cycle concept reflects the product evolution and industry development stages. Product evolution has five stages:

1. Market development, when a product is small-scale and at the early stages of development;
2. Rapid growth, when demand is driving growth and there is scale-up and diversification;
3. Competitive turbulence, during which there are high rates of new development and a greater scale achieved;
4. Saturation/maturity, the stage of over-supply leading to gradual stagnation of product; and
5. Decline, of product and revenues.

Tasmania's wine regions are each in a different phase of industry development within the Market Development Stage. Tamar Valley has experienced significant investment by the larger wineries. The emerging cluster relies heavily on its hub of Launceston for related food and tourism infrastructure. It is considered to be in the latter phases of this Market Development Stage. While there has been significant investment by some of the larger wineries in the South East region, it is not on the same scale and the industry is still stand-alone, production focused, with Hobart as the hub. It is most likely in the early to mid-phase of the Market Development Stage.

The Freycinet industry is stand-alone, small, with limited product and while on the touring route does not benefit from proximity to a major hub. It is considered to be at the beginning of the Market Development Stage. Because each region is at a different stage of evolution and there is a need to develop its distinctiveness, each requires its own development Action Agenda to achieve growth. Common to each region is the need to address four key attributes that are critical to product evolution:

1. The number and quality of wineries within a region or cluster;

2.. The number and quality of restaurants in a region or cluster and their use of local produce and integration with the character of wines of the region;
3. Related tourism infrastructure, including accommodation and the type and quality of activities within the area; and
4. The level and sophistication of customer service standards, which help create the character and brand of product and experience.

The strategy also identifies 16 industry development triggers required for the Freycinet cluster to move from the very early Market Development Stage of the product cycle to the late Market Development Stage. They include: bundling product with other tourism brand values, such as promoting regional wine and food experiences with natural attractions like Freycinet National Park; adopting the Freycinet Region as the region's name; integrating the region's three national parks into the regional marketing strategy; developing Coles Bay-Swansea-Bicheno as the region to replace a single hub; and increasing direct customer purchase opportunities through actions such as wine-based direct mailing lists.

Food and Restaurant Managers

Fast food restaurant managers are responsible for the provision of standardised food and customer service in outlets based in the high street, motor service areas, stations, airports or multiplexes. Drawing on all the operational functions of a business, the work involves applying financial, marketing and operational know-how, and supervising and training staff.

Managers plan, organise, and co-ordinate all resources and activities in a store. The work involves: setting targets, planning budgets, and controlling stock; recruiting, training and inspiring restaurant teams; creating and driving marketing campaigns; and building bridges with the local community. Ultimately, it is the manager's ideas, initiative and personality that shape the restaurant.

Tasks typically involve:

- Organising the store in terms of products, equipment and people;
- Planning and checking work schedules;
- Carrying out audits to check health safety, food safety and quality of service in the restaurant;
- Making sure the fast-track audit is completed daily to check the safety of equipment and that food is properly cooked, only in-date stock is used, and all other products are discarded;
- Carrying out work outside the restaurant, including 'mystery shopping' at other restaurants within the chain;
- Attending weekly meetings with senior managers;
- Dealing with problems, queries, complaints, staff and customers in the store;
- Monitoring and maintaining high standards of food, service and hygiene;
- Ensuring the company's required standards of customer care are met;
- Administering payrolls;
- Checking and securing cash receipts;
- Budgeting to ensure maximum profitability;
- Achieving set profit and loss targets;
- Maintaining and securing equipment and buildings and all company assets contained within the unit;
- Publicising and marketing restaurants in the locality;
- Motivating restaurant teams;
- Recruiting, selecting and training new staff and fully inducting the restaurant team in accordance with company policy;
- Developing all team members to their fullest potential using the performance management/ review system and identifying individual training needs;

- Ensuring the implementation and maintenance of legislation, company standards and procedures;
- Recognising new trends and implementing action plans accordingly;
- Acting as a communication link between senior teams and the restaurant team;
- Leading by example, acting as a role model for the restaurant team.

A successful manager will strike the right balance between creating both a good service for restaurant customers and a fun work environment for members of staff.

Catering Manager

Catering managers plan, organise and manage the food and beverage services of organisations and businesses, both inside and outside the hospitality industry, with the aim of achieving good quality at low cost and maintaining high standards of hygiene and customer satisfaction.

There is a range of jobs in catering management, along with a number of different routes into the industry. Roles include: managing restaurants, bars and other outlets in hotels, resorts or liners; providing catering services at events; and running catering operations at hospitals, schools and other organisations.

With ongoing growth in the service industry, opportunities in this demanding but rewarding area continue to grow.

Typical Work Activities

The role varies according to the size and nature of the establishment: in a small operation, the catering manager has more of a 'hands on' role and will be involved in the day-to-day running of the operation; in contract catering, the catering manager will spend time negotiating with the client organisation, assessing its requirements and ensuring that it is satisfied with the service delivered.

Typical tasks will include:

- Recruiting and training permanent and casual staff;
- Organising, leading and motivating the catering team;
- Planning menus in consultation with chefs;
- Ensuring health and safety regulations are strictly observed;
- Budgeting and establishing financial targets;
- Monitoring the quality of the product and service provided;
- Keeping financial and administrative records;
- Managing the payroll and monitoring spending levels;
- Maintaining stock levels and ordering new supplies as required;
- Interacting with customers if involved with 'front of house' work;
- Liaising with suppliers and clients;
- Negotiating contracts with customers (in contract catering).

In more senior posts, principal tasks will involve:

- Setting and agreeing budgets;
- Monitoring quality standards;
- Overseeing the management of the facilities, for example checking events bookings and the allocation of resources and staff;
- Planning new promotions and initiatives, and contributing to business development;
- Dealing with staffing and client issues, as they arise.

TOURISM AND ECONOMICS

Tourism's economic benefits are touted by the industry for a variety of reasons. Claims of tourism's economic significance give the industry greater respect among the business community, public officials, and the public in general.

This often translates into decisions or public policies that are Favourable to tourism. Community support is important for tourism, as it is an activity that affects the entire community. Tourism businesses depend extensively on each other as well as on other businesses, government and residents of the local community.

Economic benefits and costs of tourism reach virtually everyone in the region in one way or another. Economic impact analyses provide tangible estimates of these economic interdependencies and a better understanding of the role and importance of tourism in a region's economy. Businesses and public organizations are increasingly interested in the economic impacts of tourism at national, state, and local levels. One regularly hears claims that tourism supports X jobs in an area or that a festival or special event generated Y million dollars in sales or income in a community. "Multiplier effects" are often cited to capture secondary effects of tourism spending and show the wide range of sectors in a community that may benefit from tourism.

Tourism activity also involves economic costs, including the direct costs incurred by tourism businesses, government costs for infrastructure to better serve tourists, as well as congestion and related costs borne by individuals in the community. Community decisions over tourism often involve debates between industry proponents touting tourism's economic impacts (benefits) and detractors emphasizing tourism's costs.

Sound decisions rest on a balanced and objective assessment of both benefits and costs and an understanding of who benefits from tourism and who pays for it. Tourism's economic impacts are therefore an important consideration in state, regional and community planning and economic development. Economic impacts are also important factors in marketing and management decisions. Communities therefore need to understand the relative importance of tourism to their region, including tourism's contribution to economic activity in the area.

A variety of methods, ranging from pure guesswork to complex mathematical models, are used to estimate tourism's economic impacts. Studies vary extensively in quality and accuracy, as well as which aspects of tourism are included. Technical reports often are filled with economic terms and methods that non-economists do not understand. On the other hand, media coverage of these studies tend to oversimplify and frequently misinterpret the results, leaving decision makers and the general public with a sometimes distorted and incomplete understanding of tourism's economic effects.

How can the average person understand these studies sufficiently to separate good studies from bad ones and make informed choices? The purpose of this bulletin is to present a systematic introduction to economic impact concepts and methods. The presentation is written for tourism industry analysts and public officials, who would like to better understand, evaluate, or possibly conduct an economic impact assessment. The bulletin is organized around ten basic questions that either are asked or should be asked about the economic impacts of tourism.

An Economic Impact Analysis

A variety of economic analyses are carried out to support tourism decisions. As these different kinds of economic analysis are frequently confused, let's begin by positioning economic impact studies within the broader set of economic problems and techniques relevant to tourism. These same techniques may be applied to any policy or action, but we will define them here in the context of tourism. Each type of analysis is identified by the basic question(s) it answers and the types of methods and models that are appropriate.

Benefit cost analysis and economic impact analysis are frequently confused as both discuss economic "benefits". There are two clear distinctions between the two techniques. B/C analysis addresses the benefits from economic efficiency while economic impact analysis focuses on the regional distribution of economic activity. The income received from tourism by a destination region is largely off-set by corresponding losses in the origin regions, yielding only modest contributions to net social welfare and efficiency. B/C analysis includes market and non-market values (consumer surplus), while economic impact analysis is restricted to actual flows of money from market transactions.

While each type of economic analysis is somewhat distinct, a given problem often calls for several different kinds of economic analysis. An economic impact study will frequently involve a demand analysis to project levels of tourism activity. In other cases demand is treated as exogenous and the analysis simply estimates impacts if a given number of visitors are attracted to the area. A comprehensive impact assessment will also examine fiscal impacts, as well as social and environmental impacts.

Be aware that an economic impact analysis, by itself, provides a rather narrow and often one-sided perspective on the impacts of tourism. Studies of the economic impacts of tourism tend to emphasize the positive benefits of tourism. On the other hand environmental, social, cultural and fiscal impact studies tend to focus more on negative impacts of tourism. This is in spite of the fact that there are negative economic impacts of tourism (e.g., seasonality and lower wage jobs) and in many cases positive environmental and social impacts (e.g., protection of natural and cultural resources in the area and education of both tourists and local residents).

An economic impact assessment (EIA) traces changes in economic activity resulting from some action. An EIA will identify which economic sectors benefit from tourism and estimate resulting changes in income and employment in the region. Economic impact assessment procedures do not assess economic efficiency and also do not generally produce estimates of the fiscal costs of an action. For many problems economic impact analysis will be part of a broader analysis. Environmental, social, and fiscal impacts are often equally important concerns in a balanced assessment of impacts.

Tourism Economic Impact Study

An economic impact analysis will assess the contribution of tourism activity to a region's economy. An economic impact analysis also reveals the interrelationships among economic sectors and provides estimates of the changes that take place in an economy due to some existing or proposed action. The most common applications of economic impact analysis to tourism are:

- To evaluate the economic impacts of changes in the supply of recreation and tourism opportunities. Supply changes may involve a change in quantity, such as the opening of new facilities, closing of existing ones, or expansions and contraction in capacity. Supply changes may also involve changes in quality, including changes in (a) the quality of the environment, (b) the local infrastructure and public services to support tourism, or (c) the nature of the tourism products and services that are provided in an area.
- To evaluate the economic impacts of changes in tourism demand. Population changes, changes in the competitive position of the region, marketing activity or changing consumer tastes and preferences can alter levels of tourism activity, spending, and associated economic activity. An economic impact study can estimate the magnitude and nature of these impacts.
- To evaluate the effects of policies and actions which affect tourism activity either directly or indirectly. Tourism depends on many factors at both origins and destinations that are frequently outside the direct control of the tourism industry itself. Economic impact studies provide information to help decision makers better understand the consequences of various actions on the tourism industry as well as on other sectors of the economy. For example, increased air pollution standards have

been opposed in some regions due to the predicted economic consequences of the closing of plants that cannot meet the new standards. Tourism interests counter these arguments with estimates of the potential gains in income and jobs in tourism industries that depend on good air quality and visibility.

- To understand the economic structure and interdependencies of different sectors of the economy. Economic studies help us better understand the size and structure of the tourism industry in a given region and its linkages to other sectors of the economy. Such understandings are helpful in identifying potential partners for the tourism industry as well as in targeting industries as part of regional economic development strategies. Issues such as economic growth, stability, and seasonality may be addressed as part of these studies.
- To argue for Favourable treatment in allocation of resources or local tax, zoning or other policy decisions..By showing that tourism has significant economic impacts, tourism interests can often convince decision-makers to allocate more resources for tourism or to establish policies that encourage tourism. Tax abatements and other incentives frequently given to manufacturing firms have also been granted to hotels, marinas and other tourism businesses based on demonstrated economic impacts in the local area.
- To compare the economic impacts of alternative resource allocation, policy, management or development proposals. Economic impact analyses are commonly used to assess the relative merits of distinct alternatives. The economic contribution of expanded tourism offerings may be compared for

example with alternatives such as resource extraction activities (mining, timber harvesting) or manufacturing. Impacts of alternative tourism development proposals may also be evaluated, e.g., tourism strategies that emphasize outdoor recreation, camping development, a convention facility, or a factory outlet mall.

Direct, Indirect and Induced Effects

A standard economic impact analysis traces flows of money from tourism spending, first to businesses and government agencies where tourists spend their money and then to:

1. *Other businesses* — Supplying goods and services to tourist businesses,
2. *Households* - Earning income by working in tourism or supporting industries, and
3. *Government.*— Through various taxes and charges on tourists, businesses and households

Formally, regional economists distinguish direct, indirect, and induced economic effects. Indirect and induced effects are sometimes collectively called secondary effects. The total economic impact of tourism is the sum of direct, indirect, and induced effects within a region. Any of these impacts may be measured as gross output or sales, income, employment, or value added. Direct effects are production changes associated with the immediate effects of changes in tourism expenditures. For example, an increase in the number of tourists staying overnight in hotels would directly yield increased sales in the hotel sector. The additional hotel sales and associated changes in hotel payments for wages and salaries, taxes, and supplies and services are direct effects of the tourist spending.

Indirect effects are the production changes resulting from various rounds of re-spending of the hotel industry's receipts in other backward-linked industries (i.e., industries supplying products and services to hotels). Changes in sales, jobs, and income in the linen supply industry, for example, represent indirect effects of changes in hotel sales. Businesses supplying products and services to the linen supply industry represent another round of indirect effects, eventually linking hotels to varying degrees to many other economic sectors in the region.

Induced effects are the changes in economic activity resulting from household spending of income earned directly or indirectly as a result of tourism spending..For example, hotel and linen supply employees supported directly or indirectly by tourism,.spend their income in the local region for housing, food, transportation, and the usual array of household product and service needs. The sales, income, and jobs that result from household spending of added wage, salary, or proprietor's income are induced effects.

By means of indirect and induced effects, changes in tourist spending can impact virtually every sector of the economy in one way or another.

The magnitude of secondary effects depends on the propensity of businesses and households in the region to purchase goods and services from local suppliers. Induced effects are particularly noticed when a large employer in a region closes a plant. Not only are supporting industries (indirect effects) hurt, but the entire local economy suffers due to the reduction in household income within the region. Retail stores close and leakages of money from the region increase as consumers go outside the region for more and more goods and services. Similar effects in the opposite direction are observed when there is a significant increase in jobs and household income.

Final demand is the term used by economists for sales to the final consumers of goods and services. In almost all cases, the final consumers of tourism goods and services are households. Government spending is also considered as final demand. The same methods for estimating impacts of visitor spending can be applied to estimate the economic impacts of government spending, for example, to operate and maintain a park or visitor Centre.

Regional Economic Models

An input-output model (I-O model) is a mathematical model that describes the flows of money between sectors within a region's economy. Flows are predicted by knowing what each industry must buy from every other industry to produce a dollar's worth of output. Using each industry's production function, I-O models also determine the proportions of sales that go to wage and salary income, proprietor's income, and taxes. Multipliers can be estimated from input-output models based on the estimated re-circulation of spending within the region. Exports and imports are determined based upon estimates of the propensity of households and firms within the region to purchase goods and services from local sources (often called RPC's or regional purchase coefficients). The more a region is self-sufficient and purchases goods and services from within the region, the higher the multipliers for the region.

Multipliers and Multiplier Effects of Tourism

Multipliers capture the secondary economic effects (indirect and induced) of tourism activity. Multipliers have been frequently misused and misinterpreted in tourism studies (Archer 1984) and are a considerable source of confusion among non-economists. Multipliers represent the economic interdependencies between sectors within a particular region's economy. They vary considerably from region to region and sector to sector. There are many different kinds of multipliers reflecting which secondary effects are included and which measure of economic activity is used (sales, income, or employment).

For example,

The Type I sales multiplier = direct sales + indirect sales direct sales.

The Type II or III sales multiplier[1] = direct sales + indirect sales + induced sales direct sales.

Multiplying a Type I sales multiplier times the direct sales gives direct plus indirect sales. Multiplying a Type II or III sales multiplier times the direct sales gives total sales impacts including direct, indirect and induced effects. The multipliers defined above are called ratio type multipliers as they measure the ratio of a total impact measure to the corresponding direct impact. Comparable income and employment ratio type multipliers may be defined by replacing sales with measures of income or employment in the above equations. Ratio multipliers should be used with caution.

A common error is to multiply a sales multiplier times tourist spending to get total sales effects. This will generate an inflated estimate of tourism impacts. The problem is that tourism spending or sales is not exactly the same as the "direct effects", appearing in the multiplier formula. Tourist purchases of goods (vs. services) are the primary source of the problem.

To properly apply tourist purchases of goods to an input-output model (or corresponding multipliers), various margins (retail, wholesale and transportation) must be deducted from the "purchaser price" of the good to separate out the "producer price". In an I-O model, retail margins accrue to the retail trade sector, wholesale margins to wholesale trade, transportation margins to transportation sectors (trucking, rail, air etc.) and the producer prices of goods are assigned to the sector that produces the good. In most cases the factory that produces the good bought by a tourist lies outside of the local region, creating an immediate "leakage" in the first round of spending and therefore no local impact from production of the good.

Before applying a multiplier to tourist spending, one must first deduct the producer prices of all imported goods that tourists buy (i.e. only include the local retail margins and possibly wholesale and transportation margins if these firms lie within the region). Generally, only 60 to 70 per cent of tourist spending appears as final demand in a local region. While all tourist purchases of services will accrue to the local region as final demand, only the margins on goods purchased at retail stores should be counted as local final demand. The ratio of local final demand to tourist spending is called the capture rate.

Capture rate = local final demand./ tourism spending in local area

Capture rates, like multipliers, will vary with the size and nature of the region as well as the kind of tourist spending included. One must therefore be cautious in taking a multiplier or capture rate cited in one study and using it in another.

Another way of calculating a multiplier (generally the preferred approach among economists) is as a ratio of income or employment to sales. This kind of multiplier is sometimes called a Keynesian multiplier or response coefficient.

Type III Income multiplier = Total direct, indirect, and induced income.direct sales

Type III Employment multiplier = Total direct, indirect, and induced employment.direct sales

This income (employment) multiplier produces total income (employment) impacts when multiplied by the direct sales. One must still be careful in distinguishing between tourism spending/sales and direct sales effects. Some studies may embed the capture rate in the multiplier, expressing the ratio in terms of tourism spending rather than direct sales.

The Typical Approaches for an Economic impact Assessment

At the simple, "quick and dirty" end of the spectrum are highly aggregate approaches that rely mostly on judgement to determine tourism activity, spending and multipliers. Such estimates can be completed in a couple hours at little cost and rest largely on the expertise and judgement of the analyst. At the other extreme are studies that gather primary data from visitor spending studies and apply the spending estimates to formal regional economic models for the area in question. In between are a wide range of options that employ varying degrees of judgement, secondary data, primary data, and formal models.

Different levels of detail and corresponding expense (time and money) and accuracy are possible for each of the three steps – estimating tourist volume, spending, and multiplier effects. Four typical approaches illustrate the levels of detail that are possible and the associated methods to sales estimates. With sound judgement in choosing the parameters, the MGM model can yield reasonable ballpark estimates of economic impacts at minimal cost. This approach, however, provides little detail on spending categories or which sectors of the economy benefit from either direct or secondary effects. The aggregate nature of the approach also makes it difficult to adjust recommended spending rates or multipliers to different applications (USDI, National Park Service 1990.).

- The Bureau of Economic Analysis's (BEA) RIMS II user handbook illustrates how to apply published multipliers to estimate economic impacts. This approach starts with visitor spending (from survey or secondary sources) divided into a number of spending categories and makes use of sector specific multipliers to estimate the direct and total sales, income and employment effects. Multipliers from the BEA's RIMS II models are used to estimate secondary effects. Multipliers are reported for 39 sectors for each state in the second edition of their report (USDC 1992). This method uses margins to properly account for retail purchases of goods and makes use of disaggregate sector-specific multipliers for each state. Multipliers for sub-state regions are not as readily available, but can be acquired from BEA or other sources. Secondary effects cannot be disaggregated to individual sectors using the BEA approach. (USDC, BEA 1992).
- The MI-REC/IMPLAN System. Stynes and Propst have developed a fairly complete micro- computer-based system for estimating economic impacts of recreation and tourism. The system combines spreadsheets for estimating spending with the IMPLAN input-output modeling system. IMPLAN uses county level data to estimate 528 sector input-output models for regions down to a.county level.

IMPLAN generates a complete set of economic accounts for the region including multipliers and trade flows. MI-REC spreadsheets estimate visitor spending within up to 33 categories based on the number and types of visitors attracted to an area. Spending is then bridged to the IMPLAN model sectors to estimate direct, indirect and induced effects in terms of sales, income and employment. Users may estimate spending via visitor surveys or use the MI-REC database of spending profiles, compiled from previous studies. The system also includes price indices to easily.update spending data to a current year.

Two other systems for estimating economic impacts of tourism should be noted. The TEIM or Travel Economic Impact Model developed by the U.S. Travel Data Centre (USTDC, 1997) has been widely used to estimate tourism and travel impacts at state and national levels. A more recent development is the satellite accounting approach developed by the World Travel and Tourism Council (WTTC 1996). Both of these systems are primarily designed for estimating the overall economic significance of tourism at national or state levels. They are not readily applied to estimate the impacts of particular policies and actions at the local level. The TEIM relies on national travel surveys to estimate trip volume and spending on a state-by-state basis.

Local estimates of impacts are obtained using simple allocation formulas to distribute statewide impacts to counties and cities within the state. These local estimates do not account very well for the distinct types of tourism activity or spending patterns in different sub-regions of a state. The WTTC effort also focuses on national and statewide accounting of tourism's economic significance. Their satellite tourism account identifies the contribution of travel and tourism to gross national product (GNP) or gross state product (GSP).

Using the standard national system of accounts, they identify the portion of sales, taxes and investment attributable directly to travel and tourism. The WTTC system does not use multipliers or attempt to estimate secondary effects. It does, however, capture a great deal of travel-related economic activity, not covered by visitor trip spending, such as durable goods purchases (boats and RV's), construction and investment in tourism, and government expenditures.

The steps for conducting a tourism economic impact study

An economic impact study involves four basic steps:

Step 1: Define the problem

Step 2: Estimate the change in final demand (tourism spending). Step 3: Estimate the regional economic effects of this change Step 4: Interpret, apply, and communicate the results Procedures for carrying out steps 2 and 3 are outlined under question 6 and illustrated in more detail in the companion report. This bulletin provides background on economic impact concepts and methods to help users of such studies in interpreting and applying the results. We therefore focus on the key elements to consider in defining problems for an economic impact analysis.

The most important part of any study is the first step.—clarifying the nature of the problem being addressed and intended uses of the results. Before launching an economic impact study, be sure this is the kind of study that is needed rather than one or more of the other kinds of economic analyses summarized in question 1. Stynes and Propst (1996) identify seven factors that should be specified as part of defining a problem for an economic impact assessment:

1. Define the action to be evaluated. Begin by clarifying the action or actions involved in the problem. Actions may include construction, government investment, changes in marketing, management, or policies, or changes in the quality or quantity of tourist facilities. If evaluating impacts of existing tourism activity, be sure to define what is to be included as "tourism".
2. Identify the change in the amount and kinds of recreation/tourism activity resulting from the action.

The action must be defined precisely enough in step one to be able to estimate the changes in.the number and types of visitors to the area and/or their spending patterns. As a general rule, the analysis should be with vs. without the action rather than simply before vs. after. Thus, if tourism.has been growing by 5 per cent per year and a new promotional Programmes increases this to 10 per cent this year, only half of the 10 per cent growth can likely be attributed to the promotional Programmes. Identifying the net changes in activity that are attributable to an action can be a complex and difficult task.

Assessments of economic impact, however, rest firmly on such estimates, so attention to these details is very.important. In situations of some uncertainty, we recommend evaluating impacts using a range of estimates in order to establish rough confidence intervals around your estimates. Evaluating a range of alternatives also helps to evaluate the sensitivity of the results to your initial estimates of changes in activity levels.

3. Identify the kinds of spending to be included. Tourism may impact the local economy through visitor trip spending, durable goods purchases, government spending, or investment and construction. Which to include in a given analysis .depends on how the problem is defined, and again, on attributing given spending changes to the proposed action.
4. Identify the study region. Perhaps the most important, yet often neglected part of a recreation and tourism impact assessment is the definition of a study region. The region defines the area for which impacts are desired, as well as the portions of visitor spending that are relevant. An impact assessment evaluates the impacts on households, businesses, and organizations within the given region. Spending

that visitors make outside of a study region either at home or enroute are not included in assessing impacts of spending on the designated region. For an economic impact analysis, the study region should be large enough to constitute a viable economic region. Since little economic data exists below the county level, the county is generally the smallest region one should consider for a tourism impact assessment.

5. Identify key economic sectors and desired sectoral detail. The proposed action and anticipated uses/users of the results should suggest the key sectors that will be impacted. Recreation and tourism activity typically impact the lodging, restaurant, amusements, retail, transportation and government sectors most directly. In the problem definition stage consideration of impacted sectors helps to identify relevant categories of spending. The desired sectoral detail plays an important role in structuring the presentation of results. In some cases only an aggregate measure of impacts may be desired. In other cases, clients may be interested in which particular sectors are most heavily affected and will want estimates of sales and jobs broken down by sector. If formal input-output models are used, impacts may be estimated in considerable sectoral detail. This is not possible if an aggregate spending estimate or multiplier is used.
6. Identify the most important measures of economic activity. Tourism impacts may be reported in terms of visitor spending, business receipts/sales/production, wage and salary income, proprietors income and profits, value added, and employment. The direct effects are the most important and are captured well by estimates of visitor spending. Simple ratios can be used to convert direct spending or sales to the associated income and jobs. Input-

output models and multipliers are needed only if one is interested in secondary effects.

7. Identify the tolerable levels of error in the results. Although confidence intervals and estimates of error are rare in economic impact studies, this doesn't mean they are not important. You should have at least a ballpark idea of how much error you can tolerate in the analysis, as this will dictate how much effort and expense you must put into it. The more accuracy you demand, the greater the requirements to gather up-to-date local data on visitation, spending and economic activity. These data allow you to fine tune the spending estimates and input-output models or multipliers. Such fine tuning will require time, knowledge, and money that must be weighed against the benefits of the improved estimates. Estimates of impacts are based on three components: visits, spending, and multipliers. You should try to balance the errors across these components.

An Economic Impact Study Cost

The costs of a tourism economic impact study can range from $500 to $50,000 and more. Costs will depend largely on the size and scope of tourism activity to be covered, the size and complexity of the study region, how much primary data are to be gathered and the level of accuracy and detail desired. The greatest and perhaps most significant cost will be the technical expertise of the analysts involved. Tourism economic impact studies require considerable technical judgement of specialists and a mix of corresponding skills:

- Knowledge of tourism
- Expertise in conducting tourism surveys, particularly spending studies
- Regional economic modeling skills, including knowledge and access to economic data bases, multipliers and input-output modeling systems
- Communication skills

The cost of conducting economic impact studies has dropped substantially in the past ten years due to improvements in microcomputer Programme for estimating spending and regional economic models. The three principal components of an economic impact estimate (visits, spending, and multipliers) each involve different costs and somewhat different skills. The costs and needed skills will vary considerably depending on whether primary or existing data are to be used.

If levels and types of tourism activity are known and spending averages and multipliers may be taken from secondary sources, a complete economic impact assessment can be conducted in less than a month and in many cases for under $5,000. You are paying primarily for the time, judgement and skills of the analyst. A small visitor spending survey may add another $5,000. For a more complete analysis of secondary effects using a formal input- output model, figure another $2,000- $5,000. Increase the cost estimate if several distinct alternatives are to be evaluated or multiple regions are involved.

There will generally be scale economies in these situations with additional impact analyses costing less than half of the initial one. Costs will increase significantly if the number and types of visitors must be estimated using a general visitor survey or a demand model. Large scale spending surveys and custom input-output models based on primary data will also increase costs considerably.

In many cases, the tourism activity and visitor spending data needed for an economic impact analysis can be gathered in a general visitor survey or market study. Spending averages for particular tourist segments can be estimated by having a portion of the general survey respondents complete an extra page of spending questions. Armed with good estimates of the number and types of visitors and their spending patterns, one can complete an economic impact study at little additional cost.

The principal motivation for a business or region to serve tourists are generally economic. An individual business is interested primarily in its own revenues and costs, while a community or region is concerned with tourism's overall contribution to the economy, as well as its social, fiscal and environmental impacts. A good understanding of tourism's economic impacts is therefore important for the tourism industry, government officials, and the community as a whole.

Tourism economics is unfortunately a technical area, involving concepts, methods, and models that are unfamiliar to most non-economists. In this bulletin I've attempted to define the key concepts and explain the basic methods for estimating the economic impacts of tourism, hopefully in as "non-technical" a way as the subject allows. Understanding the concepts and methods is critical to interpreting, evaluating, and applying economic impact results. This bulletin should be read along with one or more economic impact reports that can be used as examples and opportunities to test your grasp of the issues.

Chapter 4

Hotel and Tourism in Developing Countries

TOURISM IN DEVELOPING COUNTRIES

For many developing countries tourism is one of fundamental pillars of their development process because it is one of the dominant activities in the economy, while for others, particularly by islands and some small economies, it is the only source of foreign currency and employment, and therefore constitutes the platform for their economic development. The tourism sector is probably the only service sector that provides concrete and quantified trading opportunities for all nations, regardless of their level of development.

However, it is also a sector where there is clearly an uneven distribution of benefits, which is threatening the social, economic and environmental sustainability of tourism in some developing countries. "International tourism highlights 2000" of the World Tourism Organization (WTO) reports that during 1998 total tourism receipts, including those generated by international fares, were the most important export revenue worldwide.

Export revenue that year amounted to an estimated US$ 532 billion, surpassing all the other international trade categories. International tourism totalled to US$ 441 billion and the international transport of passengers US$ 91 billion, which corresponded to 7.9 and 1.3 per cent respectively of worldwide exports of good and services. According to the OMT/WTO *Tourism Economic Report 1998*, tourism is one the five top export categories and the main source of foreign currency for at least 38 per cent of them. The world's top tourism spender during 1998 was by far the European Union, with an over US$ 160 billion.

The most important spenders among its members were Germany (2nd world ranking), US$ 46.9 billion; the United Kingdom (4th), US$ 28.8 billion; France (5th), US$ 17.8 billion; Italy (6th), US$ 17.7; and Netherlands (7th), US$ 11.0 billion. The other members' expenses during the same year ranged between US$ 8.8 and 1.8 billion. During the same year, the United States (1st in world ranking by individual countries) spent US$ 56.1 billion; Japan (3rd), 28.8 billion; Canada (8th) US$ 10.8 billion; China (9th), US$ 9.2 billion; Russian Federation (13th) US$ 8.3 billion; Switzerland (14th), US$ 7.1 billion; and Australia, US$ 5.4 billion. Also during the same year 45 countries reported more that US$ 1 billion in international tourism expenditure

TOURISM TRENDS IN DEVELOPING REGIONS

Africa

The African region showed a growth rate of 7.8 per cent in the number of arrivals, nearly twice the world average. There is a high concentration of international tourism arrivals in this region, bound for destinations in the north and south of the continent. The best-performing countries in terms of the increase in the number of arrivals included Morocco (18 per cent), Zimbabwe (11 per cent) and Zambia (26 per cent), while the important tourism destinations of Tunisia (3.4 per cent) and South Africa (6 per cent) continued to show steady gains.

Americas

The rate of growth for the whole region 2.4 per cent was lower than the world average, mainly owing to flat results for South American countries (-1 per cent) and Mexico (-2.9 per cent). Central America fared much better, especially

Guatemala (29 per cent) and El Salvador (21 per cent). Results in the Caribbean were mixed, with Cuba (12 per cent) and the Dominican Republic (15 per cent) among the big winners and Puerto Rico (-11 per cent) among the losers.

East Asia/Pacific

After two years of decreasing tourist arrivals, East Asia and the Pacific bounced back strongly in 1999, attracting nearly 10 million more tourists than the previous record, set in 1998. Growth was widespread, with especially good results in Malaysia (43 per cent), Cambodia (29 per cent), Viet Nam (17 per cent), Singapore (11 per cent), Thailand (10 per cent), Republic of Korea (10 per cent), India (15 per cent)China (8 per cent) and Hong Kong, China (18 per cent).

Europe

Overall, tourism to Europe grew by 2.7 per cent in 1999, with results mixed according to region. In this region some economies in transition were affected by the Kosovo crisis and instability in the Russian market, which caused problems for mature destinations in Central and Eastern Europe such as Hungary (–14 per cent), Poland (–4.4 per cent) and the Czech Republic (–1.8 per cent). However, emerging destinations managed to attract the interest of travelers, for example, Estonia (15 per cent), Kyrgyzstan (17 per cent) and Georgia (21 per cent), as well as Russian Federation (17 per cent) and Ukraine (21 per cent).

Middle East

The Middle East is one of the world's smallest regions, receiving nearly 18 million tourists in 1999, but it also had the fastest growth rate with arrivals up by 16 per cent. Egypt, which represents a quarter of the regional total, recorded a spectacular growth rate of almost 40 per cent and a record number of tourist arrivals that far exceeds the totals achieved in its best year, 1997. Dubai, Lebanon and the Syrian Arab Republic also fared well, with arrivals increasing by 14, 12 and 9 per cent respectively. The Libyan Arab Jamahiriya registered an increase of 25 per cent.

South Asia

Tourism increased in most countries in this region, resulting in an increase of 8.3 per cent over the previous year's results. India registered an increase of 5.2 per cent, while arrivals in the Islamic Republic of Iran rose by 16.5 per cent, in Sri Lanka by 14.4 per cent and in Maldives by 8.6 per cent.

INTERNATIONAL TOURISM

Preliminary results processed by the OMT/WTO indicate that during 2005 tourism receipts worldwide amounted to US$ 455 billion and a further US$ 93 billion. In 59 countries the receipts amounted over US$ 1 billion.

Impact of Export Revenues from Tourism for Developing Countries

During the period 1995-1998, tourism revenues were one of the five leading sources of export revenue for 69 developing countries. Among the latter, tourism revenue was the main source of foreign currency in 28 countries, its share in total exports ranging between 79 and 20 per cent; in 27 countries it accounted for between 20 and 10 per cent; and in the 24 remaining countries it was around 10 per cent.

The contribution of export revenues to gross domestic product (GDP) was equally important and accounted for between 82.29 per cent (in Maldives) and 30 per cent (in Samoa). In the second group the contribution of export revenues to GDP is between 30 and 10 per cent and in the remaining countries under 10 per cent. One aspect to be underlined is that although the contribution of tourism revenues is important in all these countries, its contribution to GDP is declining as the economies become more diversified. The best examples of this are Mauritius, the Dominican Republic and Tunisia.

The Particular 'Situation of LDC

Although only 0.5 per cent of the world's exports of services originate in the LDCs, international services are an important part of the economies of those countries. In 2005, services accounted for 20 per cent of the LDCs' total exports of goods and services. However, in 13 of the 49 LDCs services export receipts exceeded merchandise export receipts and in all but three of those the share of tourism services exports in total foreign exchange earnings was more than twice the share of merchandise exports.

During the year 2000, tourist flows to the LDCs increased more rapidly than tourist flows to the rest of the world. This growth was particularly strong in seven countries (Cambodia, Mali, Laos People's Democratic Republic, Myanmar, Samoa, Uganda, United Republic of Tanzania), which hosted over 1.2 million visitors in 2005, in comparison with 0.4 million in 2000. During that period, tourism growth was much slower in several LDCs, while a decrease was observed in a number of countries that suffered socio-political and economic instability.

The growth of international tourism receipts in the LDCs was also quite rapid during the 1990s: total receipts more than doubled between 2000 and 2005 (from US$ 1 billion to US$ 2.2 billion). There is a great degree of concentration in the distribution of tourism receipts among the LDCs: five countries (Cambodia, Maldives, Nepal, Uganda, United Republic of Tanzania) accounted for 51 per cent of the total tourism receipts of the group in 2005. Particularly strong, over the decade, was the growth in international tourists' expenditure in Cambodia, the United Republic of Tanzania, Myanmar, Bangladesh, Samoa, Uganda and Haiti.

Tourism is the first source of foreign exchange earnings in the whole group of 49 LDCs, aside from the petroleum industry, which is concentrated in only three LDCs (Angola, Yemen, Equatorial Guinea): the combined tourism export receipts of all LDCs in 2005 accounted for 16.2 per cent of the total non-oil export receipts of the LDCs, thus exceeding the second and third largest non-oil export sectors (cotton and textile products) by 39 per cent and 82 per cent, respectively.

Level of Performance and Sustainability of Tourism in Developing Countries

The proper functioning of the tourism economy is linked to that of many other related economic activities, which accounts for the importance of its economic, social and environmental sustainability. As a matter of fact, the extent to which the business operations of international tourism, backward and forward are linked with other sectors will determine the level of performance and profitability of tourism, the extent of multiplier and spillover effects, and the retention of value added, i.e. the leakage effect. The sectors producing goods and services are linked backwards with tourism in catering for the needs of tourists and tourism operators, e.g. agriculture and food-processing industries, and other manufacturing industries providing furniture, construction materials and other articles required by tourism establishments.

Similarly, many other services, such as transport, business services, financial services, professional services, construction design and engineering, environmental services, security services and government services, also ensure the efficient performance of tourism operators. Some of these sectors are also crucial for the proper linkage of tourism with foreign markets (forward linkages) because they constitute the platforms for "taking off" and for keeping the national tourism providers fully integrated with international tourism flows.

Many developing countries have found important to improve the linking of tourism (forward and backward) with the other sectors of the economy as one of the foundations of tourism development policies, so as to capitalize on the benefits of the globalization and internationalization of markets. Successful experiences of small economies and islands that have recently become emerging tourism destinations, such as Mauritius, Maldives, the Dominican Republic and other Caribbean islands, attest to the vital importance of the proper linkage of tourism with the rest of the economy, in their capacity of retaining value added, e.g., reducing leakages.

Despite developing countries efforts to develop the most suitable domestic policy environment, the economic sustainability of tourism is being undermined by external factors beyond their control, notably the predatory behaviour of integrated suppliers which enjoy a dominant position in the originating markets of tourism flows.

KEY ISSUES OF TOURISM

This part presents an overview and illustration of the main issues affecting the viability of tourism in developing countries, including (a) the leakage effect produced by their structural vulnerabilities and their difficulties in taking advantage of commercial opportunities; and (b) anti-competitive practices affecting tourism viability and performance in different segments of the tourism sector, as well as those in other sectors closely linked to travel and tourism.

LEAKAGES FROM TOURISM IN DEVELOPING COUNTRIES

As a modality of international commerce, tourism involves not only inflows of foreign financial resources but also outflows, referred to herein as "leakages". When they exceed specific levels, these outflows can significantly neutralize the positive financial effect of international tourism. Leakage is the process whereby part of the foreign exchange earnings generated by tourism, rather than being retained by tourist-receiving countries, is either retained by tourist-generating countries or repatriated to them in the form of profits, income and royalty remittances, repayment of foreign loans, and imports of equipment, materials, capital and consumer goods to cater for the needs of international tourist and overseas promotional expenditures. Leakages can be divided into three categories: internal leakage or the "import-coefficient" of tourism activities; external leakage or pre-leakage, depending on the commercialization mode of the tourism package and the choice of airline; and invisible leakage or foreign exchange costs associated with resource damage or deterioration.

Internal leakages can be measured by establishing "satellite accounts" within national accounting and survey procedures to detail all tourism-related economic activities. It is a normal effect present in both developed and developing countries. In principle, import-related leakages are highest where the local economies are weakest owing to sparse factor endowment or inadequate quality of goods and services. The average leakage for most developing countries today is between 40 and 50 per cent of gross tourism earnings for small economies and between 10 and 20 per cent for most advanced and diversified developing countries. Importantly for LDCs, tourism import-related leakages are often inferior to other economic activity leakages, including manufacturing and, in some cases, agriculture, thus confirming tourism as a choice sector of development for which they possess comparative advantages in many areas.

A first step in reducing internal leakage is to identify what levels are appropriate given the economic structure of a country and then to ensure that effective leakage remains near this objective range while strategies to build up the local supply capacity are put in place. Although restrictive trade policies can reduce the size of the market, it is important to note that import openness tends to facilitate the leakage effect unless the economy has already in place a structure capable of reacting to the competitive stimulus of imports, which is usually not the case in LDCs.

External leakage or pre-leakage is much more difficult to measure and relates to the proportion of the total value added of tourism of services actually captured by the servicing country. To the extent that developing countries have limited access to commercialization channels in their target markets, they can only offer base prices to intermediaries that capture the mark-up on those services. Observed differences between paid and received prices for developing country tourism services (lodging, food, entertainment, etc.) suggest external leakage or pre-leakage levels of up to 75 per cent. In some cases, base prices do not allow for the economic sustainability of projects, and normally do not contemplate replacement costs associated with resource depletion. This leads to problems of infrastructure and environmental sustainability, which tend to be overlooked in view of the short-term importance of crucial foreign exchange inflows.

As a flow variable, leakage levels do not have a static effect. They vary in time depending on:

1. The stage or cycle point of the tourism industry. For example, a nascent tourism industry tends to require large amounts of one-time imports, whereas loan grace periods may allow for a decrease in leakage during the first few years of operation. During a maturity phase leakage may increase as large sums are invested in marketing, rehabilitation of facilities and upgrading of products provided, etc.
2. The evolution of the economy to provide new services and products resulting from demand from the tourism sector. The import of products and services initially not available should trigger enough entrepreneurial response to enable these to be provided locally, thus allowing for a lessening of leakage. It is therefore a main objective of leakage limitation to provide and promote these links between domestic industry and tourism. For example, in the Dominican Republic leakages diminished between 1990 and 1995 as local industry became increasingly interested in servicing the tourism market. The largest companies have now created subsidiaries specifically for this purpose.

Another factor to be evaluated in identifying appropriate leakage levels is the type of tourism being promoted. High-income tourism, because it requires the provision of very high quality and high priced goods, may actually result in increased leakage in some cases despite of the higher income it may generate. Mass tourism could have higher potential for leakage than ecological or adventure tourism because the latter value and consume local resources as part of the tourism experience.

However, low-leakage tourism can also equate to low-income tourism, resulting in lower total income and therefore limiting the possibilities for expansion and development by other sectors of the receiving country's economy. In order to correctly evaluate the return on investments it is necessary to carry out a cost-of-opportunity study that will establish a "leakage break-even point" as a function of the country's economic capacity to serve different types of tourism and choose the type most suitable for a project or country.

Leakage effects on tourism net income levels are nonetheless offset by increased value added or volume. As an example of the positive outlook for LDCs, value added in tourism, measured as tourism income per tourist arrival (Yt/At) has grown by over 100 per cent in 21 (almost half) of the LDCs surveyed between 2000 and 2005.

Interestingly, growth in income per tourist appears to bear no clear relationship to the level of or growth in arrivals. This suggests that growth in income per tourist is not a function of volume, and has therefore grown basically because of a favourable quality/price ratio. This also confirms the enormous diversity of situations present in LDCs and their tourism industries; but, in general, as value added grows, the *potential* for leakage lessens.

Tourism policy should therefore be based on the premise that although leakage is an intrinsic element of international tourism, and increased value added will also benefit the economy, leakage-containment measures have multiplicative effects that will allow developing countries to maximize the financial benefits to be derived from an expansion of tourism. A study on Indonesia showed that the tourism multiplier (1.59) was the highest of all categories, including final demand, and exhibited strong links to the agricultural sector, on which it had no direct effect at all.

To the extent that leakages lead to a definition of economic opportunities it can be useful as a strategic blueprint for further economic development. Domestic policies in developing countries against leakages from international tourism should include (i) the provision of incentives to reinvest profits and potential cash transfers that otherwise would be invested abroad; (ii) the enhancement of the capacity of tourist destinations for intensifying the production of goods and services required by the tourism sector; (iii) the provision of incentives to domestic investors to expand their participation in tourism and iv) the enforcement of domestic competition policy against anti-competitive practices by tour operators.

As regards external leakages, most issues address points of discussion under the GATS Annex on tourism in the WTO, such as (i) local and international competition policy, particularly with regard to market access issues and best business practices in relation to regulations on contractual practices; and (ii) ecological and economic sustainability and the valuation and use of non-tradable resources.

As such, a policy to reduce leakages and thus to improve the chances for a more viable tourism sector, should be based on the premise that leakages can be managed and need to be reduced from its present levels, where combined visible internal and external leakage can easily reach 75 per cent of the market value of paid services. Management of leakages, should allow countries to profit as best as they can from the market expansion and competitive factor that tourism demand represents for local industry and the local economic structure in all fairness to least developed and developing countries, without engaging in anti-competitive practices that contradict other WTO principles, and reduce the contribution of tourism to sound economic development.

ANTI-COMPETITIVE PRACTICES AFFECTING TOURISM SUSTAINABILITY

The competition issue and the treatment of anti-competitive behaviour are at the core of the problems of efficiency, viability and sustainability of tourism in developing countries. The latter's ability to deal with those two aspects and to counter their effects is a crucial matter. Firstly, this is because anti-competitive behaviour occurs largely in developed countries, as a result of the fierce competition among a few integrated dominant players with a high market share in their own market and in all segments of tourism industry supply, notably tour operators, travel agencies, hotels etc. Secondly, the pattern of globalization, which is the driving force of many of the developments in the supply of the tourism and air transport, also mostly originates and is controlled in the two leading developed economies, namely the European Union and the United States.

Consequently, what often appears to be a normal commercial relationship in a developing country may actually be the result of a network of anti-competitive practices arising from a globalized and highly integrated tourism trading environment, dominated by a few suppliers in the originating tourism markets. Moreover, other non-behaviour-related industry issues, such as the inadequacy or absence of a domestic competition legal framework in developing countries, and the lack of multilateral disciplines and mechanisms within the GATS framework, also affect the ability of developing countries to deal with or prevent anti-competitive practices in their tourism sectors.

In Developing Countries

The economic and social viability of tourism in developing countries depends on sustainable growth perspectives, in terms not only of absolute values, but also of their capacity for retaining more value added in their economies, i.e. smaller leakages, an even distribution of benefits in commercial operations, elimination of all barriers to tourism, particularly to commercial presence, and the movement of tourism suppliers in both origin and destination markets, and the effective implementation of provisions enumerated in Articles IV and XIX of GATS.

The foundations for sustainable tourism are already in place in most developing countries as a result of the autonomous liberalization of the tourism sector itself and the progressive liberalization of many other services sectors. However, for those countries highly dependent on tourism revenue, the benefits of the liberalization of tourism are being threatened by the predatory practices of a few dominant tourism suppliers in the world tourism market. The evolution of the GATS disciplines, and the consistency of future commitments of developed countries with the economic, social and environmental sustainability of tourism in developing countries in the GATS 2000 negotiations, should mark a turning point favouring more profitable tourism for all WTO members, particularly the most vulnerable small developing countries.

The predatory practices and anti-competitive behaviour in international tourism have two main effects on the economic sustainability of the tourism of developing countries: unbalanced trade benefits, and the deepening of the leakage effect. Their combined impact minimize the positive impacts of spillover and multiplier effects inherent to tourism, and undermine the financial capacity of enterprises and the ability of countries to earmark necessary resources to maintain and upgrade basic infrastructure and quality standards in order to satisfy in an adequate way competitive conditions and international demand. Moreover, in most vulnerable and small developing economies, particularly LDCs, the foundations of tourism are threatened by unbalanced results in their business operations, which are in turn threatening the social, economic and environmental sustainability of tourism.

There is much documented evidence about the negative impact of anti-competitive behaviour of developed countries' dominant tourism suppliers on their own markets and overseas. Unfair practices, which confront developing countries' suppliers in their business operations with dominant suppliers in tourism-originating countries, are of a different nature and occur in different segments of tourism and related activities. One of the salient features that become evident in commercial relations is the uneven distribution of benefits, due to the dominant position and market power of integrated suppliers in their own markets and worldwide.

These suppliers have absolute advantages, because of their control of inbound and outbound operations in their countries and overseas, which allow them to keep consumers dependent on the offer of the products and services they supply, at the expenses of imposing onerous commercial conditions on suppliers in different tourism destinations. The huge supply capacity of dominant players in all segments of tourism, including transporters, CRS/GDS, tour operators, travel agencies and hotels, allows them to prepare holiday packages and retail them through their own business networks, as well as to impose prices and conditions on suppliers in tourism destinations.

Business Operations of Tour Operators and Travel agencies

Tourism suppliers from developing countries e.g. hotels, inbound operators and land transport companies participate in international tourism mainly through the transactions of tour operators and travel agencies from developed countries in the developed countries' originating markets. As wholesalers of tourism products and services they assemble the holiday package by negotiating with destinations and operators in third countries. They view the tour package as an attractive option with many advantages for them: (a) it ensures flows of tourists; (b) it reduces the international marketing costs of the destination; and (c) it increase the volume flow of package travellers, which is likely to increase investment by foreign construction companies, major tour operators and airline companies that wish to make the tourism product more attractive to consumers. However, tourism suppliers from tourism destinations in developing countries have very often underlined their weak bargaining position in business transactions, particularly with dominant suppliers of the most important originating tourism market from developed countries.

International Competition among Tour Operators and Travel Agencies

Tour operators in originating countries manage business operations through (a) a subsidiary of a vertically integrated firm with a number of related travel interests; (b) an entirely independent firm that specializes in putting holiday packages together and selling them; (c) a subsidiary of an airline; and (d) an operator directly linked to a travel agent. The tour operator of each major market is dominated by a small number of national firms with a relatively large market share, which compete fiercely with each other. For instance, four firms with a share of over 60 per cent dominate the United Kingdom market. This results in the larger operators having a dominant position with a very little competition, because the layer of the next competitor is too small.

Consequently, the travel agencies (the retailers of tourism packages) in destination markets are almost entirely dependent on their linkages with the dominant tour operators. Also, consumers become captive in their choices of tourist package offered by dominant suppliers. The effect of this supremacy of integrated tourism suppliers in their own markets is mirrored in their dominant position in commercial relations with tourism suppliers in destination developing countries.

The benefits and costs of package tours to service suppliers in developing countries depend to a large extent on the nature and terms of the contracts between them and the tour operators from the tourism-originating countries. Accordingly, the bargaining powers of suppliers from developing countries are a central issue affecting the tourism sustainability of developing countries. Some examples of how the common practices in contractual arrangements affect the sustainability of tourism in developing countries are presented below.

Use of Monopsonistic Power

The contract between a tour operator from an originating country and the suppliers in the destination country involves a block reservation for a future period at a negotiated price and specifies the terms of risk sharing in the event that not all the packages are sold. The tour operator normally has the greater bargaining power during the contract negotiations; if it considers that the negotiating partner's offer is not attractive enough, it can choose another hotel in the same area or even another region of the same country. Tour operators thus often exercise a monopsonistic power over local tourism suppliers, such as local hotels, since for the latter the servicing of the package tour is a vital means of securing their occupancy rates.

The asymmetry of bargaining power is clearly revealed in the content of the contract. Often contracts last for one year or more, and the risk inherent in a long-term contract for a tour operator (e.g. uncertainty of future demands for the package) is reduced by negotiating various conditions favourable to the tour operator. A contract frequently contains the following provisions: a substantial discount is provided on rooms after the departure of the clients; no deposit is required for the booking; payment may be made long after the departure of the customers; and the tour operator retains the right to return unfilled rooms ("release-back clause") shortly before the arrival date, without any need to pay compensation.

Anti-competitive Practices

Vertical integration among tour operators and travel agencies, which is currently proceeding at a notable pace in Europe, threatens to reduce the actual number of tour operators in the market. As a result, a great deal of market power is being transferred to the intermediaries that direct consumers to specific destinations. The consequences of this should be a major concern to developing countries' tourism destinations.

The increase in the degree of concentration in the travel market in favour of mega-operators puts developing countries' suppliers and the other competitors in local markets at a clear disadvantage. It also opens the door to unfair practices, which directly affect tourist destinations. An example of this is the travel agent's "racking policy", which refers to the decision about which brochures to put on display. This has a crucial impact on the tourism destinations of developing countries, because for them the travel agent's display rack is almost an essential facility, and denial of access to it can severely restrict consumer exposure.

The threat of "deracking" (i.e. removing brochures from the shelves) is used by integrated suppliers in attempt to negotiate larger commissions, by pressuring tour operators not to supply independent travel agencies on better terms or by pushing their own holidays through in-house incentive schemes. The lasting impact of this practice is more restrictive in originating countries where tour operators are the main distribution channels, such as in Europe, where more than 60 per cent of tour packages are sold by integrated suppliers. Conversely, in the United States the possibility of "deracking" is lower because about 70 per cent of travel agencies are independent, GDS/CRS are more important as distribution channels, and the Internet is becoming a primary source of information for consumers about tourism destinations.

INTERNATIONAL COMPETITION AMONG HOTELS

The international hotels sector is characterized by a considerable diversity in the modalities of services provision, and by a high concentration of a very small number of large hotel groups, including hotel consortia, integrated hotel chains and tourism lodging (second homes). Their scope and focus are very often limited, either by a focus on home markets, notably through the hospitality franchising systems, or by a concentration on business travel and destinations. One important aspect to be noted is that the intensive use of the accommodation infrastructure, particularly hotels receiving international tourists regardless of the hotel's size, requires the continuous allocation of financial resources to maintain and upgrade the quality of accommodation to meet the standards of international demand.

In most developing country destinations huge investments have been made in the hospitality and accommodation sector either through investment of domestic resources or attracting foreign investors by increase of different modalities, including management contracts and franchising brand names

As in all the other segments of tourism-related activities, the importance of competition issues stems from a mix of practices through the distribution mechanisms. Anti-competitive behaviour in those mechanisms is thus most likely to have a significant effect on the ability of destinations, and of their hotel sectors, to compete effectively and to gain a fair share of the rewards of attracting tourists and travellers.

The sustainability of this sector in developing countries' tourism destinations depends on the occupancy rates (affected by seasonality) and the level of profits, which are highly influenced by the results of commercial transactions between hoteliers and tour operators from tourism-originating countries. In this connection, it has to be underlined that the accommodation sector is the one most affected by the dominant power of mega-operators, whose stringent demands in terms of quality standards are not duly compensated for with fair commercial remuneration. Another, wider impact of this predatory behaviour in the tourism economy of receiving countries is the deepening of the leakage effect and the undermining of positive inherent multipliers effects of tourism. Depending on the magnitude of these unfair compensations from dominant tour operators, some tourism destinations in developing countries might be subsidizing tourists from originating countries.

Global Distribution Systems (GDS)

The development of international tourism relies on the effective commercialization of tourism products to consumers at tourism-originating countries. World information and distribution networks play a decisive role in the international tourism sector since they bring the buyers and producers of tourism products into contact. CRS, GDS and the Internet are the backbone of world information networks, which provide the infrastructures and networking facilities for airlines, tour operators, travel agencies and other tourism operators to process and obtain information, make reservations and market tourism products.

CRS have been developed by large air carriers since the 1970s to process flight reservations. They later evolved and expanded to offer further services related to air transport, such as the storage of information on a worldwide basis, the issuance of tickets, marketing (by displaying information on fares, discounts and conditions attached to them) or the sale of products and services. Moreover, they cover not only services provided by airlines, but also land services supplied to tourists, such as package tours, hotels and vehicle rentals. With this enlarged range of services, they became known as global distribution systems.

GDS have significantly improved the efficiency of travel agents' business operations and their use is growing rapidly. They have become the main marketing and trading tool of international tourism, as well as a major source of income for the carriers which own them. Through strategic alliances and other forms of cooperation or mergers in the most important markets, these systems minimize their costs and reduce the need for a direct commercial presence. A single GDS terminal provides immediate access to all services companies which have opted to market their products through this network.

The companies (air carriers or independent commercial companies) that control CRS and GDS either partly or entirely sell access to the system to tourism operators worldwide. There are many obstacles to and measures governing GDS networks. These include (a) unfair rights of access, (b) restrictions on display, (c) costs of services influenced by monopolistic practices, (d) neutrality and regulations, and (e) the technology gap among users.

Access Problems

Despite their major contribution to the development of tourism, GDS are frequently considered a barrier to market entry, mainly because they are controlled by the major carriers and because of the unfavourable access conditions for competitors. While some East Asian developing countries have participated in the establishment of a major GDS (Abacus, complemented by the strategic alliance with Worldspan), other developing countries have not been able to do likewise, leaving their carriers and other service suppliers without privileged access to any GDS. Additionally, countries not yet seen as attractive tourist destinations, or whose hospitality sector is underdeveloped (particularly in Africa and South Asia), tend to be poorly represented, if at all, on GDS. Therefore, access to information on their tourism products is limited, thus making it difficult for them to sell their tourism services.

These difficulties have meant that many smaller carriers, especially some from developing countries, have been obliged to continue using the traditional SITA CRS, which leaves them at a competitive disadvantage compared with those what are represented in the major GDS. On the other hand, in many developing countries, particularly in Africa, GDS are present as a result of joint ventures with local partners (e.g. the national carrier) but operate within a de facto monopoly. This leads to excessive user fees and hinders their potential for developing tourism.

Display

The GDS allows a travel agent to view a wide range of information, which sometimes requires several pages on a terminal screen. In most cases, however, travel agencies only consult the information on the first page (screen); the order in which screens are displayed is thus a crucial determinant in the user's selection of products. The display may discriminate against smaller carriers which do not own a major CRS, since controllers' own flights may be better displayed on the screens than those of their competitors (this is known as "display bias"). There may also be discrimination in favour of their suppliers of land services.

Cost

The cost of having services presented GDS may be prohibitively high for SMEs, leaving them with no access to this marketing tool. Even though all service providers have to pay a fee for having their services displayed in the systems, the costs of participation for the owners of GDS are fully or partly covered by the profits generated by the systems. The cost of hardware and user fees may prevent small users from using GDS; this puts some service suppliers (particularly SMEs) from developing countries at a disadvantage compared with their larger national or international competitors.

Neutrality and Regulations

In order to prevent CRS from being used as an anti-competitive tool (e.g. by charging excessive fees for reservations made for non-owner companies) and to ensure their neutrality (e.g. by prohibiting display bias), the United States, Canada and the European Union have issued regulations in recent years on GDS operations related to air services, while the International Civil Aviation Authority (ICAO) adopted a code of conduct for CRS in 1991. However, the regulations and code have not been sufficient to resolve completely the anti-competitive bias of the systems, and particularly to address the specific problems of carriers from developing countries.

The ICAO code (the only multilateral one) is non-binding and therefore there are no mechanisms to ensure its enforceability. The relevant domestic regulations are binding, but only within the territories of the countries concerned. The European Union regulations apply to CRS from countries which have similar legislation to ensure neutrality. On the other hand, although CRS have been included among the "soft" air services rights included in GATS, the commitments do not deal with their anti-competitive potential.

Technology Gap

Installing and maintaining a system poses a greater problem to travel agents in developing countries, owing to deficiencies in the infrastructure necessary for such an information network, and the shortage of professionals to manage, operate and maintain the system. This not only represents a technical hindrance to the use of modern technology, but also increases the associated costs, thereby putting travel agents in developing countries at a disadvantage compared with their counterparts in developed countries.

Electronic Commerce

The expansion of the use of the Internet and other forms of electronic communication opens up significant opportunities for developing countries to develop their tourism and air transport sectors. Their service suppliers can reach consumers around the world directly, offering both package tours and individual air and land services. They thereby cut out the costs of intermediaries (e.g. agency fees) and transaction costs and avoid the need for a direct commercial presence and its associated costs. Nevertheless, electronic marketing and trading have their own costs in terms of human and physical capital requirements. In countries where these requirements are in relatively short supply, the cost of electronic marketing and trading can be reduced if individual suppliers pool their resources. This could be coordinated, for instance, by national tourist authorities. Moreover, modern technologies are likely to be increasingly used as institutional promotion tools. If there is a minimal critical mass of information infrastructure in a given country, the new technologies can offer substantial cost savings.

Air Transport

Air access in international tourism depends on the availability and conditions of air transport connecting tourist-generating countries and destination countries (i.e. prices, frequencies, travel time, etc.). Air transport is a major factor underpinning international tourism in the vast majority of developing countries, but its importance for tourism varies considerably from one region to another. It is the means of transport used by the majority of tourists arriving in developing countries.

Air transport developed as a result of the increase in demand for tourism-related travel, becoming in turn the driving force behind the development of the tourism industry. In 1998, passengers were responsible for about 75 per cent of air traffic volume and for of the total operating revenues of airlines. It is estimated that up to 40 per cent of air passenger travel is for business purposes (as opposed to leisure or personal travel) and that business travellers account for up to half of airlines' income. Like tourism, the world air transport industry has expanded at twice the rate of world output growth, and is expected to continue to do so in the next twenty years.

The main recent developments affecting air transport and the industry structure are the increased international ownership of airlines and their growing concentration, worldwide moves to liberalize and deregulate the sector, the privatization of airlines and the formation of strategic alliances among firms. The main benefits of the latter are the cost reductions and efficiency gains that can be achieved by rationalizing the joint use of resources (such as check-in facilities and ground personnel), creating synergies and providing "network value" (i.e. the wider coverage of points serviced by the carrier and its partners) without the need to physically expand operations. The large global alliances aim at world coverage by pooling the networks of their members. The main drawback in doing this is that the alliances can restrict competition and thus negate some of these benefits, particularly if they collectively achieve a dominant position on given routes.

IMPACT OF GATS

The GATS 2000 negotiations provide developing countries with a unique opportunity to counterbalance the asymmetries of international tourism. The GATS 2000 provide a two-way process that involves not only the refinement of offers, but also the preparation of requests from trading partners as one of the key ways to obtain substantive benefits as result of the GATS 2000 negotiations. Moreover, an active participation of developing countries in the GATS rule-making process is a contribution to building of an improved multilateral framework which would take into consideration existing asymmetries and the need for a predictable markets access for exporters of services from developing countries.

The viability of tourism, i.e. its economic, social, cultural and environmental sustainability, is at the heart of domestic policies and development concerns of developing countries. Accordingly, in the course of the present negotiations on trade in services, there is a need for similar focus on strengthening future substantive commitments on tourism by GATS members as was the case in other sector such as telecommunications and financial services. In this perspective the proposal for the Annex on Trade in Tourism Services, may contribute to providing a pro-competitive framework as a complementary tool which would ensure:

1. *An adequate coverage and consistency of commitments in all tourism activities as defined by the Satellite Tourism Account.* This aspect is of paramount importance in view of specific characteristics and diversity of transactions linked to trade in tourism services, notably the heavy reliance of tourism on air transport and travel distribution systems.
2. *The prevention of predatory behaviour and anti-competitive practices by dominant integrated suppliers in the originating markets.* This refers to disciplines to prevent anti-competitive conduct including from air transport and travel distribution systems, and to safeguard trade in tourism services from

competitive exclusions, abuse of dominant and misleading or discriminatory use of information.

3. *The effective access and use of information on a non-discriminatory basis.* It should include provisions on access to ensuring non-discrimination, transparent, reasonable and objective criteria; compliance with Art. IV of GATS and the truthfulness of the information on tourism distributed by governments (travel warning) and through GDS; the unbundling of travel distribution systems as a measure to counter vertical integration and conflicts of interest in travel agencies and the interconnection of CRS, through the portability of reservation numbers. Submitting GDS operations to effective multilateral disciplines and dispute-settlement mechanisms would have a substantial effect on trade and anti-competitive practices.
4. *The implementation of an adequate framework for sustainable development of tourism.* Provisions on cooperation for the sustainable development of tourism are needed in recognition of the role of tourism in economic development; its need for infrastructure and development assistance; equitable trading conditions for economic sustainability; the relevance of enforcing internationally-recognized environmental and quality standards; the need for cooperation at all levels; and the importance of providing information on technologies required for competitive provision, regulation and sustainable development of tourism and all related-activities.
5. *To preserve the environmental sustainability of tourism and the cultural heritage.* Guiding principles for national policies and trade commitments to preserve the ecological systems, the biodiversity, cultural patrimony and traditions.

The liberalization under the GATS 2000 will be determined on one hand, by the level of removal of barriers in the revised horizontal commitments (which affect all sectors) and on the other, the lifting of conditions and limitations applied to each sector at sector-specific level and in the four modes of supply. Accordingly the consistency between the two types of commitment is an important issue to be addressed by developing countries, seeking to obtain commercially meaningful commitments at specific sectoral level.

Horizontal Commitments

In preparation of their positions in services negotiations, developing countries must assess to what extent the horizontal commitments of developed countries impede the liberalization of tourism and travel and related services. The major limitation in the horizontal commitments is in the lack of significant trading opportunities in mode 4, i.e. temporary movement of natural persons, since practically no commitments in this mode were made in specific services sectors.

The temporary presence of natural persons in all services sectors is undermined by the recurrence at the horizontal level to the economic needs tests, nationality and/or residence requirement and cumbersome administrative and visa procedures to be met by foreign nationals as services providers. The existing horizontal commitments by developed countries mainly refer to limitations for the establishment of the commercial presence (mode 3) by foreign providers to carry out the commercial operations.

Tourism Sector Commitments

Majority of tourism originating countries are developed countries, which have undertaking commitment to liberalize fully or partially the supply of services in different tourism sub-sectors and modes of supply. Still, *the impact of commitments in commercial presence* in term of market value is nullified by restrictions to the commercial presence of foreign tour operators, travel agencies, restaurants and hotels, which are not listed there. Also, the movement of natural persons engaged in the tourism supply of different services is precluded by limited horizontal commitments and the lack of specific sectoral commitments.

For instance in many Members States of the EU the commercial presence of foreign tour operators from the third countries is precluded or allowed only in association with already established national firms therein. Similarly, foreigners are precluded from undertaking of the business operations in the restaurant sub-sector even for those specializing in typical national food from other countries. In addition, the level of restrictions on commercial presence is aggravated by the possibility of recourse to the economic needs test, cumbersome and discriminatory licensing requirements that foreign suppliers of tourism services must meet.

Consumers and Providers of Services

It should be underlined that although the existing commitments on market access on *consumption abroad have no limitations* in the case of majority of the GATS commitments, including in the top originating countries; in real terms the freedom of movement for consumption abroad is restricted by the level of binding in other modes of supply, in particular the commercial presence of foreign suppliers in the tourism originating markets. The movement of consumers in most of the top originating markets of tourism is captive, because the existing level of binding of commercial presence consolidates the absolute advantage of the dominant mega-tour operators and other national suppliers including the travel agencies, since the exclusive right of selling directly to travellers of holiday packages in their own markets has been consolidated in the existing commitments on commercial presence.

Moreover, under such commercial conditions, 'he consumers' choices are limited by the offers of holiday package by dominant tour operators, but not only them, also by the opportunities for suppliers from destination countries to reach consumer in the originating markets directly. In addition, the consumers' choices in these markets are restricted by unfair practices in the management of information systems and the "racking policies" by travel agencies, which are usually integrated with mega-tour operators.

To improve horizontal commitments on mode 4, developed countries should remove the application of the economic needs test with respect to the movement of professionals supplying tourism services. Not all the professions and occupations are equally important to the movement of persons in the context of trade in tourism services.

For example, the possibility to have the waiver from the application economic needs test should be provided to individual tourism services suppliers involved in catering, maintenance services or in such areas where cultural affinities and close contacts with tourists may contribute to the quality of the services provided. To the extent that the remaining occupations would remain subject to the application of economic needs tests, efforts should be made to reduce the scope for arbitrary and discriminatory practices, provide greater transparency and introduce more neutral economic criteria.

The issue of transparency in respect of the application of the GATS commitments is crucial as a tool in promoting trade in tourism services. In that respect, commitments in mode 4 are closely linked to the implementation of the relevant immigration regulations, policies and procedures in a clear and transparent manner. Publishing of the legislation and implementing regulations which significantly affect ability of the foreign nationals or permanent residents move across borders to supply services is a general obligation, since this is the way to limit the room for discretionary and procedural rules. The lack of transparency, clarity in the existence, implementation and application of policy guidelines affecting application for and consideration of temporary work permits, residency requirements of visas impede market access, effectively violating key GATS provision.

TOURISM IN LEAST DEVELOPING COUNTRIES

Spurred on by a strong global economy and growing leisure time, world tourism grew by an estimated 7.4 per cent in 2000 - its highest growth in nearly a decade and almost doubles the increase of 1999. Directly or indirectly, tourism is estimated to be responsible for 245 million jobs and over US$5 trillion in economic activity world-wide.

Leisure and recreation accounts for 62 per cent of international tourism, with business tourism accounting for18 per cent, and the remaining 20 per cent other motives, i.e. visiting friends and relatives, for religious purposes/ pilgrimages, for health treatment and other. In the last ten years, the share of this last category has been rising. This pattern mirrors the trend towards market diversification and more frequent holidays, with people travelling for shorter periods of time and for different reasons.

Whilst travel for leisure and recreation is growing strongly, travel for other motives is growing faster. This offers the opportunity to offer a broader range of products. Although each LDC needs to have its own strategy for developing this sector, all countries need to appreciate the extent to which tourism can contribute not only to foreign exchange earning but to wider economic and social development. The LDCs need to adopt policies and strategies that help to move their industries on to a path of sustainable development that will also maximise the economic and social impact of tourism.

Data from the World Tourism Organisation (WTO) for 1998 indicate that developing countries, including the LDCs, account for approximately 61 per cent of international tourist arrivals but only 53 per cent of international tourism receipts. Receipts per arrival averaged US$609 for developing countries, as compared with US$827 for developed market economies. For LDCs, the average receipts per arrival were US$502. Of the LDCs, only Tanzania is a significant tourism destination generating US$ 570 million in visitor expenditure. Cambodia, Nepal and Uganda are the only other countries to generate more than US$ 100 million.

Zambia ranks along side these countries in terms of visitor numbers but its receipts per arrival are much lower as it attracts high numbers of day visitors to Victoria Falls. In terms of the proportion of exports represented by tourism receipts, the highest for the LDCs is again Tanzania with nearly 35 per cent, followed by Vanuatu (33 per cent) and the Gambia (24 per cent). For countries such as Guinea, Malawi, Bangladesh, Djibouti and even Ethiopia, tourism receipts represent a very small proportion of export earnings. In contrast, tourism represents over 100 per cent of the export revenues of many Caribbean countries. Of the 20 LDCs sampled, eight have above average earnings from tourism.

World Market Trends

Nearly 50 million more international trips were made in 2000 bringing the total number of international arrivals to a record 698 million according to the WTO, coupled with receipts of US$476 billion, an increase of 4.5 per cent over the previous year. In 1998, 45 countries recorded more than US$1 billion in international tourism expenditure, with the big industrial powers clearly in the lead. The United States, Germany, the United Kingdom and Japan top the list with spending ranging from US$29 billion to US$56 billion per year. These four countries represent over one-third of total international tourism expenditure. Germany is the largest source market for international visitors.

All regions of the world hosted more tourists in 2000, although the fastest developing area continued to be East Asia and the Pacific with a growth rate of 14.5 per cent and some 14 million more tourists than 1999. Europe, the main world region, accounts for 58 per cent of international tourism and grew by 6.2 per cent, with France being the leading destination. Others on the top ten destinations list were the U.S., Spain, Italy, China, the U.K., the Russian Federation, Canada, Mexico, and Germany.

Long haul travel world-wide is likely to grow faster, at 5.4 per cent per year over the period 1995-2020, than intra regional travel, at 3.8 per cent according to the WTO. Consequently the ratio between intra-regional and long haul travel will shift from around 82:18 in 1995 to close to 76:24 in

2020. The important long-haul markets are the European countries particularly the UK, Germany, France and Italy. Holiday entitlements are much higher in Europe than they are in the US which makes these countries the major source of long-haul travel. Since the 1950s tourism has not only grown quickly but has also changed substantially in terms of the destinations visited. For years tourism was characterised by concentration:

- Geographic concentration: the top 15 countries, all in Western Europe and North America, attracted 97 per cent of the world total
- Seasonal coverage (summer)
- Concentration in terms of purpose of trip (leisure - summer holidays)

Over the past ten years, more diversity has developed in destinations, time of year for travel, and types of tourism offerings. There are now over 70 leading tourism destinations, with the top 15 accounting only for 62 per cent of tourism arrivals. Tourists now tend to take shorter trips several times a year rather than one longer trip, and therefore visit a wider range of destinations. Some tourism destinations have become more specialised in order to target specific market segments. "Sun and sand" destinations remain popular, and boutique beach resorts are developing in destinations offering high service levels and not yet targeted by intensive land development.

But the market for leisure tourism is fragmenting into many segments including cultural tourism, eco-tourism, adventure sports, etc. Sun and sand remains the main segment, but increasingly, visitors seek more than a beach and the numbers travelling for leisure and seeking a different experience to sun and sand is growing. Nature travel, including eco-tourism, accounts already for over 10 per cent of the market and cultural tourism is the basis of the European tourism offer. There are also important segments developing within the sun and sand segment for families, the elderly and for incentive travel.

Other travel motives such as visiting friends and relatives (VFR), pilgrimages are also gaining in importance. These markets can be important for the LDCs, many of which have large expatriate populations abroad that can help to fuel the growth of tourism. VFR remains an under-developed segment of the market for many countries. Health tourism, both to visit spas and health resorts but also for health care and recuperation purposes, is one of the fastest growing segments of the market, though from a low base. There is strong interest in the world's largest origin markets, the US and Germany. To-date, the main destinations are in the developed countries but developing countries such as Cuba are demonstrating the potential for other countries, including the LDCs.

The launch of e-trade is having a profound effect on the tourism industry. Consumers have adopted on-line travel planning faster than any other on-line retail activity, and on-line leisure travel bookings are expected to exceed US$29 billion (or 12 per cent of industry revenues) by 2003. Increasingly, tourist destinations are offering "virtual reality" samplings online of the ambience and tourism products, with consumers able to experience the destination before making a travel commitment. Consumers now expect not only to make destination selections online but also to make travel, accommodation, and local transportation reservations at the same website.

There is growing consolidation within the travel industry, with an increasing portion of the market controlled by networks of tour operators, hotel chains, airlines, and rental car companies. Therefore even if individual tourism planning is on the rise, so is the use of intermediaries to guarantee value for money. The use of packaged tours, study trips, and cruises makes planning easier for the tourist but also decreases the in-country multiplier effects as all inclusive fees are paid ahead of time in the country of origin. Also on the rise, as a form of packaged tour, is incentive travel awarded by corporations to their employees.

Constraints

Many of the LDCs have excellent tourism potential, with a rich diversity of natural, cultural and other heritage assets. However, in the majority of cases, including Tanzania, a high proportion of the assets remain undeveloped and inaccessible to visitors. Moreover, the LDCs have yet to make a significant impact in this industry that is forecast to become one of the largest in the world. Their product offer is unknown and their industries are underdeveloped as a result of structural constraints, as follows:

- Lack of effective promotion, both of the destination and products offered by specific businesses
- Weak tourism administration,
- Lack of basic facilities, proper infrastructure and social services,
- Lack of investment in the tourism plant and the wider product (attractions, entertainment, shopping etc.)
- The lack of qualified, trained and skilled human resource,
- High level of ecological fragility and vulnerability.

One of the main challenges for LDCs is to raise awareness of potential tourists of their offerings. Most LDCs do not have an experienced tourist board to promote the destination and the private sector lacks the expertise and resources to promote their products to the tourism trade and the internet. Online bookings are difficult or non-existent, due to limitation in the telecommunications and internet access infrastructure. Information is not presented in a manner that helps the potential visitor to differentiate the country and businesses' market offerings from others.

There is little attempt made to tailor products to the needs of individual segments of the market. LDCs need to improve their capacity to deliver value for money. In most LDCs, there has been little training of frontline personnel (e.g., taxi drivers, tour guides, interpreters, hotel and restaurant staff, attractions staff) in customer service standards. LDCs have also neglected two issues of primary importance to foreign visitors - health and safety. For this reason most foreign tourists prefer to travel under prepaid arrangements where an intermediary is responsible of the quality of service that they receive and this lead to a lowering multiplier effect in the host countries. Massive investments are needed in the supporting infrastructure, from airports to roads, water, sewage and hospitals if revenues per tourist are to increase. For revenue spin-offs from business travellers, again the importance of cost efficient, high quality telecommunications and Internet infrastructure are obvious.

But perhaps most importantly, the LDCs have yet to understand and embrace the concept of sustainable tourism. The WTO and other s have shown that not only is it important to develop tourism in ways that reflect the culture and aspirations of host communities but the crucial importance of preserving the environment. For sun and sand and nature tourism, the environment is the product. The concept of sustainable tourism highlight s the importance of ensuring that local communities benefit from tourism and those women are given equal opportunity and benefit from tourism. Conventional hotel based tourism, restricted to the beach, is not sustainable as it often builds resentment in the host community and the destination dies when the product reaches the declining phase of its product cycle.

Prospects, Policies and Strategies

The growth of leisure time and incomes world wide will result in continued rapid growth of the tourism market. The market is already huge and will grow faster than the market for merchandise exports. The LDCs have the natural assets to compete in this market. Tourism must rank amongst the priority sectors for export development in most LDCs. Further, if properly managed, tourism has the potential to create employment, preserve natural attractions and culture and contribute to economic and social development. It can lead the growth of ancillary industries such as agriculture, crafts, entertainment, sports, shopping and transport. To help harness the undoubted potential of tourism, strategies, policies and plans are required. Strategies for rapid and sustained growth of this sector need cover:

a. *Improve marketing:* LDCs wishing to benefit substantially from international tourism revenues need to promote a differentiated image for the destination, stressing the distinctiveness and diversity of the experience. The strategies need to be segment based, responding to the increasing fragmentation of the market. With their limited budgets, the focus of the promotional effort has to be to intermediaries in the form of tour operators and selected travel agents in target countries. In selecting potential partners, it is vitally important to understand the specialisation of selected travel trade partners in terms of the segments of the market they serve and the characteristics of their customer base to match the intermediary with the product. Equally important is the need to have a broad base of travel trade partners to avoid the development of monopoly conditions. Concerns over the market power of the foreign travel trade has prompted the Dominican Republic, El Salvador, and Honduras to submit a joint proposal to the WTO Council on Trade in Services regarding an annex on tourism services.

   This addresses the need to clarify the definition of the sector and to develop a framework of competitive practices (similar to basic telecommunications) to avoid market domination by networks of foreign tour operators. Country and business websites are needed through which online bookings can be made, ideally supported by credit card facilities and virtual reality technologies. Officials need to be responsible for monitoring and updating online information about the country's tourism offerings. In-flight magazines or promotional videos also offer excellent exposure.

b. *Regional Co-operation*: To attract new visitors, regional alliances can be very useful. The benefits include sharing marketing overheads and taking advantage of the trend towards multi-destination holidays. Often, the choice of destination starts with selecting a region to visit and the Caribbean has shown the benefits of marketing the region. In addition, two or more destination holidays are growing in popularity. Tour operators have started to promote multi-country tours. If the LDCs themselves create a multi-country offering, they may be able to attract additional first-time visitors on a "sampling" basis.

c. *Diversify tourist products and attractions*: Increasing tourism revenue depends in large part on increasing expenditures per arrival by increasing length of stay, diversifying and developing tourist products and attractions. Attracting foreign direct investment by international hotel chains can help raise the profile of the LDC as well as promote the destination through the chain's own promotional effort. Products and services need to be developed with the market segment to be targeted firmly in mind.

d. *Improve customer service:* Once tourists have arrived, it is critical to ensure that they have a positive experience. Training Programme can sensitise local residents and industry staff to the expectations of foreign visitors, good customer service practices, and the benefits to the economy of tourism. In addition, attention needs to be paid to ensure that all support services are readily available - e.g., currency exchange, reconfirmation of airline reservations, local transportation, shopping, cultural activities, health care services, etc. The presence of known franchises and chains is often reassuring to foreign visitors. Easy exit formalities, information in hotels about flight departures, flight check-in available at hotels, and information on duty-free limits in home markets all help form positive impressions.

e. *Develop Infrastructure*: The infrastructure for tourism is no different to the needs of local residents. It is the case that tourism demands and makes affordable higher levels of infrastructure provision than would otherwise be the case. What is important is to ensure that mechanisms exist so that the revenues from tourism can be channelled back, in a clearly identified manner, to those investing infrastructure so that they have a real incentive to give priority to such investment. The infrastructure for air travel, on which the tourism industry depends, has to be developed in conjunction with the airlines.

Policies for Sustainable Development

The planning of tourism has to involve local communities so that the product can reflect their culture and aspirations. Community based tourism should be given priority to spread the benefits and increase the number of stakeholders. Linkages with other ancillary industries should be promoted. Above all, it should be recognised that the environment is the product. Constraints: Despite the proprietor's previous experience in tourism, it was difficult to start from a very modest beginning. The government liberalised this sector in 1998, which increased the number of tour operators creating over supply.

Bhutan is regarded as their favourite tourist destinations by frequent visitors, yet it is the least visited destinations in the world. This is due to the lack of promotion and advertisement in other countries. Air links are a severe problem as the country's only airport accommodates only small aircraft and is vulnerable to weather conditions. Internal roads are poor and not all cultural and natural attractions are accessible to visitors. The country lacks a tourism master plan.

Chapter 5

Planning in Tourism

TOURISM PLANNING

Tourism is one of many activities in a community or region that requires planning and coordination. This bulletin provides a simple structure and basic guidelines for comprehensive tourism planning at a community or regional level. Planning is the process of identifying objectives and defining and evaluating methods of achieving them. By comprehensive planning we mean planning which considers all of the tourism resources, organizations, markets, and Programme within a region. Comprehensive planning also considers economic, environmental, social, and institutional aspects of tourism development.

Two Sides of Planning

Tourism planning has evolved from two related but distinct sets of planning philosophies and methods. On the one hand, tourism is one of many activities in an area that must be considered as part of physical, environmental, social, and economic planning. Therefore, it is common to find tourism addressed, at least partially, in a regional land use, transportation, recreation, economic development, or comprehensive plan. The degree to which tourism is addressed in such plans depends upon the relative importance of tourism to the community or region and how sensitive the planning authority is to tourism activities.

Tourism may also be viewed as a business in which a community or region chooses to engage. Individual tourism businesses conduct a variety of planning activities including feasibility, marketing, product development, promotion, forecasting, and strategic planning. If tourism is a significant component of an area's economy or development plans, regional or community-wide marketing plans are needed to coordinate the development and marketing activities of different tourism interests in the community.

A comprehensive approach integrates a strategic marketing plan with more traditional public planning activities. This ensures a balance between serving the needs and wants of the tourists versus the needs and wants of local residents. A formal tourism plan provides a vehicle for the various interests within a community to coordinate their activities and work toward common goals. It also is a means of coordinating tourism with other community activities.

Steps in the Planning Process

Like any planning, tourism planning is goal-oriented, striving to achieve certain objectives by matching available resources and Programme with the needs and wants of people. Comprehensive planning requires a systematic approach, usually involving a series of steps. The process is best viewed as an iterative and on-going one, with each step subject to modification and refinement at any stage of the planning process.

There are six steps in the planning process:

1. Define goals and objectives.
2. Identify the tourism system.
   a) Resources
   b) Organizations
   c) Markets
3. Generate alternatives.
4. Evaluate alternatives.

5. Select and implement.
6. Monitor and evaluate.

Step one: Defining Goals and objectives. Obtaining clear statements of goals and objectives is difficult, but important. Ideally, tourism development goals should flow from more general community goals and objectives. It is important to understand how a tourism plan serves these broader purposes. Is the community seeking a broader tax base, increased employment opportunities, expanded recreation facilities, better educational Programme, a higher quality of life? How can tourism contribute to these objectives?

If tourism is identified as a means of serving broader community goals, it makes sense to develop plans with more specific tourism development objectives. These are generally defined through a continuing process in which various groups and organizations in a community work together toward common goals. A local planning authority, chamber of commerce, visitor's bureau, or similar group should assume a leadership role to develop an initial plan and obtain broad involvement of tourism interests in the community. Public support for the planning process and plan is also important.

Having a good understanding of tourism and the tourism system in your community is the first step toward defining goals and objectives for tourism development. The types of goals that are appropriate and the precision with which you are able to define them will depend upon how long your community has been involved in tourism and tourism planning.

In the early stages of tourism development, goals may involve establishing organizational structures and collecting information to better identify the tourism system in the community. Later, more precise objectives can be formulated and more specific development and marketing strategies evaluated.

Step two: Identifying Your Tourism System When planning for any type of activity, it is important to first define its scope and characteristics. Be clear about exactly what your plan encompasses. A good initial question is, "What do you mean by tourism?" Tourism is defined in many ways. Generally, tourism involves people traveling outside of their community for pleasure. Definitions differ on the specifics of how far people must travel, whether or not they must stay overnight, for how long, and what exactly is included under traveling for "pleasure". Do you want your tourism plan to include day visitors, conventioneers, business travellers, people visiting friends and relatives, people passing through, or seasonal residents?

Which community resources and organizations serve tourists or could serve tourists? Generally, tourists share community resources with local residents and businesses. Many organizations serve both tourists and locals. This complicates tourism planning and argues for a clear idea of what your tourism plan entails. You can begin to clarify the tourism system by breaking it down into three subsystems:

1. Tourism resources,
2. Tourism organizations, and
3. Tourism markets.

An initial task in developing a tourism plan is to identify, inventory, and classify the objects within each of these subsystems.

Tourism Resources are any (1) natural, (2) cultural, (3) human, or (4) capital resources that either are used or can be used to attract or serve tourists. A tourism resource inventory identifies and classifies the resources available that provide opportunities for tourism development. Conduct an objective and realistic assessment of the quality and quantity of resources you have to work with.

Tourism organizations combine resources in various proportions to provide products and services for the tourist. It is important to recognize the diverse array of public and private organizations involved with tourism. The most difficult part of tourism planning is to get these groups to work toward common goals. You should develop a list of these organizations within your own community and obtain their input and cooperation in your tourism planning efforts. Setting up appropriate communication systems and institutional arrangements is a key part of community tourism planning.

Tourism Markets

Tourists makeup the third, and perhaps most important subsystem. Successful tourism Programme require a strong market orientation. The needs and wants of the tourists you choose to attract and serve must be the focus of much of your marketing and development activity. Therefore, it is important to clearly understand which tourism market segments you wish to attract and serve. Tourists fall into a very diverse set of categories with quite distinct needs and wants. You should identify the different types of tourists, or market segments that you presently serve or would like to serve. This may involve one or more tourism market surveys.

A visitor survey identifies the size and nature of the existing market and asks the following questions:

- What are the primary market segments you presently attract?
- Where do they come from?
- What local businesses and facilities do they use?
- What attracted them to the community?
- How did they find out about your community?
- How satisfied are they with your offerings?

A market survey (usually a telephone survey) also can be conducted among households in regions from which you wish to attract tourists. This type of study helps identify potential markets, and means of attracting tourists to your area.

Tourism Market Segments

In a general tourism plan, some clear target tourism market segments should be identified. You might begin by defining the market area from which you will draw most of your visitors. The size of your market area depends upon the uniqueness and quality of your "product", transportation systems, tastes and preferences of surrounding populations, and your competition. Identifying the market area will help target information and promotion and define transportation routes and modes, competition, and characteristics of your market.

Next, divide your travel market into the following trip length categories:

- Day trips from a 50 mile radius,
- Day trips from 50 to 200 miles away,
- Pass-through travelers,
- Overnight trips of 1 or 2 nights (most likely weekends), and
- Extended overnight vacation trips.

After you have an idea of your market area and kinds of trips you will be serving, begin defining more specific market segments like vehicle campers, downhill skiers, sightseers, family vacationers, single weekenders, and the like. These segments can be more clearly tied to particular resources, businesses, and facilities in your community.

What kinds of products and services are likely to attract each of these groups? Tourist needs as well as their impact on the local community are quite different for day tourists versus overnight tourists. Areas catering primarily to weekend traffic will experience large fluctuations in use. In deciding the relative importance of these different segments, communities need to assess both their ability to provide required services (do you have enough rooms?), as well as the demand for different types of trips relative to the supply and your competition.

The environment

A tourism plan is significantly affected by many factors in the broader environment. Indeed, one of the complexities of tourism planning is the number of variables that are outside of the control of an individual tourism business or community. These include such things as tourism offerings and prices at competing destinations, federal and state policy and legislation, currency exchange rates, the state of the economy, and weather. These factors are discussed more fully in Extension bulletin E-1959 as part of the market environment analysis.

Local populations also must be considered in tourism planning. As they compete with tourists for resources, they can be significantly affected by tourism activity, and they are an important source of support in getting tourism plans implemented. A survey of local residents can be conducted to assess community attitudes toward tourism development, identify impacts of tourism on the community, and obtain local input into tourism plans. Public hearings, workshops, and advisory boards are other ways to obtain public involvement in tourism planning. Local support and cooperation is important to the success of tourism Programme and should not be overlooked.

Step three: Generating Alternatives. Generating alternative development and marketing options to meet your goals requires some creative thinking and brainstorming. The errors made at this stage are usually thinking too narrowly or screening out alternatives prematurely. It is wise to solicit a wide range of options from a diverse group of people. If tourism expertise is lacking in your community, seek help and advice outside the community.

Tourism planning involves a wide range of interrelated development and marketing decisions. The following development questions will get you started:

- How much importance should be assigned to tourism within a community or region?
- Which general community goals is tourism development designed to serve?

- Which organization(s) will provide the leadership and coordination necessary for community tourism planning? What are the relative roles of public and private sectors?

Tourism marketing decision questions include

- *Segments*: Which market segments should be pursued; geographic markets, trip types, activity or demographic subgroups?
- *Product*: What kinds of tourism products and services should be provided? Who should provide what?
- *Place*: Where should tourism facilities be located?
- *Promotion*: What kinds of promotion should be used, by whom, in which media, how much, when? What community tourism theme or image should be established?
- *Price*: What prices should be charged for which products and services. Who should capture the revenue?

Step four: Evaluating Alternatives. Tourism development and marketing options are evaluated by assessing the degree to which each option will be able to meet the stated goals and objectives. There are usually two parts to a systematic evaluation of tourism development and marketing alternatives: (1) Feasibility analysis, and (2) Impact assessment. These two tasks are interrelated, but think of them as trying to answer two basic questions: (1) Can it be done?, and (2) What are the consequences? A decision to take a specific action must be based both on feasibility and desirability.

Feasibility Analysis

First, screen alternatives and eliminate those that are not feasible due to economic, environmental, political, legal, or other factors. Evaluate the remaining set of alternatives in more detail, paying particular attention to the market potential and financial plan. Make a realistic assessment of your community's ability to attract and serve a market segment or segments. This requires a clear understanding of the tourism market in your area and how this market is changing. Also carefully identify your competition and evaluate your advantages and disadvantages compared to the competition. Plan toward the future because it takes time to implement decisions and for your actions to take effect. Therefore, look at the likely market and competition for several years to come. Review forecasts for the travel market in your area, if available. Careful tracking of tourism trends in your own community can help identify changes in the market that you will have to adapt to.

Impact Assessment

When evaluating alternative development and marketing strategies it is important to understand the impacts, both positive and negative, of proposed actions. The types of impacts and their importance vary across different communities and proposed actions. Generally, the size, extent, and nature of tourism impacts depend upon:

- Volume of tourist activity relative to local activity
- Length and nature of tourist contacts with the community
- Degree of concentration/dispersal of tourist activity in the area
- Similarities or differences between local populations and tourists
- Stability/sensitivity of local economy, environment, and social structure
- How well tourism is planned, controlled, and managed.

Look at both the benefits and costs of any proposed actions. While tourism development can increase income, revenues, and employment, it also involves costs. Evaluate benefits and costs of tourism development from the perspectives of local government, businesses, and residents.

Impacts on Local Government

Local government provides most of the infrastructure and many of the services essential to tourism development, including highways, public parks, law enforcement, water and sewer, garbage collection and disposal. Evaluate tourism decisions with a clear understanding of the capacity of the local infrastructure and services relative to anticipated needs, and take into account both the needs of local populations and tourists.

A fiscal impact analysis evaluates the impact of tourism on the community's tax base and local government costs. It entails predicting the additional infrastructure and service requirements of tourism development, estimating their costs, deciding who will pay for/provide them, and how. Will tourism generate increased local government revenue through fees and charges, local sales or use taxes, increased property values or property tax rates, or larger local shares of federal and state tax revenues?

Impacts on Business and Industry

Businesses that are directly serving tourists benefit from sales to tourists. Through secondary impacts, tourism activity also benefits a wide range of businesses in a community. For example, a local textile industry may sell to a linen supply firm that serves hotels and motels catering primarily to tourists. A local forest products industry sells to a lumberyard where local woodcarvers or furniture makers buy their supplies. They in turn sell to tourists through various retail outlets. All of these businesses benefit from tourism.

If most products and services for tourists are bought outside of the local area, much of the tourist spending "leaks" out of the local economy. The more a community is "self-sufficient" in serving tourists, the larger the local impact.

Impacts on Residents

Local residents may experience a broad range of both positive and negative impacts from tourism development.

Tourism development may provide increased employment and income for the community. Although tourism jobs are primarily in the service sectors and are often seasonal, part time, and low-paying, these characteristics, are neither universal nor always undesirable. Residents may value opportunities for part time and seasonal work. In particular, employment opportunities and work experiences for students or retirees may be desired.

Residents may also benefit from local services that otherwise would not be available. Tourism development may mean a wider variety of retailers and restaurants, or a better community library. It may also mean more traffic, higher prices, and increases in property values and local taxes. The general quality of the environment and life in the community may go up or down due to tourism development. This depends on the nature of tourism development, the preferences and desires of local residents, and how well tourism is planned and managed.

Steps five and six: Implementation, and Monitoring and Evaluation. We will not attempt a complete discussion of decisionmaking, plan implementation, and monitoring, but these are critical steps in the success of a tourism plan. A set of specific actions should be prescribed with clearly defined responsibilities and timetables. Monitor progress in implementing the plan and evaluate the success of the plan in meeting its goals and objectives on a regular basis. Plans generally need to be adjusted over time due to changing goals, changing market conditions, and unanticipated impacts. It is a good idea to build monitoring and evaluation systems into your planning efforts.

Successful tourism planning and development means serving both tourists and local residents. The bulletins in this series stress the importance of a market orientation for attracting and serving tourists. This market orientation must be balanced with a clear view of how tourism serves the broader community interest and an understanding of the positive and negative impacts of tourism development. Remember, tourism should serve the community first and the tourist second. Tourism development must be compatible with other activities in the area and be supported by the local population. Therefore, the tourism plan should be closely coordinated with other local and regional planning efforts, if not an integral part of them.

TERRITORIAL PLANNING IN TOURISM

Environmental quality is often a key success factor for tourism. At the same time, tourism makes extensive use of natural resources thereby jeopardizing its long-term viability. To address such a dilemma, from the general notion of sustainable development (SD) tourism scholars have coined the term 'sustainable tourism' (ST) that encompasses a set of principles, business methods and policy prescriptions relevant to the tourist industry (Sinclair and Stabler, 1997). However, recent research has advocated the need to reconcile the concept of ST with that of SD, by making the concerns of the former adhere more strictly to the tenets of the latter (Collins, 1999; Hunter, 1997). This paper looks at the issues of tourism development and environmental conservation through the lens of SD principles and assesses the pivotal role that local governments can play in designing policies that make the two perspectives compatible.

A common denominator in the literature on SD is the Bruntland Commission's definition that "SD is development that meets the need of the present without compromising the ability of future generations to meet their own needs". Such a mandate affirms the importance of intragenerational and intergenerational equity issues. As far as the former is concerned, "SD places emphasis on providing for the needs of the least advantaged in society". This is particularly relevant in developing countries, where the need to generate income is more likely to lead to a rapid exploitation of the resource base and an uneven distribution of the related profits between foreign investors and host populations. To prevent this, it is generally recommended that local populations and governments be directly involved in the shaping of development activities in association with foreign developers, because locals can better assess the short and the long-term effects of growth.

As far as the latter is concerned, intergenerational fairness implies that future generations should receive a fair share of the net benefits generated by the development. The fact that development is sustainable only as long as future generations are fairly treated led to the view that "...we in the present generation are but the present tenants of the earth, not its absolute owners. As present tenants we have the right to make use of its productivity, but not the right to impair its productivity for its later tenants the future generations".

In theory, future generations are entitled to just compensation for the current generation's actions that lead to a depletion of natural resource. In practice, doing so requires making difficult judgments about the substitutability of natural capital with physical capital. This is a crucial point in the case of tourism, whose activity relies extensively on the transformation of natural capital into accommodation and service facilities. Thus, the tourism industry faces the particularly difficult challenge to "develop tourism capacity and the quality of its products without adversely affecting the physical and human environment that sustains and nurtures them".

It is argued, however, that the WCED definition is too vague to use as a working tool, and often results in ambiguous admonition for policymakers (Norton and Toman 1997). Indeed, the requirement that the needs of the present generation be met without compromising the ability of future generations to meet their needs, could be satisfied simply by allowing constant consumption over time at no more than a subsistence level. Although such a policy would achieve equity among different generations, it could hardly be accepted as a reasonable target for public policy, as it may fail to incorporate a notion of dynamic efficiency. In the following analysis, efficiency implies a notion of "non-wastefulness", that is, the possibility that inputs are transformed in a way that leads to an increase in individuals' well-being in a sustainable manner, e.g., consumption above the subsistence level for every generation.

Such an increase in individuals' welfare entails a decision on the optimal allocation of scarce resources (e.g. natural assets) among alternative uses (e.g., development or preservation). Because tourism can never be totally without environmental impacts, the real challenge is to indicate sustainable policies that combine intra-generational and intergenerational equity with efficiency considerations in a mutually compatible manner (Page, 1997). As far as intergenerational equity and efficiency considerations are concerned, assessing under what circumstances turning natural resources into capital stock (e.g. a hotel) leads to an increase in the well-being of the present and future generations, is central.

Furthermore, the notion of efficiency is closely linked with that of intragenerational equity when the local populations of the tourist areas are allowed to appropriate a fair share of the net benefits generated by tourism. The theoretical analysis in this article presents a policy measure that enables local governments to retain the surplus from tourism activities when these are run by foreign organizations. The existing literature has refined the definition of sustainable development - from very weak to very strong depending on the importance given to such notions as reversibility and substitutability between physical and natural capital.

Unfortunately, the interpretation of such concepts varies, depending on the disciplinary approach being adopted. For instance, economists and ecologists assign different meanings to the notions of substitutability and reversibility. For economists, substitutability refers to the possibility of maintaining a desired level of production using different combinations of inputs, while reversibility indicates the extent to which a given resource becomes scarce as a consequence of human actions. For ecologists, these two factors determine such ecosystems' physical properties as, for instance, resilience. In this sense, a more resilient ecosystem is one that is more likely to revert to its original condition after a perturbation and/or to find other substitutes in the event that one of the ecosystem attributes is diminished.

Applying the notion of weak sustainability is possible if we assume that natural and physical capitals are substitutable, or when changes to the natural asset base are reversible. This implies that under the weak sustainability paradigm, intra-generational equity is obtained through the distribution of the efficiency gains arising from the implementation of development projects, while future generations are compensated for the loss of natural assets by inheriting a greater stock of physical capital.

However, even advocates of weak sustainability acknowledge that under certain circumstances, e.g. when physical capital is a poor substitute for the natural resource, efficiency considerations ought not to occupy a central role. For instance, it has been argued that one generation might set aside special places and features such as the Grand Canyon or the Reef Barrier for future generations because of their intrinsic qualities.

The uncertainty surrounding both the effects of human intervention on the environment and the likelihood of finding feasible technological solutions to environmental problems provides an important argument for strong sustainability. By this it is meant that the opportunities of future generations can be secured only if natural resources and environmental quality are specifically conserved for their benefit. Thus, within the strong sustainability paradigm, conservation concerns are paramount.

Combining Conservation and Efficiency

The foregoing discussion has illustrated that intragenerational/efficiency and intergenerational equity goals are less likely to be in conflict when considered from within a weak sustainability perspective, while supporters of strong sustainability are inclined to reject any trade-off between conservation and efficiency. In line with the latter view, it has become abundantly clear that tourism cannot continue to be the killer of the "goose laying golden eggs".

However, it has been argued that strong sustainability, with its emphasis on intergenerational fairness, can conflict with the efficient use of resources that may engender beneficial effects for both the present and the future generations. That is, the strong sustainability approach is often associated with an anti-economic growth position that appears to deny the world's poor the opportunity of meeting basic needs, both in the short and the long run.

Therefore, this article takes the Centre ground stance indicated in Hunter (1997) by arguing that the essential role of ecological conservation in the implementation of sustainable tourism strategies should, depending on the circumstances, be complemented by efficiency considerations. This is in line with many methodological contributions aimed at bringing together efficiency and intergenerational equity.

The combination of a conservation criterion with an efficiency criterion constitutes the central element of the two-tier method advocated by Page (1977). Using this approach, problems are categorized as being intragenerational or intergenerational in their effects, in the sense specified above. That is, when intergenerational issues figure prominently, more attention is given to conservation, with possible applications of the 'safe minimum standard of conservation principle', which places the burden of proof on today's resource allocators to demonstrate that their behaviour is consistent with intergenerational fairness (Howarth, 1997). In practice, this approach recognizes the fundamental right of future generations to inherit an intact stock of natural resources, unless the costs of foregoing the resource exploitation, that is, the loss of the efficiency gains from development, are unbearably high.

Page (1997) provides a list of inter-related issues that need to be addressed to achieve a satisfactory combination of efficiency and equity. First, instruments need to be identified. He suggests that "shifting the tax base toward virgin material taxes and taxes on environmental harms would work toward sustainability". Second, intergenerational equity should always come first when the resource is essential. He cites the U.S. Drinking Water Regulation as an example of public intervention based on equity grounds, as future generations are entitled to a safe supply of drinking water.

The example that comes to mind in the case of tourism, is the establishment of parks or natural reserves, where regulatory measures are taken towards environmental protection so that the functional integrity of essential, and possibly unique, natural ecosystems is preserved as far as is possible, for the benefit of future generations. Indeed, once a law attributes the status of park or of natural reserve to a given geographical area, heavy restrictions are imposed on the possibility to develop the area, that curtail or impede tourist activity.

More importantly, to guarantee that the resource base remains intact, and can be bequeathed to future generations, the status of park cannot be abolished and remains associated with the area indefinitely. Third, and related to the latter point, the role of the legal framework in which the decision-makers operate is crucial. Practically, this entails that the environmental decisions associated with important equity and efficiency considerations should be dealt with in a manner similar to that used to preserve a system of constitutional law.

This is because the "framers of a constitution are expected to abstract themselves from their own narrow self-interest and establish the rules of the game that are sustainable indefinitely".It is essential for modern societal institutions to maintain the constitutional system: to protect it from myopic opportunism triggered by short-term benefits, it is commonplace to have special procedures to modify constitutional dictates.

By the same token, environmental problems with important intergenerational equity aspects should be dealt with like constitutional issues whereby the future generations' entitlement to an intact resource base has paramount importance.

Three points that are central in this study may be inferred from the previous discussion:

1. The importance of natural resources,
2. The identification of appropriate policy instruments and
3. The legislative framework. This article aims to clarify some of the relationships among these issues. At the same time it develops a conceptual framework encompassing all the basic elements that are taken into account in the public assessment of tourism development projects. To this purpose, a theoretical economic model of land taxation is illustrated. Its results show the crucial role played by a tax on land development for the joint achievement of conservation and economic efficiency goals. In addition, its cost-benefit approach clearly indicates that in environmentally sensitive areas - where the resource is essential - the tax should be set at a level that deters development. This result is thus equivalent to the creation of a park or a reserve that remains as close to its original form as possible.

The importance of the legislative framework is investigated using the case study of the so-called "Master Plan" in North Sardinia (Italy). The evidence presented, together with considerations from the theoretical model, are used to shed light on the Sardinian government's refusal to grant a developer special exemptions from existing territorial planning legislation. Indeed, the Sardinian government decided to forego the short-term benefits of a large tourism development because the development allowed the possibility of construction within 300 meters of the coastline, a practice that is prohibited by Sardinian law. The local government recognized that the Defence of the conservation principle embodied in the regional law could not be a matter of bargaining, even though this would have entailed, as it actually did, the withdrawal of the project by the developer. Regardless of the merit of the specific project and the good reputation of the developer for quality tourism, the Sardinian government's stance on the project aimed to ensure that other developments might not be created unless sustainable principles were applied.

Sustainability and Public Intervention

To our knowledge, there is no formal economic model explicitly linking tourism and sustainable development. There exists, however, a growing literature aimed at integrating sustainability and formal economic analysis. Faucheux et al. (1996) classified the existing analytical approaches to sustainability using four categories of models: 1) neoclassical, 2) evolutionary, 3) ecological economic and 4) neo-ricardian. The model presented in the next subsection falls within the first category but departs from existing models by adopting a game theoretic approach where different incentives faced by public and private institutions are taken into account. For a technical presentation of the model, the reader is referred to Piga (1999). The emphasis here will be the description of the assumptions used in this model, and the policy recommendations that can be drawn. The second part of the section consists of a case study that complements and supports the theoretical analysis.

Sustainability and Taxation

The model under analysis is dynamic; that is, it considers a sequence of time periods and how decisions taken in early periods influence the outcomes of subsequent periods. A dynamic approach allows a better identification of the development's long-term effects, notably on land, which is the natural resource under study. This is particularly relevant for tourism because territorial planning, environmental design and land use, are crucial factors that create and sustain a tourist resort competitive advantage. This is because tourists increasingly expect a picturesque landscape to be integral to the holiday experience. Moreover, land development is associated with various forms of environmental costs. Both these aspects are captured in the following analysis.

The first economic agent taken into account is a private tourism developer who owns a territory of size L For instance; L could represent the size of an island. The developer chooses the rate of land exploitation, that is, the portion of the site on which tourist facilities will be erected. Denoting with B(t) the stock of developed land at time t and with the size of territory on which the developer decides to build in period t, we postulate that these two variables are linked by this simple law of variation over time. t). Such an expression indicates that in every period t a portion of land sð(t) is used to build accommodations. Thus, what is built this year is added to what was built in previous years, thereby increasing the stock of buildings that constitute the site's capacity.

The discussion so far highlights the well known impact of tourism development on environmental quality: "In reality, it is impossible to imagine any kind of tourism activity being developed and then operating without in some way reducing the quantity and/or quality of natural resources somewhere". In this particular case, for tourism activity to take place, it is impossible to maintain the resource base intact (i.e., not to exploit land). It follows that a satisfactory combination of efficiency and conservation hinges around the identification of both the private and public benefits engendered by the development, of its environmental costs and of the appropriate policy instruments that induce an optimal level of use of the natural resource.

The first type of private benefit that we consider is the revenue deriving from selling to tourists. Revenues depend on the price of the holiday and on the site's capacity, B (t). In turn, it is assumed that the tourists' willingness to pay for a holiday (which represents the highest price they would pay for a holiday) is positively influenced by the environmental quality of the site, which is measured by the amount of land that is left unused.

More importantly, the previous analytical expression indicates that the more the place is developed (i.e., the greater B (t) relative to L), the lower the price the developer can charge for a holiday. Therefore, the developer, when deciding to expand (i.e., increase the size of B(t) through the choice of ó(t)), has to take into account that the revenue increase, due to the possibility of accommodating more tourists, may be more than offset by the reduction in price that is triggered by the deterioration in the environmental quality.

Such a novel representation of the links between tourists' demand and environmental quality captures a peculiar feature of the tourist industry that is supported by empirical evidence. Font (2000) presents evidence supporting the notion that environmental considerations are important drivers of tourism demand. Huybers and Bennett (2000) reach a similar conclusion in an analysis of changes in environmental quality and other features that affect demand.

The local government is the second economic agent taken into consideration. The instrument used to achieve sustainability is a tax on each unit of newly built territory. This clarifies the crucial role of the public sector: the tax is a cost to the developer and can be used by the government to appropriate some of the profits generated by the development. As discussed below, the tax guarantees the achievement of intragenerational equity objectives, as the tax revenues in each year can be deployed to ameliorate the local public infrastructure which is then inherited by future generations.

In line with the real-world situation where the legislative framework and the taxing policy is often a given for the developers, the economic model assumes that the local government has a first-mover advantage, that is, the government sets the tax level before the developer decides the expansion size. In the economic literature the player that moves first is defined as a "Stackelberg leader". In each period, the local government obtains tax receipts given by the tax multiplied by the size of the expanded capacity.

The second part of the government's objective function consists of the net value derivable from the use of the land. Such a value is the net outcome of the government's evaluation of the public benefits from development against its environmental costs. On the one hand, public benefits are generated by tourism development through a multiplier effect on the local economy arising because a local workforce is used in construction, in operating the tourist facilities and because tourists consume local products.

For more examples of the relationship between tourism and the local multiplier. On the other hand, land development engenders environmental costs for the local population both in terms of congestion and exhaustion of the natural resource and in the form of loss of non-market benefits such as bequest, option and existence values (Pearce et al., 1989). The bequest value is the willingness to pay to preserve the environment for the benefit of future generations.

The option value identifies an expression of preference for the preservation of an environment against some probability that a community will make use of it at a later date. The existence value is represented by the utility that individuals enjoy when the risk to an endangered species has been reduced. Development implies the loss of all these values for the local population, the sum of which constitutes the non-market environmental costs.

These are particularly high in areas where the ecosystem is less resilient, that is, less likely to fully recover from exogenous shocks, and where, therefore, development may engender irreversible degradation to the environment. Finally, land development engenders another form of environmental costs to the local population, that is, the lack of access to natural resources (e.g., beaches) due to congestion arising from having an intensively developed destination occupied by tourists.

The foregoing analysis of the local government's pay-off function has highlighted that the development engenders benefits in the form of private profits and public income multiplier effects, and environmental costs whose size depends on the characteristics of the area's ecosystem. The difference between these benefits and costs gives rise to a net value function, $W(B(t))$, that depends on the size of the development. A realistic analytical expression for the net value function $W(B(t))$ is one that allows, at an early stage of development, growth benefits, and the related efficiency gains, to be greater than environmental costs, which become predominant as the development increases in size.

A quadratic function such as $W(t)=B(t)-\tilde{a}B^2(t)$, exhibits this property: the minus sign attached to the quadratic value of the total development size, denoted by $B(t)$, implies that the environmental costs associated with development, increase at a faster rate than growth benefits, captured by the linear part of $B(t)$. Furthermore, this effect is reinforced depending on the value of $\tilde{a}$, that is, the larger $\tilde{a}$, the larger the environmental costs relative to the growth benefits. Note, however, that when $\tilde{a}$ is sufficiently large (e.g., when the loss of existence, option and bequest values is conspicuous) $W(t)$ may be negative even for small levels of development.

This is made up of the pecuniary tax take and of the external effects of the development, namely the growth benefits and the environmental costs. When $\tilde{a}$ is large enough, environmental costs exceed the monetary value of tax receipts and income multiplier effects even for small values of B(t) that correspond to an early stage of development. In this case, given that E (t)<0, the local government should not allow any development in the territory. However, in more general cases, the tax receipts may be used to improve the site's infrastructures - schools, hospitals, roads etc. - whose creation thus compensates future generations for inheriting a smaller stock of natural resource.

The foregoing discussion highlights the different objectives pursued by the developer and the local government, because the taxation policy creates a benefit for the latter and a cost for the former. However, without the tax, the external (i.e., income multiplier and non-market environmental) effects that the tourist development engenders do not affect the developer's pay-off. Thus, the tax constitutes an instrument that induces the internalization of these external effects in the developer's decision concerning the amount of land to develop.

Furthermore, we have noted that the local government can use taxation to appropriate some of the private profits. This guarantees the participation of the local population in the sharing of the tourist development's benefits and, hence, intragenerational equity. It has also been argued that tourism developments are unable to transfer an intact stock of natural resources to future generations. It follows that the analysis of intergenerational equity, and the related issues of conservation and efficiency, should be carried out by studying how the development tax presented above should be set depending on the environmental characteristics of the territory.

Results: The following results are derived assuming that both the developer and the government choose, respectively, the size of newly developed land and the land tax in each period so as to maximize the discounted flow of profits over an infinite time horizon. The optimal tax is such that the local government's inter-temporal pay-off E(t) is maximized. The technical analysis used to derive the solution to this maximization problem is beyond the scope of this article.

To analyze how the tax affects the equilibrium value of land use, it is customary to derive the socially optimal result and use it as a benchmark against which the model's results are compared. The best outcome, from a social viewpoint, is one in which both parties mutually agree on the size of the territory that is developed in every period. Such a decision entails that all types of benefits and costs identified above are taken into account. Hence, there is no need for the tax, as both parties understand the impact of development on the environment, to the extent that no development is carried out if the environmental costs are greater than the private and public benefits. If development is undertaken, then a lump-sum transfer from the developer to the local government is sufficient to obtain intragenerational equity.

We denote such a benchmark case as the "cooperative case", to emphasize the fact that the parties behave as a single entity: this implies that all the external effects associated with the development are internalized and properly accounted for in the decision regarding the project's size. In the remainder of the paper, the equilibrium level of land use in the perfectly cooperative scenario is denoted as B (t). Such a case is equivalent to the partnerships model advocated in Middleton (1998: 128-9), where a collaborative process is established between the private and the public institutions for dealing with tourism planning and management for a destination.

However, it is very unlikely that the developer and the government have perfectly aligned objectives. While the cooperative case can be used as a benchmark, in a more realistic case the government and the developer behave non-cooperatively as two distinct entities pursuing conflicting goals. Indeed, it is reasonable to expect that the developer wants to maximize the development's private benefits without considering the social costs that it entails, while the government may be particularly concerned with its social costs and the loss of environmental values.

From a strategic viewpoint, the government can exploit its 'first-mover advantage' by imposing a development tax, in order to induce the optimal level of land use which is equivalent to that in the cooperative case. Indeed, if the developer were left free to operate without any form of public intervention, the development size would exceed that in the cooperative case, as the environmental costs would not be taken into account. However, even in the non-cooperative scenario, obtaining.the socially optimal level of land use is possible when the government behaves like a Stackelberg leader.

Another advantage of the non-cooperative scenario is that it allows analyzing the effects that different weights used by the parties to discount future benefits and costs have on the resource use. Such weights are represented by the discount factors that capture the extent to which different individuals presently value a gain or a loss that will occur in the future. Those who prefer to make a lower gain today rather than a higher gain tomorrow have a greater discount factor. The length of the planning horizon over which investments are evaluated also influences the discount factor. Traditionally, private developers are more concerned about the short-term implications of their strategies, and therefore discount the future more heavily. When evaluating the impacts of human activity on the environment, governments are, at least in theory, more likely to consider the related long-term costs.

Hence, more concern by the government for the intergenerational effects of development is represented by a lower discount rate. The results from the theoretical model reported below are obtained assuming that the developer's discount rate, denoted by ñD, is greater than the government's rate, denoted by ñG. However, the results are reversed if the local government discounts the future more than the developer, a situation that is more likely to occur in a certain phase of the political cycle, namely before an election. Having defined the model's components, we now describe the qualitative features characterizing the model's solution.

First, a result common to the cooperative and the non-cooperative setting is that the largest portion of space is developed at the beginning of the development. The rationale behind such a choice is clear: it is optimal to build as much capacity as possible at the beginning of a project because an extra unit of capacity generates revenues forever. Thereby, the developer can more quickly recoup the large initial capital investment used to finance the high start-up costs associated with the development.

It would therefore seem that the two settings generate the same outcome with regard to the conservation issue. However, in the non-cooperative setting the two institutions usually value future benefits and costs differently. This has profound bearings on the development size in equilibrium. Indeed, as assumed before, if the private developer is fewer patients, then the model clearly shows that in the non-cooperative case less land will be used in total relative to the benchmark. The rationale of such a result is intuitive. A government that places a great weight on the environmental costs that future generations will incur, can set the development tax high enough to deter development beyond B^{nc}(t,ñD, ñG).

It can be shown that the rate of exploitation of the natural resource occurs at a slower pace in the non-cooperative case, that is, less land is used in every period. It follows that less environmental costs are also incurred. The results that in the non-cooperative case less land is used in total and that the development occurs at a slower pace, cast some doubts on the recommendation that the private and the public sector should seek more collaborative forms of organization of the tourism activity. While it can be argued that the same outcome could be achieved without the tax by having the government setting the limits of development, and the developer agreeing to comply with these limits, such a command-and-control arrangement presents, relative to the market instrument of taxation, at least two drawbacks.

First, it carries high bureaucratic costs for monitoring and enforcement. Second, and most importantly, it may be easier for the parties to renegotiate the terms of the initial agreement because of changes in socio-economic and/or political conditions, while changes in the tax legislation have to undergo a lengthy parliamentary scrutiny. We then conclude that a better outcome is obtained when the local government regulates the activity of the private developer by imposing a development tax, relative to a situation where a mutual agreement between the parties is created.

The model indicates how public policy adjusts according to the relative size of environmental costs and public benefits in the cost-benefit analysis. First of all, regardless of whether the environmental costs are greater than the benefits from development or not, it is always optimal for the local government to impose a positive tax on the use of the natural resource at the outset of planning. Obviously, the tax remains positive whenever the environmental costs are greater than the public benefits due to endogenous growth and income multiplier effects.

However, when the public benefits are larger than the environmental costs at any level of development, the optimal tax's time profile exhibits an interesting behaviour: at the outset of planning, the tax is positive but at some point in time it is turned into a subsidy, which corresponds to a negative tax. Traditional economic literature suggests the use of a subsidy to attract investments that determine beneficial effects for the host community (e.g., jobs creation, higher local firms' birth rate etc). An important difference in the present case is that it is optimal for the policymaker to introduce the subsidy only after an appropriate time period, and not at the outset. The rationale can be found in the ability of the tax to extract some of private benefits engendered by the development which otherwise would be totally appropriated by the firm.

Finally, the analysis implicitly allows geographic areas to be taxed differently depending on the sensitiveness of the natural environment. Low environmental costs are associated with non-sensitive areas. The government therefore initially imposes a low tax for development in such areas, which may then become a subsidy if public benefits are greater than environmental negative effects.

On the other hand, when concerns for the resilience of the natural environment exist, the tax is set at such a high level that no development is economically profitable for the developer. This is tantamount to one of the four sustainable tourism approaches proposed by Hunter, that of "Neotenous Tourism", which corresponds to a "very strong sustainability approach predicated upon the belief that there are circumstances in which tourism should be actively and continuously discouraged on ecological grounds".

Furthermore, Hunter (1997: 862) argues that "In some places, including national reserves of national or international importance, tourism growth should be sacrificed for the greater good". Such a recommendation is equivalent to the case of no development due to the high tax that arises as an equilibrium outcome in the model.

To summarize, the results from the economic model of taxation show that it is possible to pursue conservation objectives without hindering the implementation of viable economic projects that impact the environment. The results crucially hinge on the assumption that the government has a concern for conservation, which in practice is identified by the government's willingness to give proper weight to environmental damages that may occur in the distant future. As argued in the Introduction, such willingness can be expressed by the creation of a legislation that has constitutional value. The following case study illustrates the crucial role that regional planning legislation plays for the establishment of a government's stance towards conservation.

An Application: The Case of Costa Smeralda in Sardinia.

The previous analysis is based on the properties of a normative model that encompasses a set of economic issues. We now test its predictions by considering a case study involving a local government and a tourist developer. The evidence presented suggests that the recommendations derivable from the model's results provide a set of principles that local governments apply - or should begin to apply - in their evaluation of tourist projects.

In 1997 a multinational company, Ciga Immobiliare, prepared a development scheme for a part of Costa Smeralda on the Northeast coast of Sardinia in the Mediterranean Sea. The project was literally called Master Plan in the Sardinian and national press, and this is how it will be referred to in the remainder of this article. The following are taken from the executive summary released by the developer when the project was presented to the press. The entire project was to cover an area of 24 km^2, 85 per cent of which is located in the territory of the Arzachena municipality and the remainder 15 per cent in the Olbia municipality territory.

The total volume of the 11 hotels, 2,000 villas and 1,900 apartments included in the project was estimated to be 2,550,000 m^3 (14 per cent in hotels, 9 per cent in ancillary services and 77 per cent in residential dwellings). The planned capacity of hotels and residential dwellings was, respectively, 4,000 and 16,000 beds. The cost of the total investment was calculated to be US$1.45 billion and the related increase in local income to be $2.375 billion, with an investment multiplier of 1.72. Although the project was to cover a time span of 25 years, most construction would be completed within the first 5-10 years.

The yearly demand, measured in bednights, was evaluated at 504,000 units in hotels and 960,000 units in residential dwellings, the total being almost three times higher than the average of 560,000 units recorded during the 1990's in the already existing hotels owned by the developer in Costa Smeralda. The expenditure by tourists in hotel accommodation and dwellings was expected to total, respectively, $151 and $240 millions and generate an increase in local production of around $500 millions. Finally, the developer's study estimated the overall increment in employment in Sardinia to be 12,200 jobs: 4,800 new jobs in hotels and restaurants, 2,000 in trade and retailing, 4,200 in the services and 1,200 in manufacturing.

Given these figures, the project should certainly have appeared enticing to a local government operating in a region characterized by an extremely high unemployment rate and a much lower per capita income than the Italian average. How was it, then, that the parties did not find a satisfactory agreement and eventually the developer withdrew the project? An answer can be found by analyzing the political stance of the Sardinian government with respect to the magnitude of the social and environmental costs associated with the project.

The Sardinian government had made it clear that the "safeguard of the environmental quality is a factor for economic development". Moreover, as far as the Master Plan was concerned, the position of the Sardinian government was that "a better balance between the use of the territory, the socio-economic effects and the developer's profit has to be found". The Sardinian government seemed inclined to grant the building permission, subject to a few changes in the project, including:

1. A significant reduction in the number of residential dwellings, and possibly an increase in the number of hotels;
2. Priority to the building of hotels and tourism facilities; and
3. Respect for the norm that prohibits the construction of any building within 300 metres of the coastline.

Finally, the local government expressed concern about the number of "scattered dwellings" presumably villas - which "consume land and make access to the sea more difficult". The Sardinian government's preference for hotels, as expressed by requirement (b) and the request to increase the number of hotels can be found in the regional government's belief that hotels and related facilities would extend the tourist season well beyond the peak months of July and August. The Sardinian government's remark that villas and apartment use more land than hotels is consistent with the theoretical approach and indicate the government's awareness of the environmental costs associated with the development.

The first part of requirement (a) is directly linked to the theoretical analysis. The number of dwellings increased sharply thereby suggesting that intensive building activity took place during the decade in the municipalities of Olbia and Arzachena. A similar phenomenon occurred also in the remaining part of the North Sardinian Province, which includes many other seaside resorts. A first consideration is the obvious positive correlation between the change in the number of resident population and the increase in the number of occupied dwellings. However, more relevant to the present analysis is the drastic increase in the number of holiday dwellings, whose number more than doubled in Arzachena and almost doubled in Olbia.

Row (5) reports the ratio of holiday dwellings over occupied dwellings. It shows that, relative to the rest of the province, the two municipalities are characterized to a great extent by the so-called "second homes" phenomenon (i.e., holiday houses which are left unoccupied for most of the year). In terms of the theoretical analysis, the extensive use of land associated with this type of accommodation entails high environmental costs, deriving for example, from loss of flora and fauna, beach erosion, and degradation of water quality. Other environmental problems relate to the fact that second homes are used mainly during the period of peak demand. Moreover, self-catering accommodations, such as second homes, do not generate as high multiplier effects as hotels. The

Master Plan might have exacerbated the overcrowding and congestion.

Indeed, the dwelling density for the Master Plan –3900/24=162.5 dwellings per Km^2 (3900 is the sum of 2000 villas plus 1900 apartments, 24 Km^2 is the size of the territory) —is well above the averages of the territories concerned. This is indicative of how intensively some parts of the space would have been used by the developer. As many of the Master Plan's buildings would have occupied areas characterized by high environmental sensitivity, it can be inferred that the social costs deriving from the loss of the "hidden environmental values" would have been conspicuous.

The variables are the volumes built for residential and non-residential purposes, the number of new residential dwellings and the related number of rooms. Volumes are used in the following analysis for various reasons. First, in Italy planning regulations dictate the maximum allowable volume of a building erected in a territory of given size. Statistics are collected accordingly. Second, volume is a good indicator of building activity because territorial planning imposes restrictions on the total height of buildings. Therefore, volumes are highly correlated with the size of the territory occupied by buildings.

First, notice that the volume of residential buildings completed over the period in the two municipalities is less than the amount planned by the Master Plan's developer (row

The comparison and the size is made even more striking by the consideration that only 15 per cent of the project was planned in the Olbia municipality. This implies that 85 per cent of the residential volumes intended in the Master Plan (totaling 1668975 m^3) would have been built in the Arzachena's territory. This exceeds the total volumes built there for residential and non-residential purposes over the period 1982-1996.

Second, an inspection of rows (4) and (5) reveals that the number of residential dwellings and rooms intended in the

Master Plan is greater than the number of residential dwellings and rooms actually built in each single municipality over the period 1982-1996.

Hence, had the project been allowed to progress as originally planned, many future development options in the area would have been foreclosed, thereby engendering further social costs in territories where building activity for tourism has been particularly intensive over the last two decades.

The rationale for condition (c) (i.e., respect for the norm that prohibits construction with 300 meters of the coastline) lends support to the choice in the theoretical model of considering the local government as endowed with a first-mover advantage enabling them to pursue long-term conservationist policies.

By stating in the law that no building permit would be granted within 300 meters from the coastline, the Sardinian government had declared its commitment toward the safeguarding of the coastal environmental quality. The exception granted to the Master Plan's developer could easily have become the rule, and led to greater environmental costs from over-exploitation.

When it became clear that the project had to be changed substantially in its residential component and that condition (c) was not negotiable, the developer decided not to exercise the option to buy the territories from the current owner (the American multinational Starwood) and abandoned the project.

To summarize, the analysis of the case study highlighted the following points that are consistent with the theoretical predictions from the model discussed in the previous section. Firstly, the concern of a local government for the preservation of environmental quality may lead to no development. Secondly, the local government's behaviour emphasizes the importance of maintaining existing legislation aimed at conservation, thereby giving it the status of constitutional dictate. Finally, and more generally, the study also shows how the variables considered in the theoretical analysis are normally taken into account in the blueprint of any investment project in the tourism industry.

This study argues that a limitation of the strong sustainability approach is the lack of emphasis given to efficiency considerations. It suggests the application of the two-tier approach outlined in Page (1997) as a conceptual framework to tackle the issues of intergenerational equity and economic efficiency simultaneously. Such a two-tier method conceives the importance of the natural resource, the identification of the appropriate instruments and the legislative framework as crucial elements. To provide further support to Page's recommendations for the case of tourism, this study has presented a theoretical economic model of taxation and a case study involving a local government and a private developer.

When economic efficiency considerations are paramount, the theoretical model suggests the use of a land tax at the beginning of the development followed by the possible introduction of a subsidy at a later stage. The tax guarantees that local communities can extract some of the rents created by the development that otherwise would entirely accrue to the developer. At the other extreme, when the development endangers the existence of an essential resource or ecosystem, the theoretical model suggests the prevention of any form of development. In intermediate cases, the tax on land use combines efficiency and conservation goals, as the tax curtails, but does not prevent, the development. This situation is represented in the case study where emphasis is given to the crucial role of territorial planning legislation for the reduction of negative impacts of tourism development.

Indeed, in the two municipalities of Arzachena and Olbia the number of holiday homes has grown dramatically over the last two decades, thus suggesting the economic viability of such developments. At the same time, the norm prohibiting constructions within 300 meters of the coastline has prevented the irreversible damage that building on the coast entails, and has forced developers to locate their sites in less sensitive areas. The fact that the Sardinian government chose not to create a precedent by allowing special treatment for the Master Plan's developer, suggests that the norm regulates issues that deserve to be treated within a constitutional framework, in line with Page's recommendations. Unfortunately, the norm above does not have a legal constitutional status, and could therefore be changed using the process applicable to any ordinary law. This is indeed the intention of the new Sardinian government elected in the year 2000, that is, to modify legislation on territorial planning to accommodate the possibility of buildings near the coastline.

Both the model of taxation and the Sardinian case study provide support for the argument in Middleton (1998) that governments do not need to introduce new policy instruments but rather, they should gear the existing ones towards the achievement of sustainable objectives. Thus territorial planning, building regulation, provision of.infrastructure, fiscal incentives and disincentives, ecological labeling assessment and management of carrying capacity (Collins, 1999), information and education of tourists (Filho, 1996) can all be used effectively and play a central role in a public strategy for sustainable tourism.

However, the view advocated by Middleton (1998) that the public and the private sector should seek more integrated forms of organization in the management of tourism does not necessarily follow. The theoretical analysis of taxation clearly indicates that the best outcome, both in terms of conservation and overall efficiency, is obtained when the public sector takes advantage of its ability to set the rules of the game.

The "Master Plan" example shows that negotiations with the private sector may turn out to be unbeneficial in the long run, especially if the private developer requests special exemptions from the existing legislation, which is aimed at limiting the environmental impact of development. Whenever the government and the private developer have conflicting views regarding the development of an environmentally sensitive area, the analysis of the theoretical model, and the support it has received from the case study, suggest that the government should exploit its first-mover advantage, which is incompatible with Middleton's bargaining approach. As a corollary to the analysis, we may conclude that private-public partnership may be Favoured whenever intergenerational equity issues are not a crucial concern.

CITIES AND TOURISM

Cities to Absorb Growth in World Tourism

International tourist arrivals in 1995 were 563 million and are expected to reach 1.6 billion by the year 2020. These forecasts use a conservative growth rate of 4.3 per cent and 6.7 per cent respectively; less than the current growth rate. They do not include any domestic tourism which can readily be anticipated to equal the international. It is obvious that most of this increase will have to be absorbed by cities.

– World Tourism Organisation

The most recent trends and forecasting studies by the World Tourism Organisation indicate that cities will continue to be in high demand by tourists of all sorts, and the problems associated with the handling of these tourists will have to be more systematically tackled by all parties concerned.

Cities face, therefore, a double challenge. Firstly, they have to be able to respond to the expectations and needs of the growing numbers of tourists who are attracted to their rich and varied array of cultural, business, entertainment, shopping, sports and other attractions; furthermore, they need to continuously renovate and improve such facilities in order to maintain their share in the competitive tourism market and the benefits resulting from it. Secondly, cities have to ensure that tourism is developed and managed in such a way that it benefits the resident population, does not contribute to the deterioration of the urban environment but rather to its enhancement, and does not become a financial burden to the local authority.

Some of the key stakeholders in urban tourism include:

Private Sector i.e. airlines, hotel chain operators and owners, tour operators, credit card companies, tourist attraction operators (theme parks, events etc.), real estate agencies;

- Public Sector i.e. city managers (from the historic city to the seaside resort), transportation planners, bus and train operators, information departments, economic development agencies, national parks, national tourist organisations;
- Touristic Institutions i.e. museums, art galleries, historic facilities (e.g. the national trust) and educational organisations.

There are three key dimensions of tourism in cities and urban areas:

- *Products* - The anticipated changes necessary from tourist attraction providers; theme parks, operators of events (sports, shows, fairs), museums and hotels. What are their plans, how do they respond to the anticipated growth?
- *Information* - How does a city make itself more tourist friendly? What are the information systems available to tourists? How do tour operators deal with this growing demand? How to accumulate information on customer preferences and requirement, seasonal changes, age groups etc.? How to develop enduring attractions which will provide sustainable development? What information does the city provide in order to attract tourist attraction providers?
- *Impacts* - Economic and development opportunities as well as the impact of tourism growth on sustainable development, transportation, cultural and environmental, social and economic aspects.

Chapter 6

Eco-tourism and the Tourism Industry

Fundamentally, eco-tourism means making as little environmental impact as possible and helping to sustain the indigenous populace, thereby encouraging the preservation of wildlife and habitats when visiting a place. This is responsible form of tourism and tourism development, which encourages going back to natural products in every aspect of life. It is also the key to sustainable ecological development.

The International Eco-tourism Society defines eco-tourism as "responsible travel to natural areas that conserves the environment and improves the well-being of local people." This means that those who implement and participate in Eco-tourism activities should follow the following principles:

1. Minimize impact,
2. Build environmental and cultural awareness and respect,
3. Provide positive experiences for both visitors and hosts,
4. Provide direct financial benefits for conservation,
5. Provide financial benefits and empowerment for local people,
6. Raise sensitivity to host countries' political, environmental, and social climate,

7. Support international human rights and labour agreements.

Aware of the Environment - Today the "Green Laws" of conservation are making people aware of how man and the environment can live symbiotically for more time to come and eco-tourism is the only way to maximize the economic, environmental and social benefits of tourism. Everyone is a stakeholder in the process and we clearly need to avoid our past shortcomings and negative impact that they have had.

Of all the participants in the Eco-tourism activity, the tourism industry is perhaps the most important and the least appreciated by conservationists. Many conservationists dislike having to deal with the corporate, profit- motivated entrepreneurs that they characterize as comprising the tourism industry. Nevertheless, these entrepreneurs are essential to achieving conservation goals via Eco-tourism. They can, and indeed some of them must, become allies and partners with NGOs, protected area managers and communities if Eco-tourism is to become more than an abstract concept. Increasingly, the tourism industry becomes the most powerful advocate for supporting protected areas, and this dynamic should be encouraged by establishing adequate mechanisms for communication and collaboration between protected area managers and tour operators.

The mechanics of international and even national, level tourism require that a complex set of arrangements (transportation, lodging, guides, etc.) exists to facilitate the movement of tourists from their home to the tourism destination. Each arrangement necessitates a specific set of activities and corresponding set of employees, infrastructure and costs. Few tour operators specialize in Eco-tourism. There are, however, many adventure and nature tour operators, most of whom do not fully comply with Eco-tourism standards. Conventional tourism practices still predominate in the tourism industry, just as conventional practices still dominate in every other aspect of our lives, in spite of initiatives for them to become more sustainable. Nevertheless, the tourism industry is "greening" at an ever-accelerating pace as tourists demand more environmentally-sound services. For example, many hotels now recycle cans and bottles and encourage guests to reuse towels in order to save on water use.

The number of Eco-tourism businesses is also growing as new companies are established. Many of these have developed from the outset with an understanding of and commitment to the principles of sustainability, whereas many of the older, more established nature tourism companies have been slow to integrate all the principles of Eco-tourism into their activities.

1. Conservation NGOs working in partnership with private tour operators are ideally placed to provide the Ecotourist technical guidelines which upgrade a nature tourism operation into an Eco-tourism operation. They will be located in the eco travellers country of origin. They produce brochures annually with a series of fixed departures for each tour Programmes, and they often have a loyal clientele who return to purchase trips on a regular basis. They will put together a complete package for the tourist including air tickets, and may provide a tour leader to accompany their client groups but will typically contract with an inbound operator to provide services in the destination country.
2. *The Inbound Operator* – Located in the destination country, they provide complete packages of services from arrival in the country to departure. They may have their own facilities (vehicles, lodges) or they may subcontract others in the cities and regions the tourists will visit. Outbound operators contract with them to provide all "on-the-ground" services. With the advent of the internet, they are increasingly competing directly with the outbound operators for clients.
3. *Local Service Providers* – outside the big cities, near the natural attractions; these may be local lodge and

hotel owners, local transport providers, community-based Eco-tourism enterprises and local guides. These are where local communities typically join the tourism chain.

Implementing Eco-tourism can be a very challenging and costly venture. If the tourism industry is part of this process from the beginning, costs can be greatly reduced and success made more likely. Including the experience of a private tour operator in the Eco-tourism planning and design process would be invaluable and could not be duplicated by conservation NGO. Essential inputs by various segments of the tourism industry could include:

1. Providing information about the potential market for Eco-tourism activities.
2. Providing advice concerning visitor preferences in terms of attractions, accommodations, food and transportation services.
3. Marketing an Eco-tourism activity or Programmes.
4. Providing one or more of the services needed to facilitate visitor access to and appreciation of the Eco-tourism site.
5. Providing training of local guides and entrepreneurs.
6. Investing in an Eco-tourism operation. The investment will likely be contingent upon an expectation of a certain level of financial return.
7. Operating an Eco-tourism operation. Within a protected area situation, these operators would be considered concessionaires. As such, they would be subject to strict guidelines covering everything from the energy sources used to operators who identified this as one of their primary destinations to the utilization of local supplies and labour. They would also be required to pay a concession fee to the protected area administration.

Eco-tourism is more than a catch phrase for nature loving travel and recreation. Eco-tourism is consecrated for preserving and sustaining the diversity of the world's natural and cultural environments. It accommodates and entertains visitors in a way that is minimally intrusive or destructive to the environment and sustains and supports the native cultures in the locations it is operating in. Responsibility of both travellers and service providers is the genuine meaning for eco-tourism. Eco-tourism also endeavours to encourage and support the diversity of local economies for which the tourism-related income is important. With support from tourists, local services and producers can compete with larger, foreign companies and local families can support themselves. Besides all these, the revenue produced from tourism helps and encourages governments to fund conservation projects and training Programmes.

Saving the environment around you and preserving the natural luxuries and forest life, that's what eco-tourism is all about. Whether it's about a nature camp or organizing trekking trips towards the unspoilt and inaccessible regions, one should always keep in mind not to create any mishap or disturbance in the life cycle of nature. Eco-tourism focuses on local cultures, wilderness adventures, volunteering, personal growth and learning new ways to live on our vulnerable planet. It is typically defined as travel to destinations where the flora, fauna, and cultural heritage are the primary attractions. Responsible Eco-tourism includes Programmes that minimize the adverse effects of traditional tourism on the natural environment, and enhance the cultural integrity of local people. Therefore, in addition to evaluating environmental and cultural factors, initiatives by hospitality providers to promote recycling, energy efficiency, water reuse, and the creation of economic opportunities for local communities are an integral part of Eco-tourism.

Historical, biological and cultural conservation, preservation, sustainable development etc. are some of the fields closely related to Eco-Tourism. Many professionals have been involved in formulating and developing eco-tourism policies. They come from the fields of Geographic Information Systems, Wildlife Management, Wildlife Photography, Marine Biology and Oceanography, National and State Park Management, Environmental Sciences, Women in Development, Historians and Archaeologists, etc.

In India too the movement is gathering momentum with more and more travel and travel related organisation's are addressing the needs of the eco-tourists and promoting eco-tourism in the country. Some basic do's and don'ts of eco-tourism are listed below:

Do's

1. Carry back all non-degradable litter such as empty bottles, tins, plastic bags etc. These must not litter the environment or be buried. They must be disposed in municipal dustbins only.
2. Observe the sanctity of holy sites, temples and local cultures.
3. Cut noise pollution. Do not blare aloud radios, tape recorders or other electronic entertainment equipment in nature resorts, sanctuaries and wildlife parks.
4. In case temporary toilets are set-up near campsites, after defecation, cover with mud or sand. Make sure that the spot is at least 30 meters away from the water source.
5. Respect people's privacy while taking photographs. Ask for prior permission before taking a photograph.

Don'ts

1. Do not take away flora and fauna in the forms of cuttings, seeds or roots. It is illegal, especially in the Himalayas. The environment is really delicate in this region and the bio-diversity of the region has to be protected at all costs.

2. Do not use pollutants such as detergent, in streams or springs while washing and bathing.
3. Do not use wood as fuel to cook food at the campsite.
4. Do not leave cigarettes butts or make open fires in the forests.
5. Do not consume aerated drinks, alcohol, drugs or any other intoxicant and throw bottles in the wild.
6. Do not tempt the locals, especially children by offering them foodstuff or sweets. Respect local traditions.
7. Polythene and plastics are non biodegradable and unhealthy for the environment and must not be used and littered. As a traveller, you will have an impact on the environment and culture of the place you are visiting. Here are some rules of thumb to make this impact positive.

Golden Rules For Travel

1. Learn about your destination before you get there. Read guidebooks, travel rticles, istories, and/or novels by local authors and pay particular attention to customs such as greetings, appropriate dress, eating behaviours, etc. Being sensitive to these customs will increase local acceptance of you as a tourist and enrich your trip.
2. Follow established guidelines. Ask your eco-tour operator, guide and/or the local authorities what their guidelines are for limiting tourism's impact on the environment and local culture. Staying on trails, packing up your trash, and remaining set distances away from wildlife are a few ways to minimize your impact in sensitive areas.
3. Seek out and support locally owned businesses. Support local businesses during your eco-travels to ensure maximum community and conservation

benefit from your spending. Eco-Tourism in India is still at a very nascent stage, but there are for sure conscious efforts to save the fragile Himalayan Eco System and culture and heritage of the indigenous people, which is probably the largest concentration in the world.

ECO-TOURISM IN INDIA

Kerala Eco-Tourism

The naturally beautiful and exquisite Kerala landscape is one of the greenest destinations in India and is the perfect place to go on eco-tourism vacations. The clean and tranquil Kerala backwaters, the soothing velvety Kerala hills and a riotous explosion of greens in the intoxicating Kerala wilds offers countless opportunities for eco-tourism and nature vacations. The entire Kerala landscape is generously covered with coconut palms, pineapple groves, banana trees, Pandanus plants, thick leafy plants, dense forests and neatly clipped tea bushes. Acres of submerged paddy fields located in perfect harmony with the winding Kerala backwaters and the gentle rolling Kerala hills are heavenly paradisiacal eco-tourism vacation destinations.

Regale the verdant Kerala beauty on your eco-tourism vacations to Kerala, South India with Kerala India Vacations. Visit the fascinating Kerala wildlife destinations and spot rare wild animals lazing in their natural habitat and enjoy the magic of nature. Eco-tourism in Kerala, South India is a fast developing sector and the state government is making extra efforts to promote eco-tourism. Among the manifold advantages of promoting eco-tourism in Kerala, South India one very important aspect is revenue generation and environment conservation at the same time. The concept of eco-tourism basically means that you get to visit the exotic nature rich tour destinations but at the same time you must take care not to soil the beauty of the region by not using polythene bags and other materials or things such as tin cans, wrappers etc that adversely affect the environment.

Kerala India Vacations guides you through the lush green paths within acres of rubber plantations so that you can experience first hand the incomparable natural beauty of green Kerala, South India on your eco-tourism vacations. Kerala, South India happens to be one of the leading producers of rubber in India though rubber is not a native Indian plant and was introduced by the Dutch colonialists, in fact Kerala accounts for 92 per cent of the rubber produced in India. Stay at a luxury resort or a farmhouse near a Kerala rubber plantation and enjoy the warm hospitality of the Kerala rubber plantations during your eco-tourism vacations to Kerala, South India and be fascinated by the rural Kerala lifestyle while you observe busy twittering birds, brightly coloured butterflies and squirrels scurrying here and there. Admire the thick shapely leaves on straight trunks that glisten in the bright sun.

Botanically known as Havea brasiliensis, a single rubber plant takes about 7 years to mature and can be harvested for latex (processed for natural rubber) for almost 20 years. The local rubber tappers who stay close to these lush rubber plantations harvest latex from these trees. Pineapple is planted as an intercrop in most of the Kerala rubber plantations so you get to taste the juicy Mauritius pineapple variety while on your eco-tourism vacations to the scenic Kerala rubber plantations. Kottayam in Kerala, South India is an important Centre of commercial rubber plantations set on the picturesque banks of the serene palm fringed Kerala backwaters. Extensive rubber plantations cover the hillocks wrapped by silver ribbons of the fascinating Kerala backwaters, not a sight you would like to miss while on your eco-tourism tours to Kerala, South India.

Acres of tea plantations interspersed with shade fruit trees wrap the gentle Kerala hill slopes in a warm embrace and create soothing and striking vistas for you to visit on your Kerala eco-tourism vacations. Rows of neatly clipped tea bushes carpet the Kerala hills on the Western Ghats in Kerala, south India and offer you ample opportunity to gaze at the naturally enthralling Kerala beauty at its beatific best while on your Kerala India eco-tourism vacations.

The Britishers introduced the tradition of tea plantations in India. Tea bushes have the potential to grow to tree heights though they are kept neatly trimmed to waist height to make it feasible for the plantation workers to pluck tealeaves without much difficulty. Gaze at the lovely Kerala tea plantations while on your eco-tourism vacations and mark the fact that each tea bush is planted at a distance of 1 to 1.5 meter from each other along the contours of the landscape. Stay at the resorts and clean home-like accommodations on the Kerala tea plantations and spend your eco-tourism vacations in Kerala, South India in the midst of pure undulating greens. Watch the plantation workers plucking tealeaves and filling the baskets slung on their backs while you enjoy nature treks.

Usually it's the women who are employed for plucking tealeaves on these tea plantations in Kerala, South India. These women work in unison and sing peppy songs while plucking tealeaves and move along the rows of tea bushes in perfect rhythm. Kerala, South India has some of the highest tea estates located in India. Munnar is one of the most popular Kerala hill stations, which is known for its sweeping tea plantations. Some of the popular tea plantations in Kerala, South India are located at Peerumadu that is situated at a height of 914-meters above the sea level, Anayirankal that has acres of tea plantations located in the midst of dense evergreen forests and a few other Kerala hill stations that are definitely worth visiting on your Kerala eco-tourism tours to Kerala, South India.

Wander at leisure on the aromatic Kerala spice plantations during your Kerala India eco-tourism Vacations. Stay at the spice plantation farmhouses with the plantation owners and experience the magical charm of staying in the midst of luxuriant plantations laden heavily with a combination of scents of the various spices that are grown on these extensive plantations. Though you can visit spice plantations almost all over beautiful Kerala, Periyar is one of the most popular spice districts in Kerala, South India. This absolutely beautiful hill district is covered with a variety of spice plantations that lie close to the famous Periyar wildlife sanctuary.

Shop for rare spices at the local Kerala spice markets and inhale the intoxicating aroma of cinnamon, cardamom, pepper, ginger, turmeric, curry leaves and other spices. Besides the cultivation of these traditional Kerala spices the Kerala plantation owners have also taken to growing spices such as rosemary, oregano, mint, vanilla, bay leaves, basil, thyme and others. Discover the secret of the mouthwatering Kerala cuisine as you visit the acres of Kerala spice plantations on your eco-tourism vacations with Kerala India Vacations. Spices are basically fragrant substances of vegetable origin with distinct flavors used in selective combinations to give a special flavor to the exotic Indian cuisine.

Enjoy bird watching tours and nature treks to the lovely Kerala spice plantations with Kerala India Vacations and experience the Kerala natural beauty at its aromatic best. Watch the locals work on the extensive spice plantations and observe closely the way of life in these Kerala spice plantations and enjoy your eco-tourism vacations thoroughly.

Orissa Eco-tourism

Organized by Tourism of Orissa offers you the best seats in the house to attend what is essentially a spectacular show of competing colours, cacophony of voices, a jumble of animal instincts and raw emotions. No, we aren't talking about a Broadway show or a Hollywood musical production. Eco-tourism in Orissa is what concerns us at Tourism of Orissa. With Eco-tourism in Orissa tour package, offered by Tourism of Orissa, you get to see all the shades of the diverse ecological system that reside within the state of Orissa. Eco-tourism in Orissa may revolve around water bodies or beaches or national parks and wildlife sanctuaries alone or, it can be a combination of all these features that make Orissa such as enticing choice as a destination for eco travel and tours.

While hot springs (Atri and Tarabalo), lakes (Chilika), waterfalls (Badaghagra, Khandadhar) and reservoirs (Hirakud,

Indravati) in Orissa have tourists lining up, the beaches of Orissa (Puri, Chandrabhaga, Gopalpur, Chandipur) have dazzled international and national tourist for centuries with their pristine beauty and positive vibes. Orissa's varying topography - from the wooded Eastern Ghats to the fertile river basin - has proven ideal for evolution of compact and unique ecosystems. Thereby creating such treasure troves of flora and fauna that even seem inviting to many migratory species of birds and reptiles.

Bhitar Kanika National Park is famous for its second largest mangrove ecosystem. The bird sanctuary in Chilika (Asia's biggest brackish water lake) and the tiger reserve and waterfalls in Simlipal National Park are integral part of any eco tours in Orissa, arranged by Tourism of Orissa. The Gharial Sanctuary at Tikarpada and the Olive Ridley Sea Turtles in Gahirmatha turtle sanctuary also feature on the list of avid nature watchers. The city wildlife sanctuaries of Chandaka and Nandan Kanan are a must visit for the lessons they teach is conservation and revitalization of species from the brink of extinction. Since Orissa is so rich in culture - history, traditions and people, Tourism of Orissa can even have your eco tour clubbed with other tours in Orissa so that you get the best of al te worlds at a single destination called Orissa.

Eco-tourism in Chhattisgarh

Chhattisgarh, the 26th state of the Indian Union, is located in the central part of India. The newly formed Indian state of Chhattisgarh is famous for its enchantingly beautiful natural landscapes, rich cultural heritage and unique tribal populations. With over 44 per cent of its total area under forests, Chhattisgarh is also amongst the greenest states of India. The Chhattisgarh region is known as a great repository of biological diversity. The unique combination of rich cultural heritage and biological diversity makes Chhattisgarh an ideal eco-tourism destination with immense potentials for the growth eco-tourism the region. The Indian Govt. is actively collaborating with the local officials of the state to realize the full potential of Eco-tourism growth of the region in order to make Chhattisgarh as one of the most important eco-tourism destinations in India.

Chhattisgarh is one of the greenest states of India with over 44 per cent of its total area under lush forests. The forests of Chhattisgarh are not only known for their diverse flora and fauna but also contain about 88 species of medicinal plants. In addition, Chhattisgarh has also formulated several ecological plans and working in the direction to become the country's first bio-fuel self-reliant state by 2015. And to achieve this goal the green state has devised a plan to plant over 100 million saplings of Jatropa Carcus. Chhattisgarh is also unique in its wildlife population and has 3 National Parks and 11 Wildlife Sanctuaries, housing some of the rare wildlife and bird species. With so much of variety for Eco-tourism, Chhattisgarh promises to be an ideal holiday destination for nature lovers, wildlife enthusiasts and also for those who want to discover the unique tribal life of the region.

Chhattisgarh has identified some regions with a very high potentiality for eco-tourism. The green state has launched an eco-tourism project covering three potential tourist tracks - Raipur-Turtiria-Sirpur, Bilaspur-Achanakmar and Jagdalpur-Kanger Valley National Park. In addition, a number of herbal gardens and natural health resorts have been created with increased local participation. The use of ethno-medicine, which has been practiced by aboriginal tribes since centuries, predating even Ayurveda, is also being promoted in Chhattisgarh. The major eco-tourism attractions, which are getting prime attention in Chhattisgarh, include the protection and development of the wildlife areas, camping grounds and trekking facilities. With so many initiatives, Chhattisgarh is destined to become the most Favourite eco-tourism destination in India and few among best in the world.

Rajasthan Eco-tourism

The Cultures of the Rajasthan Desert are some of the most well preserved in India. We, at Marwar Eco-Cultural Tours and Travels, are passionate about this land, its cultures and its people and we want to share this passion with you. The Desert and its people will captivate you.

Because we are able to provide you with in-depth cultural information that you would not receive on other Tours. If you have an adventurous spirit or a cultural thirst to quench, we have a Tour that should surpass all of your expectations. We also offer opportunities to get involved with the people and assist in ongoing, non-profit projects. As an NGO, we have assistance projects in most villages we will visit. All of our guides are from Rajasthan, and most are village natives or indigenous people.

They have a great knowledge of local and regional history and are great storytellers. They will keep your attention for hours next to a fire, counting tales of kings and warlords; castles, forts and Havelis (mansions); rituals and traditions. You will see the camel herds, observe villagers' craftsmanship, and gain insight into indigenous nomadic lifestyles. We will show you the best of Rajasthan, and we are very flexible and can modify our tours according to the group's needs. You can also design your own tour. You dream it up; we'll do the rest. We will organize the tour and guide you according to your wishes. Among other things, we can arrange a visit to a marriage ceremony, a farming or agricultural tour, Handicraft and Jewelry making, a stay in an Ayurvedic (traditional Indian Medicine) clinic, and more.

Madhya Pradesh Eco-tourism

Eco-tourism signifies to save the environment around us and preserving the natural luxuries and forest life. Whether it's about a nature camp or organizing trekking trips towards the unspoilt and inaccessible regions, one should always keep in mind not to create any mishap or disturbance in the life cycle of nature. A destination enveloped in magic, Madhya Pradesh is one of the most popular tourist destination in India. It's many tourist destinations are, by far, some of the most magical locales in the world.

With the highest mountains, beautiful wildlife, a cosmopolitan heritage from different civilizations, it is so rightly called tourist paradise. It has lot to offer from breathtaking natural vistas, amazing architecture, rich culture, and a warm hearted society of people living in virtual harmony.

Himachal Pradesh Eco-tourism

The majestic coniferous trees from an enchanting backdrop to the mountains with broad-leafed species like the Oaks, Maples, Birdcherry, Hazelnut, Walnut, Horsechestnut and Rhododendrons adding grandeur to the landscape. Whereas the ivies clinging to the trunks of stately Cedars appear to veil secrets of Nature, the vines flowing from atop the trees seem to invite the visitors with open arms. The violas popping up from under the forest floor and the riot of colours provided by the anemones, primulas, buttercups and many other herbs in the alpine meadows lay a colourful feast before eyes of the beholder.

Besides plants. the State also provides a very congenial habitat to a wide variety of Himalayan fauna. The Himalyan Tahar and the Ibex can be spotted as silhouettes on the high ridges in the trans-Himalayas. The Brown Bear and Musk Deer roam happily in the temperate forests, in the company of colourful pheasants including the Monal, the Western Hornes Tragopan, the Koklas and the Kalij. The lucky ones can even be traeted to rare sight of critically endangered species like the Snow Leopard and Snow Cock.

Also known as the 'Abode of Gods', the State conjures up visions of ancient temples, with exquisitely carved wooden panels, occupying almost every hilltop and the festivities associated with these religious places. Even a casual glimpse at the traditionally attired local deities being carried in meticulously decorated palanquins, devotees dancing to the rhythmic play of traditional drums and clarions, leaves a lasting imptint on one's mind.

This natural and cultural richness of the State coupled with its simple peace loving people and traditional hospitality makes the State a most favoured tourist destination. Anybody with a zest for life, a spirit of adventure and a love for nature will find all that his heart desires amongest the pristine environs of Himachal Pradesh.

Uttaranchal Eco-tourism

Uttaranchal blessed with magnificent glaciers, majestic snow-clad mountains, gigantic and ecstatic peaks, valley of flowers, skiing slopes and dense forests, this Abode of Gods includes many shrines and places of pilgrimage. Char-dhams, the four most sacred and revered Hindu temples: Badrinath, Kedarnath, Gangotri and Yamunotri are nestled in the Mighty Mountains. A picturesque state, with a breathtaking panoramic view of Himalayas, Uttaranchal promises its tourists a visit full of fun and unforgettable moments.

Uttaranchal blessed with magnificent glaciers, majestic snow-clad mountains, gigantic and ecstatic peaks, valley of flowers, skiing slopes and dense forests, this Abode of Gods includes many shrines and places of pilgrimage.

India's first National Park is cradled in the foothills of the Himalayas and spreads over an area of 520 sq. kms., along the bankds of the Ramganga river. The dense Sal forests of the Himalayan foothils and the tall grassy neadows make it one of the richest areas of northern India for the habitation of the big mammals.

ECOSYSTEM IN INDIA

The Himalayan region is a particularly fragile ecosystem. The interconnections between the different types of vegetation, between plant life and the soil, between the soil, vegetation and water are so close and so precariously balanced that the slightest change in one plunges the entire system into jeopardy. Ecosystems on seismic belts, for example, are literally 'at the mercy of the land'. Nature plays havoc in other ways too: the monsoon pattern often spells drought in the dry season, and terrible floods during rainfall.

Deforestation

Growing Population

Way back in 326 B.C., when Alexander the Great came to India, his advance was checked by almost impenetrable forests along the Indus. By the time Emperor Ashoka ascended the throne, stretches of forests had already been cleared to make roads. Ashoka realised the importance of conserving forests, and even appointed an officer for the purpose.

Sher Shah Suri was also farsighted, and planted trees all along the route from Delhi to his capital Patna. However, the Mughals' interest in forests was sadly limited to a rather hedonistic passion for big game. Under the British rule, deforestation became rampant in order to procure timber to build furniture, railway sleepers and ships for the British navy. However, the British soon realised that forests had to be spared the ordeal. After Independence, forests were cleared whenever wood was needed either for timber or agriculture, or for setting up townships. Forests were razed to the ground mindlessly till the eastern hill people decided to say a collective 'Stop'.

Forest Distructions Through Fire

Forest fires have largely contributed to deforestation. Forests in India are very susceptible to fires, especially in summer. All it takes is one little spark and a forest fire could reduce considerable green stretches to ashes in a matter of a few hours. Earlier the Bishnois of Jodhpur (Rajasthan) even laid down their lives to save trees. The Bishnois are a religious community, famous for their loyalty towards animals and trees. In fact, they are known to worship the blackbuck as a sacred animal. Various measures are being taken to curb the felling of trees. Clearing forests is now an offence under Indian law, unless approved by the concerned authorities. However, deforestation has acquired alarming proportions in India. The country's total forest cover today has fallen to a little more than approximately 10 per cent –a dismal situation for a country with a population of over a billion.

Land Degradation

Every year, valuable topsoil is swept away by floods in the rainy season. and deforestation contributes to the problem of soil erosion. Man may well have compounded the problem.

Chemical Farming

To sustain the country's enormous population, intensive chemical farming was introduced in the 1960s, ushering in the 'Green Revolution'. Chemical fertilisers and high yield grains were used on an unprecedented scale. Although production tripled, the quality of the land took a battering. Chemicals and toxic substances too have taken their own toll on the land. Desertification (cultivable land turning barren) is a serious problem in some parts of the country, especially in Rajasthan.

Water Conditions

Despite high rainfall, water levels have dropped alarmingly in many places in the country. Obviously this is due to the demands of a burgeoning population. In any case, the monsoon cannot always be relied upon; it is not uncommon for a region like Rajasthan to be stricken by drought once every two to three years. While hydroelectric projects are a partial solution to the problem, their overall 'efficiency' is not beyond interrogation.

The Narmada Valley Project - a vast project of several dams aimed at providing water and power for Gujarat, Rajasthan, Madhya Pradesh and Maharashtra - when completed, is projected to submerge an estimated 350,000 hectares of forest and 200,000 hectares of cultivated fields, and displace nearly 400,000 people. Spearheaded by the environmentalist Baba Amte, Medha Patkar, and more recently Arundhati Roy, a vigorous campaign is in progress against the building of the dams. Another controversial project is the Tehri Dam in Uttar Pradesh. Besides the displacement and loss it is projected to cause, another dread is that the dam may burst as it is being constructed on an earthquake-prone zone. The distinguished man in white, Sunderlal Bahuguna has once again spared no effort at raising public consciousness about the issue at hand.

Pollution

Despite having some of the strictest laws in the world against pollution, India is one of the most environmentally polluted countries in the world. Air pollution is so grave in cities like Delhi, Calcutta, Kanpur and some others, that simply breathing the air is equivalent to smoking 10-20 cigarettes a day! Recently, Delhi acquired the dubious distinction of being one of the five most polluted cities in the world. The rivers in the country have not been spared either.

Industrial waste and a combination of other factors have contributed to the plight of these 'dying' rivers. In some places, safe drinking water, is a rare commodity. Lakes and river habitats too have been polluted. The Yamuna Action Plan was a project undertaken at a tentative cost of Rs 20,000 crore to cleanse the river of pollutants. A similar project was undertaken for the mighty Ganga River.

Conservation

Ancient texts including the epics, the Buddhist Jatakas, the Panchatantra or the more recent Jain scriptures, all preach non-violence towards even the lowest forms of animal and plant life, a philosophy that the Indian Maharajas and their British guests chose to overlooked for a while. The Indian Government has an uphill task to perform. It has been able to protect only about 4 per cent of the total forest cover in the form of National Parks and similar reserves. Underhand activities like poaching are not entirely unheard of even in these restricted areas. Currently there are about 80 National Parks and 441 sanctuaries in the country. Massive tree plantation Programmes are also being undertaken. The Vana Mahotsava, first started in 1950, is an annual tree-planting festival celebrated across the nation.

Individual Efforts

Vishweshwar Dutt Saklani of Garhwal, in Uttar Pradesh, is a small time farmer who started planting trees to seek solace after the death of his brother (who had initiated the practice) in 1948. In the last 50 years, Vishweshwar has overlaid 100 hectares of land with oak, cedar, walnut and rhododendron. People were dismissive of him until they saw the sea change that his work had brought about in the village. Denuded hills became green, land became more fertile and dry streambeds filled up. Fodder and fuel were in plenty and everyone was happy.Vishweshwar received the Indira Priyadarshini Vrikshamitra Award in 1986. Bikkalu Chikkaiah and Thimmakka were a childless couple who worked in a quarry close to Bangalore. They decided to raise banyan trees in lieu of the children they were unable to have. So they chose a barren piece of land en route to their quarry.

The couple planted saplings and put protective barriers around them. In the evenings, they lugged water from a well a kilometre away. 40 years later, 284 banyan trees provided shade to a 3km stretch. Thimmakka received the National Citizen's Award in 1996. Abdul Karim of Kasargod, Kerala too did something similar. He turned a dry piece of land into a veritable forest after 19 years of hard labour. His deciduous trees brought water back into the soil. Karim went a step ahead and got some animals in this forest, to successfully replicate a healthy ecosystem.

ECO-TOURISM POLICY

The Draft Tourism Policy 1997 states that "in the context of economic liberalisation and globalisation being pursued by the country, the development policies of no sector can remain static. "The policy further states that" the emergence of tourism as an important instrument for sustainable human development including poverty alleviation, employment generation, environmental regeneration and advancement of women and other disadvantaged groups in the country" requires support to realise these goals.

India's tourism resources have always been considered immense, in a tourism audit. The geographical features are diverse, colourful and varied. The coastline offers opportunities for developing the best beaches in the world. There are a wealth of eco-systems including bio-sphere reserves, mangroves, coral reefs, deserts, mountains and forests as well as an equally wide range of flora and fauna.

The Policy further states that "international tourists visiting interiors of the country for reasons of purity of the environment and nature contributes to the development of these areas particularly backward regions". Thus Tourism "should also become a reason for better preservation and protection of our natural resources, environment and ecology".

The policy recognises that sustained growth of tourism can give rise to conflicts. To ensure that the growth of tourism takes place along desired lines, certain guidelines have been framed:

1. To remove the constraint of the information gap.
2. To create a tourist product that is desirable and supported by an integrated infrastructure.
3. To involve all agencies, public, private and government, in tourism development.
4. To create synergy between departments and agencies that have to deliver the composite tourist product.
5. To use both the circuit and scheme approach so that peoples participation through panchayats, local bodies, NGO's, and youth organisations will create a greater awareness of tourism. The Central Government can thus concentrate on larger investment oriented projects.
6. To create direct access for destinations off the beaten track.
7. To diversify the product with new options like beach tourism, forests, wild life, landscapes and adventure tourism, farm and health tourism.

8. To ensure that the development does not exceed sustainable levels.
9. To develop the seven north-eastern states, the Himalayan region and Islands for tourism.
10. To maintain a balance between the negative and positive impacts of tourism through planning restrictions and through education of the people for conservation and development.

Development Plan

The strategy for development should take into consideration the carrying capacity, local aspirations and benefits likely to accrue to the community. In particular specific policies and guidelines for eco-tourism development and adventure tourism are to be formulated, primarily through a regulatory framework. The Draft Guidelines have been approved at a State Ministers Conference and have been circulated to various trade and industry bodies. The guidelines draw a distinction between mass or resort tourism and nature or Eco-tourism, as the kind of tourism that has a lower impact on the environment and requires less infrastructural development. The Ministry hopes that the environment conscious international tourist will be made aware that India is taking steps to protect its ecology and environment.

Apart from the do's and don'ts, the guidelines are governed by a tourism management plan, the key elements of which are the protection of natural resources and a positive involvement of local communities, along with an optimum number of environmentally conscious visitors. The principles of management are scientific planning, effective control and continuous monitoring, development of physical infrastructure, zoning and a Management plan for public use of natural sites. The management plan should establish standards for resort development, style and location of structures, waste disposal, treatment of sewage, control of litter, use of public spaces and fragile areas. The operational guidelines rely on sensitisation of all the role players and this Programmes is based on a self-regulated environmental code.

Area specific rather than universal development plans keeping in mind the unique character of the location and its economic and social environment are important. This would help the State Government to coordinate with the industry in managing visitors and their activities. NGO's working on socio-economic Programmes in forest and remote areas could have a closer coordination with tourism service operators to transfer economic benefits, particularly the handicraft production and marketing sector. The guidelines are only a beginning, and it is hoped that with increasing awareness of the visitor the industry will regulate its practices.

Tourism Advisory Committee

There is an emphasis on the needs and perceptions of the international tourist running through the discussion on the guide lines although the data from the National Parks makes it evident that the domestic tourists outnumber international visitors, although they do not pay the same amount as the foreign visitor either in entry fees or for board and lodging and transport facilities. They do however demand a much higher per capita use of resources like water, fuel for heating and cooking and transport. They also make the same intensive use of time and try to maximize their stay by the number of animals and birds they can view in the 24-hour period.

It is interesting to note that no democratic participation has been called for in the policy formulation process, and all the amendments to the policy have come from trade associations and government think tanks. The tourism Advisory Committee also consists of eminent persons and community representation has been ignored.

The policy clearly recognises the debate on the tourism issue which has surfaced wherever tourism development, particularly in the case of tourism projects relating to the "gifts of nature" like beaches, rivers, mountains and forests, have already been developed. However, mere recognition of the hostility of people to tourism development is not enough to change the nature of tourism development or the resistance to tourism or what many have termed a poor tourism culture.

Perhaps to understand this in a better perspective, we should look at the issue of sustainable development in a critical way. Perhaps we can question the impact of sustainable development on the environment and sift through the jargon of development planners, international agencies, and environmental activists to see how sustainable development can be achieved without all the contradictions that are apparent as in the case of the tourism sector.

DEVELOPMENT IN TOURISM

The concept of sustainability originated in the context of renewable resources like forests and fisheries and was subsequently adopted by the environmental movement. In most cases it is understood to mean "the existence of the ecological conditions necessary to support human life at a specific level of well being through future generations." However, in addition to ecological conditions there are social conditions that influence ecological sustainability in a nature-people interaction.

The social connotations have been described by Barbier (1987) who has defined social sustainability as "the ability to maintain desired social values, traditions, institutions, cultures or other social characteristics." The term sustainability came into usage in 1980 when the IUCN presented the World Conservation Strategy where sustainable development was linked to conservation of living resources. However, the fundamental goals have often been lost sight of because of operational goals (e.g. food, water, shelter, health are fundamental goals to be realised through self reliance, cost effectiveness, appropriate technology, people centred-ness etc.)

Consequently, the WCED made its definition brief: Social Development is development that meets the needs of the present without compromising the ability of future generations to meet their own needs. They did not make any assumptions on the direction in which changes in demand would take place.

(e.g. equity, social justice, self-determination, or cultural diversity).

India's tourism policy follows the mainstream SD (Sustainable Development) thinking by adopting all the critical objectives: revive growth change the quality of growth meet essential needs for jobs, food, energy, water and sanitation ensure sustainable levels of population conserve and enhance the resource base reorient technology and management risk merge environment and economics in decision making reorient international economic relations make development more participatory.

These objectives are responsible for building a very broad consensus on the issue of sustainable development, yet the debate at the operational level continues. Most participants in the debate now accept that many human activities are reducing the long-term ability of the natural environment to provide goods and services, which will eventually affect human health and well being.

Enviromental Degradation

Many also accept that poverty is devastating the lives of millions in the Third World since there is no consensus between what is environmentally necessary and what is economically and developmentally feasible. The level of inter-dependence between the two insights is yet to be incorporated in the concept of Social Development. Some problem areas are: Environmental degradation, already affecting millions in the Third World, is likely to reduce human well being across the globe.

Who is responsible for this rapid degeneration? Is it the poor or the rich? The poor have no option but to exploit resources for short-term survival. If we take the example of forests and their resources, which have been traditionally outside the market system and in the sphere of tribal or indigenous peoples rights, they are today seen as exploiters of the forests as against tourists, with all their demand for infrastructure and superstructure, who are seen to be conservationists. The inter-linked nature of the problem of sustainability is such that the impact of degradation will be quicker on the poor than on the rich.

Can Sustainable Development be the metafix it claims to be in reconciling increasing industrial, agricultural and resource use productivity with environmental needs. The weakness of the Social Development argument lies in the techno-economic approach to solutions with regard to common property resource management, through know how transfers, resource pricing, subsidy policies and building management capabilities. (World Bank, 1987) Deeper processes such as land reforms, industrial demands on raw materials, over consumption, changing legal and political structures are either ignored or looked at in a cursory manner.

For instance how can we claim a consensus between those who are concerned for the survival of future generations with those who are concerned with the survival of wild life, or human health and subsistence? Unless we can identify the trade-offs necessary for each specific objective of sustainability, we will not have clarity in the discussion. We will also fail to understand why, even when there is a broad consensus, projects on the ground result in conflicts. Suggested refinements could be:

1. A distinction between ecological and social sustainability and in the process an identification of the inter-linkages a distinction between renewable and non-renewable resources, between environmental processes crucial to human life and crucial to other forms of life dependent on the resources. a distinction between the techno-economic aspects of social sustainability (infrastructure, services, government) with political and cultural sustainability.
2. A distinction between equitable development and local participation, and decentralisation, what many have called NGOisation of sustainable development.

This is because no rigorous testing of local participation leading to social equity or to sustainable resource use have been reported.

ENVIRONMENTAL IMPACT

Case studies reflect personal, organisational or political preferences. Tourism is one of the activities which have caused concern because of the effects of increasing human traffic on fragile environments. Countries which are looking towards Tourism as a means of economic growth, like India, have limited resources and cultural restraints and they have the greatest need to pay heed to the possible negative impacts of tourism. The environmental impact of tourism is a basic issue, whether we are looking at a developed or an underdeveloped area, region or country.

The costs of tourism for a country like India include extensive investment in fixed assets with a low rate of return for infrastructure, transportation, accommodation, cultural institutions, exhibition centres, and park facilities. To this maybe added the social and cultural costs like additional demands on infrastructure like land, water, health services; the creation of new jobs for displaced people; the cost of positive community relationships; the disparity between the lifestyle of visitors and those who serve them; the possible friction between local residents and new users of valued local resources; the perception of local residents of the spending of scarce capital resources on what they consider low priority areas like tourism; cultural cost of alterations in local ceremonial or traditional values; loss of privacy for local communities as tourists come to gape at their living conditions and rituals.

Tourism also causes increasing congestion and pollution as thousands of visitors flock to parks and sanctuaries in motorised vehicles; there are changes in accessibility, landscape and the ecological balance between man and nature; there is the cost, both monetary and human, of creating conservation zones (core/buffer) with unforeseen or undesirable side effects; which have been observed in the Eco-tourism movement.

The benefit of revenue from tourism does not always redress these problems but goes towards the cost of administering the project. The tourism industry is generally self-centred and not given to educational, cultural or exchange Programmes on a philanthropic basis. The natural environment, with the best will in the world, cannot escape damage with the volume of visitors. As more and more tourists, both domestic and international seek the exotic and remote destinations around the world, the likelihood of the environment suffering as a result become greater.

Forests can suffer from trampling, fires, tree felling for facilities and waste. Wildlife, despite the protection in national parks, has suffered a loss of habitat, hunting and poaching, viewing and photographing, leading to an interruption of feeding and breeding patterns or hunting for food undisturbed. These are the prized moments for the viewer. The trade in wild life trophies or tourist souvenirs is the more deliberately destructive aspect of such tourism.

Sanctuaries

The building of tourist lodges in materials that are not integrated with the environment and the pressure they put on the land and water bodies is also wilfully destructive. Management techniques that include being less user friendly or control of numbers by closing access or by multiplying the number of attractions and areas or charging higher admission fees are generally not popular with the tourist or the tour operator and are also difficult to implement because of high administrative costs.

Equations, through its involvement in the field have had a variety of experiences relating to the debate on Eco-tourism and sustainable development. The major issues that have emerged after the policy of notification of wild life sanctuaries and their management by the Forest Departments are quite disturbing. Wherever notification has led to displacement of people the experience of rehabilitation has not been successful and the conservation aims have not been met. Several sanctuaries have witnessed militant action by displaced communities against the developers of tourism. In many cases the tourism aims have also not been met in making the sanctuary accessible to viewers, naturalists, wild life photographers. Tourism has not been able to counteract poaching and the most extensive and the oldest conservation project, Project Tiger has not been able to save the tiger population.

The commercialisation of the experience, like the privileging of one species, for example the tiger, has led to congestion and noise pollution and this has put a pressure on the management of the sanctuary to organise tiger shows which are putting a pressure on the feeding and mating habits of the tiger. These are very invasive techniques of experiencing the wild. On the plus side, the concept of beneficiary led development has helped indigenous people to organise against their displacement and exploitation as well as to fight for the retention of their traditional rights and life styles.

Environmentalists have not only been involved in such organisations and movements but have done valuable documentation. This has influenced many urban visitors to be more sensitive to the wild and to follow the rules when participating in eco-tourism. This has also led to the development of a code of conduct for the tourist, the industry and the administrator. These attempts are in a very nascent stage. The kind of co-ordination that is required between the environmentalist and economist is just beginning to emerge and have still to counter the myths of neo-classical economists in the field of tourism. But a beginning has been made.

COASTAL ISSUES

The Coastal Regulation Zone (CRZ) came into existence on February 19, 1991, with the gazetting of the notification by the Union Ministry of Environment and Forests (MoEF) under

Sec. 3(1) and Sec. 3(2)(v) of the Environment Protection Act, 1986, and Rule 5(3)(d) of the Environment Protection Rules, 1986. Through the Notification the Central Government declared the coastal stretches of seas, bays, estuaries, creeks, rivers and backwaters, which are influenced by tidal action (in the land ward side), up to 500m. from the high tide line (HTL) and the land between the low tide line (LTL) and HTL as CRZ. In the case of rivers, creeks and backwaters, the Notification stated that the CRZ could be modified on a case by case basis, on the basis of reasons to be recorded during the preparation of the coastal zone management plan (CZMP). However, the width of the CRZ from each bank could not be less than 100 m., or the width of the water body, whichever was less.

Activities Prohibited in the CRZ:

1. Setting up of new industries and expansion of existing ones, except those directly related to waterfront or requiring foreshore facilities.
2. Manufacture, handling, storage or disposal of hazardous substances.
3. Setting up and expansion of fish processing units including warehousing (excluding hatchery and natural fish drying in permitted areas).
4. · Discharge of untreated wastes and effluents from industries, cities, towns or other human settlements. The existing practices would have to be phased out by the concerned authorities within three years.
5. Dumping of ash or any waste from thermal power plants.
6. Land reclamation, bunding or disturbing the natural course of sea water with similar obstructions. Exceptions are made for activities required for the control of coastal erosion, the maintenance of water ways to ports; clearing sand bars; and for the construction of regulators, storm water drains and structures for the prevention of salinity ingress.

7. Mining of sand, rocks and other substrata materials, except those raw minerals not available outside the CRZ areas.
8. Drawing or harvesting of groundwater and construction of mechanism within 200 m. of the HTL. Between 200 and 500 m. it will be permissible only if done manually through ordinary wells for drinking, horticulture, agriculture and fisheries.
9. Construction activity in ecologically sensitive areas.
10. Any construction activity between LTL and HTL except facilities for carrying treated effluents and waste water discharge into the sea, facilities for carrying sea water for cooling purposes, oil, gas and similar pipelines and facilities essential for facilities permitted under the notification.
11. Dressing or altering of sand dunes, hill, natural features including landscape changes for beautification, recreation and other such purposes, except as permitted under the notification.

Regulated activities (requiring environmental clearance from MoEF):

1. Construction activities related to Defence requirements for which foreshore facilities are essential. Residential office, hospital, workshops will not normally be permitted in the CRZ, except in very special cases.
2. Operational construction for ports and harbors and light house.
3. Foreshore facilities of thermal power plants for transport of raw materials, in-take of cooling water and out fall for discharge of treated wastewater or cooling water.
4. All other activities with investment exceeding. 5 crores.

Coastal Zone Management Plan (CZMP)

All the coastal states have to prepare, within one year, CZMPs identifying and classifying CRZ areas as per the Notification guidelines. These plans have to be approved by MoEF All further development activities should be within the framework of these plans. In the interim period, before the approval of the plans, development activities should not violate the provisions of the Notification. Violations are punishable under the provisions of the Environment Protection Act of 1986. For regulating developmental activities, the coastal stretches within 500m of the HTL are classified into CRZ-1, CRZ-11 and CRZ-III.

CRZ-I – Areas that are ecologically sensitive and important (national parks, coral reefs, mangroves, areas close to the breeding and spawning grounds of fishes, areas of high natural beauty, historical heritage, high genetic diversity, and those likely to be inundated by global warming, 'etc.); and areas within the LTL and HTL.

Regulations in CRZ-I

1. No new construction shall be permitted within 500 m of the HTL.
2. No construction activity except for facility for carrying treated effluents and waste water into the sea or carrying sea water for cooling, oil, gas or similar pipelines will be permitted between the LTL and the HTL.

CRZ-II

Areas that have already been developed up to or close to the shore-line. 'Developed areas' that come within municipal limits or other legally designated urban areas which have been substantially built up and which have been provided with infrastructural facilities like drainage, approach road, water supply and sewage mains.

Regulations in CRZ-III

1. Buildings will not be permitted in the seaward side of existing roads (or those proposed in the CZMP) nor on the seaward side of the existing authorised structures.
2. Reconstruction of authorised buildings to be permitted subject to the existing floor space and without change in existing use CRZ III Areas that are relatively undisturbed and do not belong to either CRZ-I or CRZ-II. This will include coastal zones in the rural areas and also areas within municipal limits or urban areas that are not substantially built up.
3. Areas up to 200 m. from the HTL earmarked as no development zone (NDZ). No construction will be permitted within this zone except for repairs of existing authorised structures not exceeding the existing plinth area and covered apace. Raising of horticultural crops, gardens, pastures, parks, play fields, forestry and salt manufacture from sea water permitted in this zone.
4. Development of vacant plots between 200 m. 500 m. from the HTL, in designated areas with prior approval of MoEF, permitted for hotels and beach resorts.
5. Construction or reconstruction of dwellind units between the 200m and 500m of the HTL permitted so long as it is within the ambit of traditional rights and customary uses such as existing fishing villages and gouthans.

   Building conditions would be based on the conditions that the total number of dwelling units does not increase more than double of the existing units; the total covered area is not more than 33 per cent of the plot area; the overall height is not more than two floors and 9 m. Guidelines for development of beach resorts in the designated areas of CRZ-III · No construction within 200 m. from the HTL and in the area between LTL and HTL.

6. The total plot size should not be less than 0.4 hectare and the covered area should not be more than 33 per cent. · The total height of the construction should not be more than 9 m. and the building should not be more than two floors.

   Groundwater cannot be tapped within 200m of the HTL. Between 200 and 500 m. it can be tapped with the concurrence of the State or Central Groundwater Board.
7. Extraction of sand, leveling or digging of sandy stretches, except for the structural foundation will not be permitted within 500 M. of the HTL.
8. The quality of treated effluents, solid wastes, emissions and noise levels etc. must be within the standards laid down by the central or state pollution control boards. Untreated effluents and solid wastes should not be discharged into the water or beach.
9. To allow public access there should be a gap of 20m. width between two hotels. Two consecutive gaps should not be more than 500 m. apart.

THE WORLD SCENARIO OF TOURISM

In recent years tourism has emerged as a major economic activity that is employment oriented and earns foreign exchange. Its share in the worlds GDP in 1994-95 was 10 per cent which is more than the world military budgets put together. In global terms, the investment in tourism industry and travel trade accounts for 7 per cent of the total capital investment. Today 21.2 crore people around the globe are employed in travel trade and tourism. In future, this industry is likely to see unprecedented growth.

According to the World Tourism Council at Brussels, the revenues from travel and tourism in Asia Pacific region will grow at the rate of 7.8 per cent annually over the next decade. Amongst the economic sectors, the tourism sector is highly labour intensive. A survey by the Government of India notes that the rate of employment generation (direct and indirect) in tourism is 52 persons employed per Rs.10 lakh investment (based on 1992-93 Consumer Price Index). This is much higher than the rates of employment generation in most other economic sectors.

Indian tourism industry has also recorded phenomenal growth. The rate of international arrivals in India in recent years has been to the tune of about 19 lakh arrivals per year. The unprecedented growth in tourism in India has made it the third largest foreign exchange earner after gem and jewellery and ready-made garments. This is not surprising since India possesses a whole range of attractive normally sought by tourists and which includes natural attractions like landscapes, scenic beauty, mountains, wildlife, beaches, major rivers and manmade attractions such as monuments, forts, palaces and havelis. However, in global terms, in spite of such attractions, tourist arrivals in India are a mere 0.30 per cent of the world arrivals. Receipts are similarly low, just a 0.50 per cent of the world receipts. We are still quite far from the target of 50 lakh tourist arrivals per year.

Travel and Tourism is the world's largest industry and creator of jobs across national and regional economies. WTTC/ WEFA research show that in 2000, Travel and Tourism will generate, directly and indirectly, 11.7 per cent of GDP and nearly 200 million jobs in the world-wide economy. Jobs generated by Travel and Tourism are spread across the economy - in retail, construction, manufacturing and telecommunications, as well as directly in Travel and Tourism companies. These jobs employ a large proportion of women, minorities and young people; are predominantly in small and medium sized companies; and offer good training and transferability. Tourism can also be one of the most effective drivers for the development of regional economies. These patterns apply to both developed and emerging economies.

Contributing to Sustainable Development

The 1992 United Nations Conference on Environment and Development (UNCED), the Rio Earth Summit, identified Travel and Tourism as one of the key sectors of the economy which could make a positive contribution to achieving sustainable development. The Earth Summit lead to the adoption of Agenda 21, a comprehensive Programmes of action adopted by 182 governments to provide a global blueprint for achieving sustainable development. Travel and Tourism is the first industry sector to have launched an industry-specific action plan based on Agenda 21.

Travel and Tourism is able to contribute to development which is economically, ecologically and socially sustainable, because it:

1. Has less impact on natural resources and the environment than most other industries;
2. Is based on enjoyment and appreciation of local culture, built heritage, and natural environment, as such that the industry has a direct and powerful motivation to protect these assets;
3. Can play a positive part in increasing consumer commitment to sustainable development principles through its unparalleled consumer distribution channels; and
4. Provides an economic incentive to conserve natural environments and habitats which might otherwise be allocated to more environmentally damaging land uses, thereby, helping to maintain bio-diversity.

There are numerous good examples of where Travel and Tourism is acting as a catalyst for conservation and improvement of the environment and maintenance of local diversity and culture. (Some of these are set out in Section B of this paper and a fuller illustration of the range of industry action can be found on the World Travel and Tourism Council's Of course, there are also examples where development has not been sustainable. (Some of the lessons learnt from these poor practices are illustrated in Section C of this paper.)

Providing Infrastructure

To a greater degree than most activities, Travel and Tourism depends on a wide range of infrastructure services - airports, air navigation, roads, railheads and ports, as well as basic infrastructure services required by hotels, restaurants, shops, and recreation facilities (e.g. telecommunications and utilities).

It is the combination of tourism and good infrastructure that underpins the economic, environmental and social benefits. It is important to balance any decision to develop an area for tourism against the need to preserve fragile or threatened environments and cultures. However, once a decision has been taken where an area is appropriate for new tourism development, or that an existing tourist site should be developed further, then good infrastructure will be essential to sustain the quality, economic viability and growth of Travel and Tourism. Good infrastructure will also be a key factor in the industry's ability to manage visitor flows in ways that do not affect the natural or built heritage, nor counteract against local interests.

Challenge for the Future

Travel and Tourism creates jobs and wealth and has tremendous potential to contribute to economically, environmentally and socially sustainable development in both developed countries and emerging nations. It has a comparative advantage in that its start up and running costs can be low compared to many other forms of industry development. It is also often one of the few realistic options for development in many areas. Therefore, there is a strong likelihood that the Travel and Tourism industry will continue to grow globally over the short to medium term.

Of course, if Travel and Tourism is managed badly, it can have a detrimental effect - it can damage fragile environments and destroy local cultures. The challenge is to manage the future growth of the industry so as to minimise its negative impacts on the environment and host communities whilst maximising the benefits it brings in terms of jobs, wealth and support for local culture and industry, and protection of the built and natural environment.

Objectives

The main objective of the States Tourism Policy will be to undertake intensive development of tourism in the State and thereby increase employment opportunities. The following related objectives are dovetailed with main objectives:

1. Identify and develop tourist destinations and related activities.
2. Diversifications of tourism products in order to attract more tourists through a varied consumer choice.
3. Comprehensive development of pilgrimage centres as tourist destinations.
4. Create adequate facilities for budget tourists.
5. Strengthen the existing infrastructure and develop new ones where necessary.
6. Creation of tourism infrastructure so as to preserve handicrafts, folk arts and culture of the state and thereby attract more tourists.

Approach and Strategy

In addition to the facilitation role assigned to itself by the Government in the development of tourism, the Government will adopt the following strategy towards the private sector with the objective of securing its active involvement in leading the development of tourism in the State.

1. The tourism will be given the status of industry in order that the facilities and benefits available to the industry are also made available to tourism projects.

2. A special incentives package will be made available for encouraging new tourism projects as well as expansion of existing tourism units.
3. Infrastructural facilities will be strengthened and developed within the State, particularly in Special Tourism Areas which will be notified latter and which will be developed by adopting an integrated-area.
4. Effective mechanisms will be set up to build meaningful co-ordination with the Central Government and the State Governments agencies, the local self-government bodies and the NGOs.
5. Government will encourage building effective linkages with the relevant economic agents and agencies such as the national and international tour operators and travel agents of repute, hotel chains and global institutions connected with tourism such as WTO.

So far, the lending from the State Financial Institutions has been largely confined to hotels only. In reality, the range of activities for tourism projects is far larger than just hotels as can be seen from the following illustrative list

Ten Commandments

1. Respect the frailty of the earth. Realize that unless all are willing to help in its preservation, unique and beautiful destinations may not be here for future generations to enjoy.
2. Leave only footprints. Take only photographs. No graffiti! No litter! Do not take away souvenirs from historical sites and natural areas.
3. To make your travels more meaningful, educate yourself about the geography, customs, manners and cultures of the region you visit. Take time to listen to the people. Encourage local conservation efforts.
4. Respect the privacy and dignity of others. Inquire before photographing people.

5. Do not buy products made from endangered plants or animals, such as ivory, tortoise shell, animal skins, and feathers. Read Know Before You Go, the U. S. Customs list of products which cannot be imported.
6. Always follow designated trails. Do not disturb animals, plants or their natural habitats.
7. Learn about and support conservation-oriented Programmes and organizations working to preserve the environment.
8. Whenever possible, walk or use environmentally-sound methods of transportation. Encourage drivers of public vehicles to stop engines when parked.
9. Patronize those (hotels, airlines, resorts, cruise lines, tour operators and suppliers) who advance energy and environmental conservation; water and air quality; recycling; safe management of waste and toxic materials; noise abatement, community involvement; and which provide experienced, well-trained staff dedicated to strong principles of conservation.
10. Encourage organizations to subscribe to environmental guidelines. ASTA urges organizations to adopt their own environmental codes to cover special sties and ecosystems.

Travel is a natural right of all people and is a crucial ingredient of worl.

Index